Foreword

The problem of extracting knowledge, actionable information, and understanding from large and complex data sets is one of the fundamental intellectual and scientific problems of our time. Many different methodologies are being brought to bear on it, but it is clear that the problem is far from being definitively solved. There are many questions around *"how to"* compute with large data sets, but there are also fundamental questions concerning *"what to"* compute. At a very high level, the term *Machine Intelligence* denotes a set of methodologies for addressing both these needs. One such methodology is topological data analysis (TDA), which is seeing striking applications within many domains, including healthcare, life sciences, and financial services.

TDA was initially developed under the auspices of a Defense Advanced Research Projects Agency (DARPA) grant, which provided resources for a multi-university initiative during the period 2005-2010. A great deal of very interesting research came out of the project. In particular, the Stanford "node" in the project developed methods for creating network models for arbitrary data sets. This idea has turned out to be extremely powerful, and indeed creates a new method of modeling data, orthogonal and complementary to standard algebraic modeling of data. The potential of the idea became clear to Gunnar Carlsson, Gurjeet Singh, and Harlan Sexton, members of the Stanford node, and they formed the startup company Ayasdi Inc. to bring these methods to bear on the important problems facing society and the economy.

Applications of Machine Learning and TDA are maturing just in time to meet the needs of healthcare and life sciences. Over the past ten years great strides have been made by physicians and hospitals to adopt electronic health records (EHRs). Now health systems across the U.S. are creating large data warehouses and data lakes to store these data on millions of patients and hundreds of millions of transactions per year. After 25 years of great promise, the ability to test patients for genetic information is now nearing widespread application. Patients are increasingly able to monitor their own health at a very granular level with the use of smart phones and wearable monitoring devices. The challenge is to store, integrate, analyze and communicate meaningful insight from the enormous quantity of information now available. We predict that Machine Intelligence will become a necessary part of the information infrastructure for most every healthcare system in coming years. Standard analysis will include routine evaluation of thousands of real world surgical cases to understand and rapidly adopt best practices. Machine Learning will enable early identification of patients developing sepsis with predictive algorithms tailored to an individual hospital's microbiological flora, antibiotic resistance patterns and the patient population served in that community. In the new information world, every hospital and medical group will become a part of a "learning healthcare system" as envisioned by the Institute of Medicine.

The availability of Machine Learning tools is already transforming clinical research. Leading health systems are now collaborating in large scale precision medicine enterprises which share data across millions of patient lives. This is accelerating the discovery of specific genes responsible for diseases such as cancer and diabetes. Advanced analytics will help map results from whole genome testing with phenotype characteristics found in patient histories and clinical EHR data. The same is being done for the discovery of new protein and small molecule biomarkers such as patient microbiome and immune system data. New opportunities exist for analysis of large data sets now available from advanced imaging such as CT scanning and functional MRI, particularly in the field of chronic neurological disease. There is no doubt that Machine Learning software will help enable researchers involved in the recently announced "moonshot to cure cancer".

As the promise of medicine has never been more exciting, the reality of providing healthcare services for a growing and aging population is challenging governments around the world. In the U.S., we have embarked on new healthcare financing methods to foster "value based care." Traditionally, provider organizations of doctors and hospitals have been at odds with health insurance companies, but now there is a new mandate for collaboration and cooperation to achieve the best possible patient outcomes at the lowest possible cost. Machine Learning and TDA are now being used to analyze the needs of populations of patients, improve insurance plan design and identify individual patients at highest risk of medical problems. There is great potential for real efficiencies, improved patient outcomes and patient experience through predictive analytics and the reorganization of resources through payer-provider collaboration.

Machine Intelligence software was created to help solve these difficult problems. Its methods are very general, and so in addition to addressing the problems in healthcare, they can also solve problems in financial services, energy, security, and all domains in which the interpretation and utilization of complex data is of central importance. This book gives an introduction to the principles and methodology of Machine Intelligence, as well as to many of the use cases to which it has been applied. We hope that it will be a guide for software users and for dreamers of what is possible. We look forward to work with collaborators to bring the real potential of information to improve the lives of patients and communities across the globe.

Machine Intelligence for Healthcare

Published by: Francis Campion & Gunnar Carlsson

iv

Machine Intelligence for Healthcare

First Edition

Francis X. Campion, MD, FACP
Instructor, Department of Population Medicine, Harvard Medical School

Gunnar Carlsson, PhD
Professor Emeritus, Department of Mathematics, Stanford University

Acknowledgments

This book is a natural development of our work and discovery in the field of Machine Learning. We are fortunate to be surrounded by extraordinary colleagues at Stanford and around the country. Ayasdi was founded 10 years ago, answering a call to universities for assistance from DARPA for the exploration of very large datasets. Over the years, the Ayasdi team has worked with colleagues in academia, industry and government to refine the software, user interfaces and applications for solving real world problems. In this book we are taking a deep dive into the world of healthcare and life sciences. We believe that the insight and answers to many of the challenges facing healthcare in the U.S. and around the world will be found through the use of Machine Intelligence.

We would like to express our thanks to many people who helped refine the topics and case studies for the book. These include Gurjeet Singh and Harlan Sexton, co-founders at Ayasdi. Gurjeet has provided an ambitious vision for the use of Machine Intelligence and Harlan led the data science efforts to select and fine tune the algorithms needed for many of the healthcare applications. We are indebted to Vance Moore, Todd Stewart, MD, Seth Barbanell, MD and Ursula Wright, FNP from Mercy Health System, St. Louis, MO, for their continuous efforts to apply the Ayasdi software to solve real world problems. Our colleagues at Intermountain Health in Salt Lake City, UT have shared that vision and extended the work tremendously; a special thanks to Todd Dunn, Lonny Northrup and Bill Adams at Intermountain Healthcare Transformation Lab and to David Skarda, MD in the Department of Surgery.

This book would not have been possible without Devi Ramanan who managed the large number of collaborators with case studies nominated for inclusion in the book. She worked directly with the researchers, completed the writing and assisted with final selections.

Ajith Warrier, Jennifer Kloke, Alan Lehman, Dev Ghosh and Jen Gamble led much of the technical and data science efforts underlying the case studies and successful software applications now in use. Prashanth Kini provided sections related to data preparation and product development. Sangeeta Chakraborty and Diljit Singh gave review and guidance on implementation methods. Ajith Warrier gave outstanding advice concerning various parts of the manuscript. Dan Druker also made a number of excellent suggestions.

Acknowledgements

We are ever grateful for editing and production assistance from Vince Guaglianone, Gloria Consola and Adrian Kane.

With great expectation, we look forward to meeting new healthcare and life science colleagues who may be introduced to the promising world of Machine Intelligence through this book project.

Table of Contents

Chapter 7: Clinical Variation and Hospital Clinical Pathways167

Chapter 8: Population Health Management............................197

List of Tables

Table of Figures

Introduction to Machine Intelligence

In the beginning…

Since prehistoric times, humankind has been devoted to the pursuit of minimizing the need for physical effort in all the tasks and processes required for survival and for improving human existence. Initially, progress was made in augmenting and amplifying human effort, through simple devices such as the wheel and the lever. Over time, the devices became more complex and were able to address increasingly complex tasks and replace more and more human effort. Devices such as the steam engine and the automobile greatly increased productivity and allowed for possibilities that previously could not even have been contemplated. Huge advances in this direction were made during and after the Industrial Revolution, which not only developed devices but also found how to use them at scale, to obtain the full benefit for society.

With the advent of modern computing, an effort has been underway to similarly replace and augment human cognitive and analytic effort, when desirable. It might not always be desirable – the task of balancing a check book is clearly one that should be replaced, while it is not so clear that one should automate the task of reviewing a movie. The effort has been labeled *Artificial Intelligence* (AI). In its most ambitious form, it attempts to create machine models for all aspects of human intelligence. Defined in this way, we are not very far along the path of realizing this vision, since there are many aspects of human intelligence and emotions that we simply don't understand very well. However, there is a less ambitious goal toward which we have made enormous progress, which we will call *narrow AI*. Narrow AI focuses on the modeling of simple, well defined cognitive tasks, such as balancing a check book or guiding a caller through options for billing, rather than the grander vision of more general AI. The development of solutions to narrow AI problems usually proceeds by (1) careful analysis of a human process, followed by (2) the subsequent building of software models to accurately mimic what a human performing the task would do.

Where it's leading…

To begin to realize the vision of broader AI, one must add additional components to the process. We will sketch a framework that can accomplish the full range of tasks needed for the construction of applications. Applications will be constructed using four layers.

1. Analysis
2. Prediction/Classification
3. Action
4. Justification

The analysis layer is the analytic component, which can be addressed directly by various methodologies. The prediction/classification layer ingests new data points and determines where they fit within models constructed in the analysis layer, and determines likely consequences from that placement. The action layer takes as input the output of the preceding two layers and performs actions based on it. Finally, the justification layer takes the results of the preceding three layers and in some form or another describes them. The output of the justification layer can then be used as a rationale for performing new calculations, as a monitoring tool for processes, or simply as an explanation for what has taken place to give a user confidence in the outcomes. Here are three situations that can serve as exemplars for this notion.

1. Automated Classifier Generation: The input to his type of application is data concerning a population of some kind (customers, patients, movie goers, users of Facebook, etc.), and has four objectives. The first is to create a taxonomy or segmentation of an existing population about which one has data. The second is to devise a scheme by which one can accept data about a new member of the population and determine where it fits in the taxonomy, i.e. to what segment one believes it belongs. The third is to actually place the new member within the taxonomy, and the final task is to report the segments that have been constructed, together with an explanation of each of the segments in terms of the features of the data being used. Within this volume, we provide numerous case studies, several of which are examples of this task. These include cases on breast cancer genetic marker analysis (Chapter 1), the use of cell phone data to study Parkinson's disease (Chapter 8) and the subtyping of Type 2 Diabetes and asthma (Chapter 9).

2. Emergent Phenomena Detector: This type of application supposes that we have a data source that is producing data over time, and should report about what the most recent "trends" in the data are. Things that might trend are developing topics on Twitter or other social networks, or they could be newly emergent forms of disease. In Chapter 10 we have included three cases studies relating to the detection of payment denials, Medicare overpayments and fraud, waste and abuse of health insurance claims which nicely exemplify this concept. The analysis layer should in this case be an explicitly time dependent form of

segmentation. The prediction/classification layer should in this case be a time varying classifier which assigns new data points to one of the existing groups if appropriate, and reports that it is not possible if not. The action layer then either places the point in one of the existing groups, creates a new group and assigns the point to it, or ignores the point as not being meaningfully attached to an existing group and not part of any "trend". The reporting layer would be a dynamic form of the reporting layer in (1) above, in which groups would be reported, with characterizations or explanations. Additionally, one might like to report on the appearance of new groups, vanishing of earlier groups, splitting of existing groups, and merging of existing groups.

3. Process Monitoring and Intervention: This kind of application would collect data from a complex process, automate the analysis and take steps to stabilize or improve the process. Examples could include an industrial process or perhaps from the power grid which needs protection from "going off the rails". In Chapter 7 we have provided case studies from hospital systems using Machine Intelligence to improve high volume surgical cases, total knee replacement and colon surgery. The analysis would include both knowledge about what states are to be regarded as anomalous or "off the rails", as well as identification of novel improvements. In the surgical example, we seek to find characteristics which make the surgery better. The prediction/classification layer observes a new state and determines if it is anomalous. The action layer then takes the corrective action that was learned by the analysis layer. The reporting layer informs the user of the anomalies found, as well as what corrective actions were taken in order return to a normal state. It should also give a characterization of the anomaly, in terms of variables that characterize it.

We refer to this view of the transition from narrow AI to broader AI as *Machine Intelligence*. In this volume, we will describe a new methodology that can be used to address all four layers in the process. To explain this contribution, we will need to discuss and important set of ideas related to AI, called *Machine Learning*.

Machine Learning (ML) has been in existence since roughly 1980. It provides tools for the analysis layer described above. In some cases, the analysis portion can be performed entirely manually and without reference to any data concerning the process to be modeled. However, it is increasingly the case that this portion of the solution requires a great deal of analysis of observed data concerning the process and the goals of the process. ML supplies a set of data analytic tools, and often a solution for the prediction/classification layer. The methods of ML are very mathematically sophisticated, and often work remarkably well. They are discussed in more detail in Chapter 5.

The new approach that we introduce in this volume is called *Topological Data Analysis* (TDA). It adds to the capabilities of ML both in accuracy and efficiency. It is motivated by observations concerning human intelligence, and adds them to the ML capabilities. To understand the importance of the new methodology, we discuss some concrete ways in which ML can be improved.

- ML proceeds via sophisticated mathematical techniques, whose output is usually not readily interpretable by humans, especially humans who do not have advanced training in mathematical technique. For example, the output of linear regression analysis on high-dimensional data is typically a very long vector of coefficients, the entries of which are not readily interpretable. The same remarks apply to other techniques in the ML toolkit, such as Principal Component Analysis and Multidimensional Scaling. Although such methods can be used to create accurate predictors and classifiers, the fact that they are not interpretable means that there are many domains in which they do not give the most useful results. For example, in the creation of risk models for stress testing of banks, such complicated models are often not regarded as convincing. The reason is that although they give good predictions on existing data, they do not give confidence because one cannot understand what they are using and what they are ignoring. This is important, because one does not believe that the existing data is always a perfect or very good predictor of the future, and wants insight into how it is operating so as to be able to assess whether one believes the results. In this case, it is more desirable to have outputs that augment human intelligence, and allow a human to reason about the outputs.
- Because of the algebraic nature of many of its algorithms, and the fact that it is designed to produce simple binary or numerical outputs, ML will often focus exclusively on the strong "signals" in a data set, and ignore weak signals. Sometimes this is desirable, but often one wants to understand both strong and weak signals. The weak signals might, for instance, represent *emergent* phenomena, namely phenomena the scale of which is currently small, but may be growing. Understanding such phenomena is of critical importance in many situations, for example in risk forecasting.
- ML techniques work extremely well when the tasks at hand, such as prediction and classification, permit simple and readily understood solutions. For example,

in problems that arise in physics, they are typically very effective because the answer is in the end represented well by a simple algebraic mathematical model. Many real world problems, though, do not admit such simple solutions. For example, the analysis of fraud of various types or cyber security problems typically produce complex answers, where there are many different types each of which has its own distinct explanation. Here again, the problem is the nature of the output, which is often too simplistic to represent the complex phenomena and the reasons behind them.

- There are unsupervised techniques within ML, in the form of *clustering techniques* that produce a partitioning of a data set into disjoint groups that often have conceptual meaning. They are typically based on a similarity measure on the collection of data points, and operate in an automatic fashion on the similarity measure to produce the partitioning. There are many such techniques and it is often problematic to decide which one to use. A way to resolve this problem is to produce a model in which one can quickly understand the results of the various methods, and in which one directly defines partitions or segmentations of various types by inspection of the model.

- In designing narrow AI applications based on data analysis, it is desirable to have as much ability to reason about the data as possible. One can sometimes achieve this by clever and highly iterative ML analysis of data sets, but a more flexible model that still retains information about the similarity measure would be very desirable. It will speed up the process in that it may not require iteration or will lessen the number of necessary iterations. It will also permit the kind of reasoning about the problem that is more difficult to achieve with standard ML techniques alone.

The key feature of TDA is the nature of the model or output that it produces. Rather than producing a model whose output is a collection of algebraic equations, it produces a *topological network*, a collection of nodes and edges between pairs of nodes that represents effectively a similarity measure present in the data. The model may be laid out on the screen and operated on in ways similar to those used in image editing software, or they can be used directly from a command line to extract useful information. The network model also possesses a rich functionality, including the capability of coloring by quantities of interest, selecting subgroups, and finding "explanatory variables" for groups that have been selected. It is this functionality that allows one to reason about the data, and to build transparent models in which one understands how the model operates. The TDA methodology makes the work of data analysis quicker, easier, and more intuitive. In some cases, one can even regard the analysis as automated. Provided is a detailed description of this method in Chapter 4.

Why it's important…

The general idea of Machine Intelligence is to produce models of data that (a) are more flexible than standard ML methodology, permitting more accurate modeling of complex data and (b) have additional functionality permitting reasoning about the data and providing interpretability and transparency in the data analysis process. It is therefore an important step toward "broadening" AI, and therefore toward automating cognitive tasks that are either difficult, tedious, or impossible for humans to perform.

In summary, we have identified some of the requirements for enabling the transition from narrow AI towards broader AI, as well as a technology that can begin to fill some of those requirements. The rest of this volume will move from the general to the specific, while emphasizing the general problem of large and complex data sets. We explain the role of TDA as an enabling technology for the transition from narrow AI to broader AI, and the wide variety of applications of Machine Intelligence in healthcare.

Chapter 1: Machine Intelligence and Shape

"I paint with shapes."
-Alexander Calder

1.1 Chapter Preview

- As data accumulation grows explosively, the importance of topology and topological data analysis in managing and interpreting datasets is discussed.
- Defining topology as the study of shape; a study of qualitative rather than quantitative properties of shape.
- A brief history of topology; the movement of Mathematics toward the study of more complex qualitative problem.
- A brief discussion of topology and classification.
- A brief discussion of the practical application of topology to real world problems.
- Case Studies:
  - Case Study 1: *World Values Survey.*
  - Case Study 2: *Analysis of Twitter and the 2013 Presidential Inauguration*

1.2 Introduction

In this chapter, a high-level introduction to the concepts of topology is presented, illustrating why these are powerful tools for the analysis of large and complex data sets.

The notion of shape is a very fundamental one in the study of human perception. Shape recognition and analysis is a fundamental part of human intelligence and cognition, and attempts to mimic these tasks are a fundamental part of Machine Intelligence. Shapes exhibit many complex phenomena and intricate features. Consider, for example, a ring, the surface of a baseball, a cross, and a doughnut. These are all distinguished very effectively and rapidly by humans, and we are also able to characterize the differences between them more or less immediately. Topology is the branch of mathematics that studies shapes, and attempts to perform automatically the tasks of distinguishing shapes and characterization of the differentiating features. The rapidity with which humans analyze and recognize shapes is something one would want to mimic in other cognitive tasks. For example, the study of large data sets is a very important task which can be extremely time consuming. Data sets exhibit a great deal of complexity, and the observations above suggest the possibility that one can encode large and complex data sets by shapes to obtain models in which one can rapidly obtain understanding of them. This premise is the starting point of *Topological Data Analysis* (TDA), the adaptation of the methods of topology to the study of complex data. It should be viewed as an important part of Machine Intelligence, since it adapts a capability of human intelligence to solve problems different from those normally addressed by that capability.

Consider the magnitude of the problem of data analysis. Google receives more than 4 million search queries every minute.[1] Humans are generating over 2.5 exabytes (quintillion bytes) of data every single day.[2] Ninety percent of the world's data has been created in the last two years alone.[3] By 2020, humankind's collective data will reach 40 zettabytes (trillion gigabytes), 57 times more than all the grains of beach sand.[4] We are drowning in a sea of data; **data that can't be analyzed is opportunity wasted.**

TITLE	AUTHOR	WORDS	MB
Artamène/Cyrus the Great	Georges de Scudéry/Madeleine de Scudéry	2,100,000	10.50
A la recherche du temps perdu / In Search of Lost Time	Marcel Proust	1,267,069	6.34
Mission Earth	L. Ron Hubbard	1,200,000	6.00
Der Mann ohne Eigenschaften / The Man Without Qualities	Robert Musil	1,153,100	5.77
Zettels Traum	Arno Schmidt	1,100,000	5.50

Table 1.1: Five Longest Novels Ever Written[5]

The brain can process an image consisting of many megabytes in a mere 13ms[6]. By way of comparison, the world champion speed reader reads text at 4700 words (~30kB) per minute[7]. This observation suggests that visual approaches, when available, are much more efficient in transmitting information. Given the rate of data growth, visual methods are imperative if we are going to stay ahead of the data we are storing.

Michelangelo once noted about sculpture, "every block of stone has a statue inside it and it is the task of the sculptor to discover it." Within every dataset is the potential to cure disease, find undiscovered efficiencies and provide a solution to any problem the human mind can conceive. Topology and Topological Data Analysis are powerful mathematical tools that will aid in the analysis of large and complex data sets.

1.3 Topology Defined: Qualitative vs. Quantitative

In mathematics, topology is defined as the study of shape. Topology concerns itself with the properties of shapes that are qualitative, rather than quantitative. To understand the significance of this distinction, consider the problem of distinguishing the letter "A" from the letter "B". Assume that all the letters to be distinguish are in the same font, i.e. that all A's and B's are identical to all other A's and B's respectively, then one could develop a method for recognition by simply overlaying each candidate letter with a letter template, and checking for a perfect match. This approach is called a quantitative approach, since it does not deal with qualitative properties of the shape but rather the quantitative measurement of the positions of individual pixels.

Unfortunately, usually all versions of the same letter are not typically identical. Often hand printed letters, letters in varying fonts and sizes, letters seen at an angle, or letters drawn on a round surface such as a soccer ball must be recognized. Humans are very good at pattern recognition, because we are able to quickly and robustly recognize qualitative properties of the letters that don't depend on the font or the angle at which the letter is being viewed. In the case of letters, one can distinguish the letters A and B by recognizing that the letter A has a loop and two "legs", while the letter B has two loops. These properties are qualitative properties. The alphabet was doubtless designed to take advantage of the ability to recognize qualitative properties of symbols to perform recognition tasks such as this.

To look at this from the more complex stand point of data analysis, in order to quantitatively analyze high-dimensional data, it requires a data scientist and researcher with intimate knowledge of the data to hypothesize what the data means, so that a model can be created, where the data can be fitted to the model. On the other hand, topological analysis creates groups of data and forms them into shapes, which allows researchers to qualitatively visualize commonalties and formulate questions not even conceived of prior to analysis.

1.3.1 Brief History of Topology in Mathematics: "Where's that Confounded Bridge?"[8]

Table 1.2, below summarizes and abbreviates a very rich history of topology and the newer subdiscipline of applied topology. What's important to note, prior to the conception of topology and the study of shape, mathematics was generally considered the science of quantitative measurement, and did not address more qualitative properties that are difficult to define.[9] [10]

YEAR	NAME	WORK
1736	**Leonhard Euler**	Königsberg Bridge problem– the solution of a problem relating to the geometry of position.
1752	**Leonhard Euler**	Polyhedron formula v-e+f=2 published.
1848	**Carl Friedrich Gauss**	Gauss-Bonnet theorem published by P. Bonnet, relating curvature and connectivity.
1857	**Bernhard Riemann**	Studied connectivity of and defined manifolds, higher dimensional analogues of surfaces.
1871	**Enrico Betti**	Investigated "higher connectivity" and defined numerical quantities that measure shape.
1895	**Henri Poincaré**	Published "Analysis Situs' introducing homology and therefore made Betti's numbers more rigorous. Applications to physics.
1934	**Marston Morse**	Developed Morse theory. Uses functions on spaces to describe them combinatorially.
1944	**Samuel Eilenberg**	Introduced "singular homology", shows homology can be applied to all spaces.
1999 --	**Applied Topology, TDA**	See detailed timeline.

YEAR	NAME	WORK
1999		NSF runs exploratory meeting, "Workshop on Computational Topology."
1999-2004	**V. Robins, P. Frosini, A. Zomorodian, H. Edelsbrunner D. Letscher, G. Carlsson**	Persistent homology introduced and computational methods developed. Analogues for point clouds of Betti's numbers.
2001-2010		Various NSF funded projects in Computational Topology including two focused on Topological Data Analysis at Stanford.
2004-2010	**G. Carlsson, H. Edelsbrunner, J. Harer, P. Diaconis, G. Sapiro, B. Mann, G. Singh, H. Sexton, S. Holmes**	Multi-university DARPA initiative on Topological Data Analysis is centered at Stanford.
2006-2011	**B. Mann, R. Ghrist, F. Cohen**	DARPA "STOMP" program, engineering applications of topology.
2007	**G. Carlsson, G. Singh, F. Memoli**	MAPPER algorithm conceived and implemented. Motivated by Morse's theory.
2008	**G. Carlsson, G. Singh, H. Sexton**	Ayasdi founded to commercialize work from DARPA project, creating functionality for MAPPER.

Table 1.2: Brief Histories of Topological and Topological Data Analysis

1.3.2 Euler's Brilliance[11]

What Leonhard Euler is officially credited with is being the father of Topology and Graph theory. What he is unofficially (mythologically?) credited with is motivating the building of an 8th bridge over Pregel River in 1875.

Prior to 1736, when Leonhard Euler published, *"The Solution of a Problem Relating to the Geometry of Position"*[1], a solution to, *"the Königsberg bridge problem"*, mathematics did not possess methods for studying the flexible and qualitative properties of shapes. Euler's work was revolutionary in that he solved such a problem by a process of abstraction to remove unnecessary detail.

In his paper, Euler took up the challenge posed concerning the seven bridges crossing the river Pregel in Königsberg, Prussia. The following graph is Euler's original abstraction of the bridge problem.

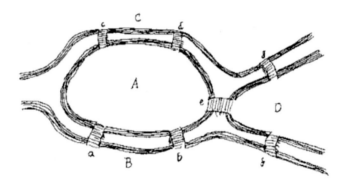

Figure 1.1: Königsberg Bridges

The Königsberg bridge problem asks whether it is possible for a person to take a walking tour crossing each bridge once and only once. Of course, swimming, boating, and vaulting over the river was not allowed, restricting one's access to the islands only by way of a bridge.

Euler studied this problem by first observing that there is a great deal of irrelevant information. For example, the length of the bridges, the path on the island, the size of the islands, and the depth of the water have no relevance to the question being asked, so it is useful to ignore these properties in order to focus one's attention only on the sequence of crossings of the bridges. Euler recognized that there is an abstraction, in the

---

[1] English translation of the Latin title "Solutio problematis ad geometriam situs pertinentis"

form of what is now called a *"topological network"* or "topological graph", which permits one to reason about the problem visually, enabling one to solve it.

Below, the figure on the left is a topological representation of the bridge problem and the one on the right is a map of the configuration of the bridges. The reader is left to judge which is the more efficient representation of the problem and which is the better tool to solve the problem of the path dilemma.

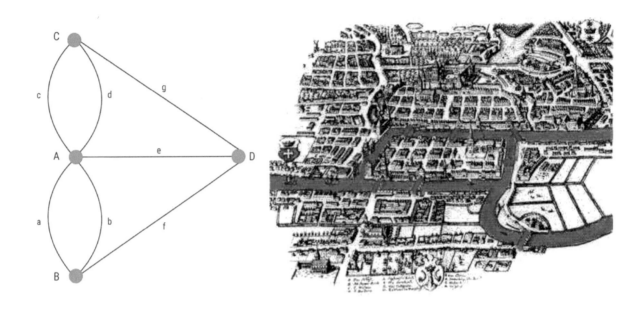

Figure 1.2: TDA Representation and Konigsberg Bridge Image

Euler was slightly annoyed that the Mayor of Danzig, who brought the problem to Euler's attention, would waste his time with such a trivial problem. Perhaps for that reason, Euler's conclusions didn't go much beyond concluding that it was impossible to walk the route by only crossing each of the seven bridges only once, though he did create a general rule for the relationship of land masses to bridges. The value of what Euler did was the graphical nature of the method that yielded conclusions, not the conclusions themselves; ***the path that brought him to the conclusion is what's important.***[2]

It turns out that problems of this kind are actually quite common within the real world. Many attributes describing real world events are qualitative in nature, and one often finds meaning in these events by representing them by shapes.

---

2 Pun Intended.

1.4 Analysis of the Network

In the graph above (left), the islands have been replaced by nodes (A and D), as have the river banks (B and C). Each of the bridges is replaced by an edge (connections a-g). The nodes are all of equal size, since the size of the islands has no relevance, and the lengths of the edges have nothing to do with the length of the bridges. Therefore, the graph can be distorted in any way as long as the node and edge information remain intact. The network is a qualitative representation of the original, more complicated situation.

Since only the connection path (edge) information is relevant, the positions of the nodes within the graph may also be modified in any way without changing usefulness of the graph itself. Only preserving the edges and the degree of each node is relevant, not whether the edges are on the left or the right, curved or straight. The degree of a node is the number of edges emanating from it.

Though Euler's result was not practically useful, the result has been generalized for networks exhibiting specific node and edge characteristics. Carl Hierholzer posthumously published a proof of some of Euler's results in 1873. The terms *"Eulerian path"*, as the term for a solution of the bridge problem, and *"Eulerian circuit"*, to describe the different problem of starting and ending in the same spot, were introduced, extending Euler's fundamental work.

Following Euler's paper, the mathematical subdiscipline of topology, which is the study of shape, grew at a moderate pace throughout the 18th and 19th centuries, and then much more rapidly in the 20th. This growth was driven by numerous problems in calculus, motivated by questions arising from theoretical physics. By the end of the 20th century, the subject was clearly appreciated as one of the central subjects within pure mathematics. However, with the exception of some work in theoretical physics, it had not crossed the boundary from pure mathematics to a discipline that could be used in applications.

Topology was viewed as "the purest of the pure", and for many years there was open skepticism that the subject in fact had applications. Around the year 2000, though, the realization that topology *should* be applicable became current, and initiatives taken within the U.S. scientific funding agencies helped make that a reality.

1.4.1 Topology as a Theoretical Field

Topology is the study of shape, but it is the study of what might be called "generalized shape", in that it deals with mathematical objects that do not necessarily belong in the world of two or three dimensional shapes, but instead belong in very high (or even infinite) dimensions. For example, there are mathematical surfaces called n-spheres, each of which is the analogue of the standard sphere in $n+1$ *dimension*. Of course, one cannot actually visualize any of these higher dimensional surfaces, but they exist as mathematical objects and thinking about them geometrically and topologically is very fruitful mathematically.

A very important topic in topology is classification. Classification being defined in the simplest terms as creating shape analogies to a set of standard surfaces, i.e. classifying all possible higher dimensional surfaces, or classifying transformations between members in known families of surfaces, such as the family of all ellipses, which are topologically identical. These questions are of fundamental intellectual importance, but it is difficult to find immediate applications to real world problems. One fully expects that the kind of understanding obtained from this work will eventually be of value as the problems confronted in applications become more complex, but there is clearly a compelling interest in finding applications of topological methods in the here and now.

1.4.2 Applying Topology to Real World Problems: Topological Data Analysis

There are now numerous applications of topological methods in science and engineering. A very important one of these is in the study of large and complex data sets. Even within this area there are several threads, but the most directly applicable of these is what are called the *mapping thread*. This method at its core is an extension of Euler's idea described above in the bridge example, where one replaces a fairly complex domain problem with a simplified network which aids reasoning about the problem.

Consider the following example from pure mathematics.

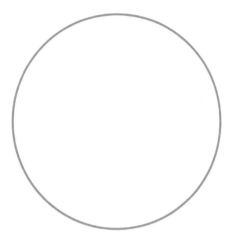

Figure 1.3: Simple Geometric Object, Circle

The circle is one of the simplest of geometric objects, but it is defined by infinite amounts of information, namely an infinite list of points and pairwise distances. On the other hand, we can consider the hexagon below.

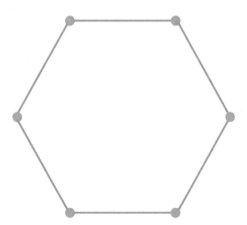

Figure 1.4: Simple Geometric Object, Hexagon

It has roughly the same shape as the circle. One could map each vertex of the hexagon to a point on circle and each edge to an arc. A hexagon could be thought of as a circle but in a different "font". However, the amount of data required to represent a circle is infinite, namely the positions of an infinite set of points, yet a hexagon can be completely described by a collection of 6 nodes and 6 edges, together with the information about which node belongs to which edge. From a computational point of view, the information content of a hexagon, our analogy to a circle, can fit into a couple of bytes. **So, if one is willing to sacrifice detail, one can represent the circle very compactly as a hexagon.** The hexagon is an example of a *topological network* or a *topological graph*. A topological network consists of a collection of *nodes* or *vertices* and a collection of edges, each edge connecting a pair of nodes. Topological networks will be very useful in topological data analysis, as a model for describing data sets. The simplification of the circle into a network can also be applied to data sets, where we are often happy to sacrifice a bit of detail to understand the overall picture. Thus, topology can be used to make efficient representations of data sets, which often clarify the structure of the data set and permit higher level reasoning about the data set. In addition, the representation is quite flexible, which permits additional accuracy for many problems relevant in data science. We will discuss how this is carried out later, but for now we will give some examples.

In each case, a picture of the data itself will be pictured in the center, the outcome of standard modeling techniques will be **on the left**, and the topological model network will be **on the right.**

Figure 1.5: Linear Regression vs. Topological Modeling

Looking at this data, we see clearly that it appears to lie along a line. Linear Regression will produce the line on the left, together with an equation describing the line. Of course, as in any modeling mechanism, there is loss of information in that many different data sets give rise to the same line. Nevertheless, in this case the algebraic model provides many capabilities, including prediction of one variable given another.

On the right is the topological network model. It is a schematic version of a line, described by a collection of nodes with edges connecting them. Each node represents a group of data points, grouped by some commonality, such as position on the graph. We notice, though, that the TDA model does not contain information about the placement or slope of the line. That information can be encoded by coloring each node of the network with the average value of the x and y coordinates of the data points contained in the node.

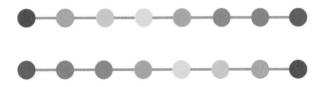

Figure 1.6: TDA Model Colored by X&Y Axis

The upper network is colored by the y-coordinate, and the lower one by the x-coordinate. The process of coloring the network by various interesting quantities is an extremely useful capability of the TDA method. Note that topological model does not contain information about the placement of the points, only information about which points are near which other points. This kind of information is very useful for the interrogation of data sets.

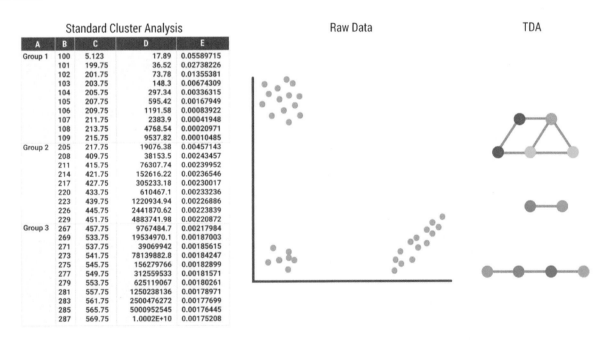

Figure 1.7: Standard Regression vs. Topological Models

Next, a data set that naturally breaks up into clusters is shown. There is a wide variety of algorithms for clustering. They produce as output a collection of non-overlapping groups of data points, so that every data point is in one of the groups. These groups can be displayed in a spreadsheet table, as we see above on the left. On the right-hand side, we see the TDA model, colored in this case by the y-coordinate. Notice that we see the decomposition into three groups, but also some reflection of the shape of each of the groups. The lower right hand cluster within the data is shown as a segment, namely the lowest connected component of the network on the right. The TDA representation of the data illustrates the clusters and the relationship between data and clusters, where the cluster chart is nothing more than a compilation of the group members, leaving interpretation to a skilled (expensive) eye. For a more detailed discussion, refer to the paper, "Why Topological Data Analysis Works"[12]

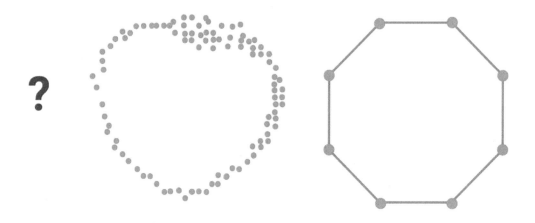

Figure 1.8: Topological Models with Loops

Periodic or recurrent behavior in a data set is a property that often results in networks such as the ones above. The data set has the shape of a kind of loop, although it is not perfectly round, or evenly distributed. There is no standard methodology for dealing with data having this shape, but the topological model on the right captures the "loopy" behavior.

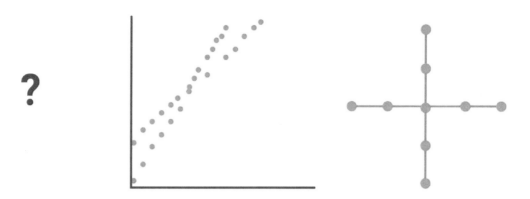

Figure 1.9: TDA for Two Lines Crossing

The data set in the middle is roughly decomposed into two crossing lines. Again, no standard methodology handles this kind of data well. For example, linear regression will produce a line that looks like this.

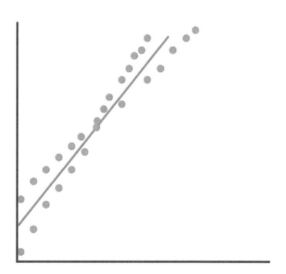

Figure 1.10: Linear Regression Plot of Two Lines Crossing

The linear approximation does not capture the fact that there are two lines, and instead only finds a kind of average between the lines. On the other hand, clustering will not find this decomposition either, since the lines overlap. The topological network on the right clearly identifies the decomposition and data shape.

In later chapters, it will be apparent that topological models have numerous capabilities that allow one to extract knowledge from real world data. A huge benefit of TDA is that much of the algebra that is usually used to analyze data is replaced by point and click operations of the network model on a computer screen.

1.4.3 Topology Meets Computer Science: Big Data Meets its Match

As part of pure mathematics for many years, most of topology has been carried out by hand, which is not very efficient for large problems. In order to make topology useful in the real world it's important to automate calculations; *seven bridges and two islands as opposed to 50 terabytes of data per second*. Although we might see a loopy data set such as the one above, and by hand construct a network approximation as shown above, one needs to find systematic methods to construct the networks automatically.

There are a number of aspects to topology that lend themselves to automation:

- Scalability: The creation of topological models is highly parallelizable in very simple ways, which allows one to deal effectively with very large data sets. Fundamentally, the time issues involved in dealing with large data can be effectively mitigated by supplying more computing resources.
- Flexibility of analysis parameters: A well designed user interface allows topological models to operate by constructing an abstract network of high-dimensional datasets, laying it out on the screen for the user, and permitting the user to operate on it with point and click gestures. This flexibility allows the user to configure analyses, find local groups of interest, color by quantities of interest, display explanatory variables for groups, and easily incorporates new information into the analysis as initial results are returned.
- Acts on the data not on hypothetical outcomes: The network construction requires very primitive information concerning the data, namely a quantitative measure of similarity of data points, rather than a more specialized model; often these specialized models are based on hypothesis, skewing the analysis toward what the user thinks they know. By acting on data, it permits the analysis of many different data types, provided one can construct simple measures of similarity of data points. This has been carried out with very good results in the analysis of clinical variation. See the case studies below.

1.5 Application to Different Industries

Because of its flexibility and its power to handle complex data, as described above, TDA is able to deal with data coming from all industries. The data is not required to be numerical, and is not required to be well summarized by spread sheet tables. For this reason it is appropriate for data for the highly variable data types that arise in different industries. For example:

- Electronic medical records
- Clinical care path time series
- Free text as arises in reporting or sentiment analysis
- Log files occurring in cybersecurity data
- Survey data

This same flexibility permits TDA to merge and compare data of different types associated to the same subjects, and ultimately to see what information about the subjects are carried by the different data types.

The following case studies are real world examples of topological modeling illustrating the concepts discussed in this chapter.

Chapter 1

1.6 Case Study 1: World Values Survey

1.6.1 Case Study Highlights

- Data from the World Values Survey is analyzed to gain understanding of responses to questions concerning a population's values and beliefs.
- Illustrates how multidimensional complex data can be represented in a 2-dimensional graph.
- Demonstrates how the highlighting of data characteristics through color, position and shape.

1.6.2 Introduction

The *World Values Survey* is a research project conducted by a worldwide network of social scientists, who survey people around the world concerning their values and beliefs. The surveys consist of approximately 250 questions which are designed to assess respondent's values and beliefs, as well as other conditions, such as personal well being. It began in 1981, and has been carried out in six "waves", with a seventh one to begin in 2017. Data from this survey has been used in numerous publications, and gives many interesting insights into how values vary across cultures. It is a very natural data set for the application of Machine Intelligence.

1.6.3 Results

Within the data set are a number of questions that concern the respondent's trust in particular institutions. The question asks the respondent to indicate the degree of confidence he/she has in an institution, on a scale from 1 to 4. The institutions include the federal government, churches, labor unions, the press, and numerous others. Selecting these questions produces a data set which populates a small spreadsheet, with 11 columns. Selecting the respondents from the United States gives approximately 2000 rows. A topological model of this data looks like this.

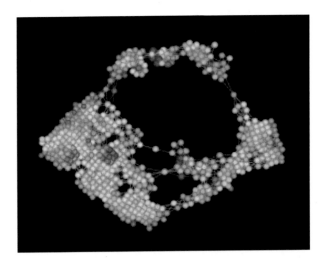

Figure CS1.1: Example of Topological Model

One of the capabilities in the topological model is to interrogate it by selecting groups of nodes using standard lassoing techniques. In this way, we can select groups in the four "corners" of the model, North, South, East, and West. They turn out to be very different from each other. For example, the group in the western corner has elevated trust in all institutions. The group in the southern corner has elevated trust in the police, the armed forces, and the churches, the eastern corner has elevated trust in only the churches, and the northern group has generally low trust in all institutions. The topological modeling methodology also permits coloring the model by other quantities. For example, there is another question in the survey that asks for the respondent's assessment of his/her placement on left/right, liberal/conservative scale, on a scale of 1 to 10. One can also color the topological model by this quantity, and the resulting coloring looks as follows.

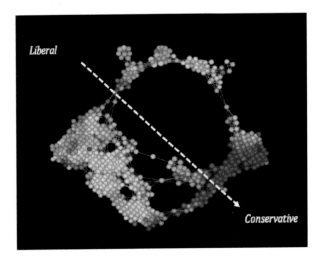

Figure CS1.2: How Coloring Highlights a Topological Model –Example A

Red coloring corresponds to positioning on the right side of the scale, blue to the left. In this case, one sees that it roughly corresponds to movement from the upper left to the lower right. One can also color by the aggregate value of trust in all institutions, and the resulting coloring is displayed below. We describe those with high aggregate trust in institutions as "establishment", those with low trust as non-establishment.

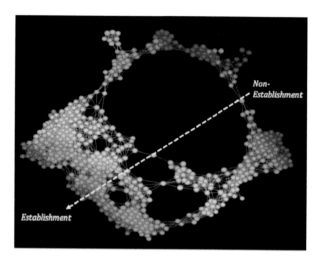

Figure CS1.3: How Coloring Highlights a Topological Model – Example B

In this case, this quantity describes an upper right to lower left motion. We see that ones left/right status is independent of one's establishment/non-establishment status. Another question asks to what extent a respondent has control over his/her life. Coloring by the response to this question is shown below.

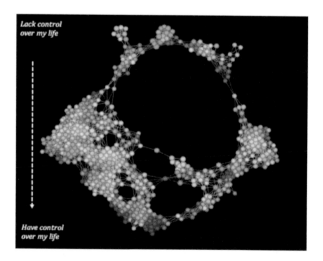

Figure CS1.4: How Coloring Highlights a Topological Model – Example C

In this case, the movement appears to go from top to bottom, with the north corner having relatively low control of their life, and the south corner having a good deal of control.

1.7 Case Study 2: Analysis of Twitter and the 2013 Presidential Inauguration

1.7.1 Contributors:

Damir Herman, Alexis Johnson, Jesse Paquette

1.7.2 Case Study Highlights

- Twitter feeds from the 2013 Presidential Inauguration are analyzed by topological methods.
- Demonstrates how TDA can be employed to segment complex data.

1.7.3 Introduction

A collection of 12,000 tweets including reference to the word "inauguration" were collected, and analyzed using Machine Intelligence. Several interesting segments were found.

1.7.4 Results

A collection of 12,000 tweets referencing the inauguration were collected. The most frequently occurring 56,000 words occurring in the corpus were selected, and each tweet was then assigned its vector of "word counts" for each of these words. The normalization procedure known as tf-idf (term frequency-inverse document frequency) was applied to account for the fact that occurrences of infrequently occurring words are more significant than more frequently occurring words. With this vector representation, standard metrics and lenses produced the topological model shown below.

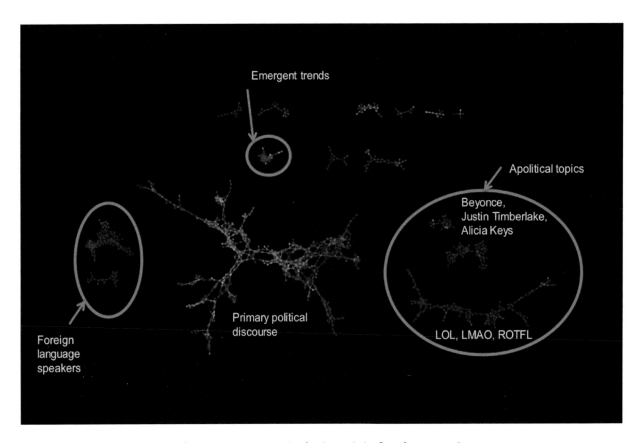

Figure CS2.1: Topological Model of Twitter Feeds

There are several interesting features. There is a group on the right labeled "apolitical topics" that consist of discussions of non-political events going on around the inauguration. The middle structure labeled "primary political discourse" contains discussion of political matters surrounding the inauguration. There is, however, a smaller group labeled "emergent trends", that consists entirely of tweets concerning Rand Paul's filibuster, which was then in the very early stages of discussion. Soon after the inauguration it became a much larger subject of discussion, and ultimately took place in March of 2013. Finally, there is a group on the far left labeled foreign language speakers. Although the tweets are in English, usage by foreign language speakers can be significantly different from that of native speakers of English, and this is reflected in this group. One can select this group, and perform analysis exclusively on it, to obtain a more fine-grained analysis, which separates different language groups, and separates political tweets from non-political ones for Spanish language speakers.

This case study demonstrates the ability to segment data into coherent groups, as well as the capability of obtaining higher resolution analyses by selecting subsets.

Chapter 2: What is Data? Complex Data vs. Big Data

"It is a capital mistake to theorize before one has data. Insensibly one begins to twist facts to suit theories, instead of theories to suit facts."
-Sherlock Holmes[13]

2.1 Chapter Preview

- Discussion of the origins of large data sets with examples of rapid growth and the need for automated analysis
- Define the meaning of data and data sets
- Define Big Data and analytics and how they are related to data science
- Describe data science and the various aspects of its components
- Define data complexity and how it relates to data analysis, with an introduction to methods of dealing with some aspects of complexity.
- Case Studies
  - Case Study 3: Financial Services Anti-Money Laundering
  - Case Study 4: Cybersecurity

2.2 Introduction

The terms used to describe data and the analysis of data are thrown around loosely by marketers and journalist, leaving some words used to describe technical specifics in an ambiguous state. Talking about "collecting data" and "analyzing data" seems to be in vogue, but what do these terms actually mean and to what end? The following chapter explores various practical aspects of data, Big Data (and big data), analytics and data science.

2.3 Origin of Large Data Sets

Our capability to collect very large amounts of data has increased tremendously over the last quarter century. The general population, whether knowingly or unwittingly, appears to accept the collection of a great deal of data concerning their lives in databases (Facebook™, Google™ search, Fitbits™, etc.). The end result is the creation of many very large data sets in a wide variety of domains awaiting analysis to extract useful knowledge.

Here are some examples of large data sets.

- The SETI program (Search for Extra-Terrestrial Intelligence) monitors electromagnetic radiation for signs of transmissions from other planets. It is constantly collecting data at very fine time intervals, with very high spatial resolution, and very high frequency resolution. In 2008, it was collecting 100 terabytes per year. The most recent version of the project, which begins in 2016, will be collecting petabytes of data per *day*.

- In August of 2013, Salesforce™ was processing 1.3 billion transactions per day. Amazon™ alone averaged 26.5 million transactions per day in 2012. In either case, the data set of all these transactions is obviously of a great interest, and clearly an opportunity awaiting new ways of mining it.

- There are an estimated 1.2 billion visits to physician offices, hospital outpatient clinics, and emergency rooms in the United States per year. By law, under the American Recovery and Reinvestment Act, each such visit must be electronically stored and generates electronic data about the clinical condition of the patient, what interventions were performed, and billing, among other things.

- The German Climate Computing Center in Hamburg maintains an archive of more than 40 petabytes of climate data. This archive is expected to grow at a rate of roughly 75 petabytes per year for the next five years.

- Twitter's collection of tweets can be viewed as a very rich data set, which can be very informative about trends in society, as well as information about attitudes and sentiment. There are around 6,000 tweets per *second*, and around 200 billion tweets per year. One expects this rate to grow, but even if the rate remains constant, the accumulated data will be growing at an enormous rate.

These are only some of the most obvious examples. It is clear that throughout society, and within all areas of endeavor, data collection is growing and the problem of making sense of it is a fundamental one.

2.3.1 Definition of Data

Starting with a definition of data, according to Merriam-Webster[14], data is

1. factual information (as measurements or statistics) used as a basis for reasoning, discussion, or calculation
2. information output by a sensing device or organ that includes both useful and irrelevant or redundant information and must be processed to be meaningful
3. information in numerical form that can be digitally transmitted or processed

For our purposes "raw data" and "data" are the same thing and refer to unanalyzed data. Data in its raw form is inundated with noise, irrelevant information and misleading patterns that need to be removed in order to apply the data set to useful purpose.

A data set is a collection of stored information. IBM initially coined the term to mean a computer file. For the purpose of this book it assumes data sets are in electronic storage. A data set could be data, the transitional results of analysis awaiting more analysis, or the final results.

2.3.2 Definition of Big Data: There is a Difference Between Data and Big Data and it's Not Just Size.

The term, "Big Data" is not very well defined. It can refer to very large spreadsheets, but also to data of many different types where there are many data points and/or many features describing the data. For the purpose of this book, "Big Data" will mean any data set for which the simplest modes of analysis fail either because of the scale or complexity of the definition of the data.

Some say the term Big Data is a truncated form of Big Data Analytics, largely vendors of data analytic tools. For our purposes, though the notion of Big Data is the characteristic of the data set. The analysis of data is the province of data science which will be discussed in the next section.

All data (Big or otherwise) has four characteristics[15][16][17] volume, velocity, variety and veracity. There is an additional notion, that of complexity, which is an informally defined idea depending on the other four. Complexity of a data set comes in two forms, namely its *structural complexity* and its *format complexity.* The complexity of data sets is discussed in more detail later in the chapter.

CHARACTERISTIC	DEFINITION
Volume	The physical size of the data set.
Velocity	How fast the data set is growing or changing. Note that this applies only when the data is varying (increasing, perhaps) over time.
Variety	The specificity of the data and the number of different types of features describing the data.
Veracity	The quality of the data set. Refers to the biases, noise, continuity and abnormality in data. Also, the data's relevance to the problem being analyzed. *Some add a fifth and sixth "V" for volatility and validity, which refers to the timeliness or shelf life and the relevance of the data, but volatility and validity are included in veracity, so it seems redundant to list them as unique characteristics of the data set
Complexity	An informally defined property depending on the other four properties.

Table 2.1: Characteristics of Data

2.4 Defining Analytics and Data Science

2.4.1 Analytics

Analysis and *analytics* are old words, predating data science by many centuries. The first known use of analytics is ~1590, as adjective forms of analysis.[18] These words have recently been co-opted by marketing departments as nouns and now are part of the data vocabulary. Analytics as a noun describing a data product maybe first appeared in 2002, with the joining of "Predictive" to "Analytics", coined as means to differentiate a data product from its competitors.[19] In 2005, Google coined, "Google Analytics", and others have followed with Amazon Mobile Analytics, Energy Analytics, Products Analytics Manager, etc. Since "analytics" is being widely linked with branded products, its meaning, as with all marketing terms, is dependent on how the product marketing department wishes to define it. Analytics has become a "mushy" word for descriptive purposes, because the meaning is highly volatile.

For our purposes the word "analytics" is synonymous with the real-world functions within data science of analyzing and modeling data, with the caveat, "exclusively by computer analysis". It's not analytics if the analysis is performed by insight alone, "eying it". Since data science can be both practical and theoretical, analytics refers to practical applications exclusively.

2.4.2 Data Science is Analytics and Much More

When considering all areas of employment, data science is one of the fastest growing fields. According to a McKinsey study, the demand for data scientists is increasing so rapidly, there will be a 50-60% gap in the supply of data scientists versus demand by 2018.[20] This makes perfect sense in that with the explosive growth of data, the need for people to analyze it is also growing explosively.

The Harvard Business Review calls data science, *"the sexiest job of the 21st century."*[21]

New York University defines data science as[22]

"...an evolutionary step in interdisciplinary fields like business analysis that incorporate computer science, modeling, statistics, analytics, and mathematics.

At its core, data science involves using automated methods to analyze massive amounts of data and to extract knowledge from them. With such automated methods turning up everywhere from genomics to high-energy physics, data science is helping to create new branches of science, and influencing areas of social science and the humanities. The trend is expected to accelerate in the coming years as data from mobile sensors, sophisticated instruments, the web, and more, grows. In academic research, we will see an increasingly large number of traditional disciplines spawning new sub-disciplines with the adjective "computational" or "quantitative" in front of them. In industry, we will see data science transforming everything from healthcare to media."

The need for data science described in more poetic terms:

- Data science is the Dutch boy with his finger in the dyke of data.
- We are generating so much data we better figure out ways to automate our way out of the hole we are digging for ourselves.
- We are so data rich, yet so insight poor.

Data science has its theoretical aspects to it, as does physics and mathematics, but for this book on Machine Intelligence, we'll restrict our definition of data science to the practical application to solve real world problems.

The categories of tasks performed in data science are the cleaning, analyzing, modeling and building useful tools from data. These categories are described in the table below.

CATEGORIES	DEFINITION
Cleaning	Also known as "data wrangling," "data munging" and "data janitor work." It involves making sure that data is consistently formatted and conforms to some set of rules. Fixing formats, filling in missing values, correcting erroneous values and standardizing categories are all aspects of cleaning. Cleaning is the most labor intensive aspect of data science and can represent 50% to 80% of the effort.
Analyzing	Building the hypotheses in an attempt to understand what the data is saying. Data visualization, segmentation and clustering are all aspects of analysis. Also included are exploratory data analysis (EDA), and confirmatory data analysis (CDA), where EDA focuses on discovering new features in the data and CDA on confirming or falsifying existing hypotheses.
Modeling	The means by which a prediction or forecast is possible given the data set. Also included in modeling is a measure of forecast error.
Building Useful Tools	The practical application of the model. The building of a chart, dashboard, or an application that packages the model as a useful tool.

Table 2.2: Practical Data Science Tasks

2.5 Components of Data Complexity: Size Doesn't Matter...much

Although we have made a compelling case that the amount of data available for analysis is growing at an accelerating rate, the difficulties in gaining actionable understanding from that data are not all, or even mostly, about the size of the data. Size is only one smaller aspects of data complexity and seems to be the smallest factor of difficulty, among other data characteristics, such as member structure and format, even ranking below data variety, veracity and velocity.

As introduced above, complexity is a superset characteristic of a data set. How one gets from a data set to actionable understanding is though data science. How and what aspect of data science is employed to any aspect of the data set is determined by the complexity of the data set.

An often-overlooked characteristic of data set complexity relates to degree of difficulty to develop strategies for analyzing the data. Potentially, due to a lack of tools or insight, a "non-prognostic" data set is data whose predictive power will remain a mystery. Further, even if one can develop strategies for the analysis of portions of a difficult data set, a "*piecewise prognostic*" data set may provide results that are ambiguous or inconclusive, which is uninformative. Though one may view "difficulty of analysis" as a failure of data science, it most certainly is a characteristic of the data and is a data type that is worthy to note, if for no other reason as a warning to the users of a model to step carefully.

2.5.1 Data Complexity Defined

To determine whether a data set is of *high or low* complexity, we'll first divide the notion of data complexity into two categories:

- Format Complexity
- Structural Complexity

2.5.1.1 Format Complexity

Format complexity, also known as data type complexity, encompasses volume, velocity and variety. Format complexity can be exhibited in a number of different forms.

- A very large number of columns in a spreadsheet.
- Time varying nature of a data set.
- A large number of different types of columns in a spreadsheet.
- Failure of the data to be adequately represented by a spreadsheet.

So, a spreadsheet with numerical entries of the same data type and with a moderate number of columns would be considered a data set of low complexity. Complexity if of course a relative description, so "high" and "low" complexity may mean different things in different contexts. The most important and challenging high complexity data sets are those for which the last type occurs, i.e. in which the data set is not naturally faithfully represented in a spreadsheet.

To get an idea of the kinds of data that might be regarded as high complexity, here is a list of some datasets exhibiting a complex data type.

- Molecular structures are a quite complex data type. They can be described as lists of positions of atoms and lists of bonds, but such a list cannot be analyzed effectively with standard methods since positions for the same atom might be different depending on the viewpoint of the imaging technology.
- Imaging technology can produce databases of images. These images are often stored as lists of pixels with gray scale values, but the desired information is not usually very transparent from this representation. Analyzing and even searching such databases is a very difficult task due to the complexity of the data.

- Databases consisting of visits to a webpage are a very complex data type. The length of the visit is variable, as are the possible behaviors within the session. Data sets of such sessions present substantial difficulties in analysis.
- A data set of "shopping baskets", i.e. collections of products available for sale in a store, has a complex data type.
- Any data set of documents of free text is a complex data type. We have mentioned the Twitter set above, but even much smaller corpora of text are of interest.

2.5.1.2 Structural Complexity

The other component of data complexity is structural complexity. Structural complexity refers to the nature of the mathematical interrelationships among the data points, i.e. linear, logarithmic, spherical, time dependent, etc. Structural complexity encompasses the veracity of the data set. Validity and volatility are other "Vs" used to describe structural complexity, though for our purpose we've included these in the term veracity. Sub-components of structural complexity also include data completeness and data quality.

Even data sets that are small in size and that have a simple data type, low format complexity, can exhibit structural complexity, making the data set complex.

The following are several examples that have the format of a spreadsheet with 2 columns and <100 rows, that are considered "structurally complex".

Example 1:

Figure 2.1: Example of Structurally Complex Data

This is a data set from a gene expression study of rheumatoid arthritis[23]. Notice that it does not have a simple form, such as a line, which describes it. Instead, it requires the case by case analysis of the various regions.

Example 2:

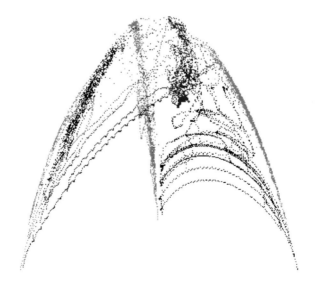

Figure 2.2: Example of Structurally Complex Data

This data set comes from a study of certain quantities produced in mathematical experiments with cellular automata. The intricate structure does not lend itself to simple geometric descriptions.

Example 3:

Figure 2.3: Example of Structurally Complex Data

This data set comes from a study of sugar consumption compared to body mass index. The complexity of the picture comes from the fact that the study was done in different countries, and that each country had incomplete information. Each of the arcs corresponds to a different country.

2.5.1.3 Data Completeness

Data completeness specifically concerns itself with missing data and is a component of veracity. Even highly structured data can be rendered complex if there is a great deal of missing data. For example, a spreadsheet with many empty cells can be quite difficult to deal with. This happens with many kinds of data, and it is very important to have strategies to deal with it. The first thing to observe is that missing data occurs for different reasons, and the reason may affect how one deals with it. One can divide the different situations into four groups.

1. Missing completely at random (MCAR): The data is missing because of a completely random process, unrelated to any systematic phenomenon. This would for example be the case if one had a spreadsheet, and simply removed the entries in cells, where the cells are chosen completely at random, regardless of the nature of the data.

2. Missing at random (MAR): The data is missing because of a random selection, related to something systematic concerning the source of the data, but unrelated to the specific variables in the data. For example, one might suspect that boys might be more careless in filling out a survey than girls, and therefore that although both genders would include some missing data it would be much more heavily concentrated among the boys, even though gender might not appear as a field in the data.

3. Missing not at random (MNAR): The missing data might be strongly correlated with specific features of the data. One example, would be data consisting of measurements of a collection of sensors, in which all the sensors but one always produce a result, with the remaining one occasionally producing no response.

4. Censored data: This occurs when for one reason or another one is not able to obtain a precise numerical value of a variable, but a description of a range in which the value lies. For example, it might be specified as greater than some fixed value, or less than a fixed value. This might occur in a study where one of the variables is survival, and a subject leaves the study at some point.

There are a number of ways of dealing with missing data. We will describe some, but the whole problem is a very fundamental one in the field of statistics and is the subject of intensive study in the statistics community.

- Drop data points: Given a data set with some missing data, one can remove all data points for which any data is missing. When the data set is a spreadsheet, this means dropping any rows with empty cells. This is a very natural approach, but in situations where there is a great deal of missing data, one loses a great deal of information this way. As mentioned in (2) and (3) above, this could be problematic if the data missing correlates with features of the data points, or with some underlying "populations" within the data which might themselves be correlated with features, because in that situation one is skewing the analysis by removing these points. One therefore tends to adopt this method when one believes that one is in situation (1) above.

- Drop columns: One might alternatively drop all columns that include some missing data. Of course, this is only practical if there are only a small number of columns that include missing data. One would also tend to adopt this approach if one is convinced that the column to be dropped is not one of *the* driving features in the data.

- Imputation of numerical features: *Imputation* refers to a process that assigns a value to the missing data based on properties of the other points and columns in the data set. It can be done when the data is structured as a spreadsheet, so that the notions of rows and columns make sense. Also, it is done differently depending on whether the values are numerical or categorical. For numerical features, there are a number of straightforward approaches. The first would be to replace each missing cell by the mean or median of all the values appearing in the column containing it. A more sophisticated approach would replace the value by the output of a regression procedure based on some or all of the other variables. One would perform a least squares regression that treats some or all of the other variables as independent variables, and the column containing the missing data as an outcome variable.

- Imputation of categorical features: If one has a binary (0/1) feature, one can modify the data so as to make the feature have a continuous value lying between 0 and 1. In some situations, one can also retain the binary property of the variable by approximating it by logistic regression using continuous variables in the data together with a 0/1 classifier. Another method is to use *discriminant analysis* for the imputation. There are methods that permit using categorical variables as the independent variables as well. This is very rich and complicated area of study. For further information, please consult, "Regression with SPSS."[24]

- Creating a new value: In dealing with categorical variables, one can add a value "missing" to the possible values of the variable, and simply assign each cell with missing value this new value. A related method additionally creates a binary variable attached to the given variable that takes the value 0 when the cell has a value and the value 1 when the data is missing. In situations where there are many missing values, this can be useful.

- Survival analysis: This is an area of study that, among other things, concerns itself with methods to deal with censored data. An excellent reference to this complicated can be found in "Survival Analysis: Techniques for Censored and Truncated Data"[25].

2.5.1.4 Data Quality

Another component of veracity and a related problem to completeness, concerns itself with the detection of errors within the data, and the correction of such errors. There are a number of ways to locate likely errors.

- In a situation where rules apply, one can locate errors by searching for data points where one or more rules are not satisfied. For example, if a company has a maximum salary of $200,000, any salary entry which is reported to be higher than $200,000 or less than $0.00 is obviously in error.
- For numerical values, one can describe the distribution of all values taken by the variable, and determine which values appear to be outliers. Such data elements can then be checked to see if they in fact are in error.
- In many situations, it is an important constraint that some fields have the property that the values must be unique, i.e. that no two different data points have the same value in that field. This would be the case for unique identifiers, social security numbers, and serial numbers for various kinds of items.
- When one has data sets consisting of text, there are often syntax errors which can be detected, and for which it is clear what the error is, so that they can be corrected.
- Sometimes an entry given in a cell is not among the permitted values for the column containing the cell.

Chapter 2

2.6 Case Study 3: Financial Services Anti-Money Laundering (AML)[26] [27]

2.6.1 Case Study Highlights:

- How AML efforts are hampered by data incompatibilities, data obfuscation, reliance on manual processes, and poor use of Machine Intelligence.
- How Machine Intelligence techniques could be applied to the current manual processes to increase efficiency of detection.
- How microsegmentation techniques could be applied.

2.6.2 Introduction

Money Laundering is the illegal concealment of money by individuals or entities (Money-transfer firms, foreign institutions, non-profits, etc.) using global financial systems to blur the audit trail. Anti-Money Laundering (AML) is a mitigation process implemented by large banking institutions to detect, prevent and report instances. Failure by financial institutions to have adequate protection processes can result in massive regulatory fines totaling in the billions of dollars.

The data relevant to money laundering cases are incredibly complex, consisting of many different types of data:

- KYC (customer) data
- SWIFT (Wire-Transfer) Transaction time-series
- SAR (Suspicious Activity Report) Filings
- External Customer Data, Watch Lists
- Analyst Notes (typically unstructured text)

By definition, "successful" money launderers are very good at hiding their tracks. Money laundering takes place using three components:

- Placement, which is the movement of cash from its source. It is characterized by cash smuggling, blending funds with other legitimate funds or asset conversion.
- Layering, which is the practice of converting cash into other financial assets then selling those and buying different assets, to make the cash difficult to trace.
- Integration, which is using the laundered money for legitimate purposes, such as buying a business or purchase of an asset.

Once laundered, it is very difficult for law enforcement officials to track and seize funds. Assets may be sold to other customers or customer's customers, forming pseudo customers, to further obfuscate the transaction flow. Moreover, using shell corporations and pseudonyms, employing data storage in multiple source systems and incompatible data structures, the data tracks of laundered money are increasingly difficult to reconcile.

2.6.3 Results

Current AML processes typically have hand-coded money laundering rule patterns to evaluate each transaction for each geographical or type of business. Subject matter experts encode established patterns such as high repetitive number of small transactions, money flows in and out of high-risk countries, etc. The process of setting these rules is biased, time-intensive and fragmented across geographies. The transactions that have been flagged are then sent to analysts to manually dispose of individual cases in a series of escalation steps termed L1/L2/L3. Large analyst teams can lead to lack of uniformity and potential for insider threat in review processes. In current AML processes, the segments that emerge are typically static and coarse since they only consider a limited set of factors. Moreover, they are done manually and separately for customer data and transaction data and have trouble effectively capturing the complex feature interactions. This has a massive effect downstream as the rules are applied on a set of coarsely defined segments. This can make rules difficult to tune as too low of a threshold triggers too many alerts (and people to review), too high of a threshold brings more regulatory scrutiny.

Machine Intelligence can make the AML process much more efficient. Micro-segmentation is done upstream on the various input data streams, taking into account complex transaction and entity relationships to relate similarities across customers and transactions. Rules can be tuned to provide analysts with feedback on false positive and false negatives rates. Finally, a consistent interface for escalating and disposing of individual cases can be automated with the drivers surfaced clearly.

2.7 Case Study 4: Cybersecurity[28] [29]

Title: Cyber Attack Analyses Using Ayasdi

2.7.1 Contributors:

Dr. Frederick W. Kagan, PhD, Director, Critical Threats Project, American Enterprise Institute & Institute of the Study of War

Tommy Stiansen, CTO, Norse Networks

2.7.2 Case Study Highlights

- Machine Intelligence is used to find patterns within Cyber Attacks.
- Using MI, similarity analysis is performed identifying clusters and nodes of suspect source and destination IPs, ports, protocols and timing.

2.7.3 Introduction

In a study of a cyber attack on Sharif University's Norse System, Machine Intelligence tools are used to identify and segment details regarding the source, time and other dimensions of the cyber attackers.

2.7.4 Results

Individual events are likely to appear in more than one cluster or node. This is because there is a diversity of elements within the event that may be similar to certain events in some ways and to other events in others. An event could be placed in a node with other events that happened at around the same time, but it could also appear in a different node with events using the same IP address or ports that occurred at different times.

The figures below are colored according to IP address, with each node taking on the color assigned to the IP address to which most of the events in that node belong. The graph reveals one large and complex group of nodes (group 2) dominated by IP addresses tightly concentrated in three ranges (red, teal, and blue), with a few nodes in other ranges or with intermingled IP addresses. It also shows a second dense group of nodes (group 1) with many colors spread all through it, indicating that a number of events with very different IP addresses are all linked by some other factor. The smaller groups repeat this phenomenon with many fewer events.

Examination of the underlying data shows that all of the events in group 1 used the same source port: 53. The 249 events in this group are, in fact, part of a port scan conducted by systems on several IP addresses trying to find vulnerabilities by trying many destination ports to see if any are open. The larger and more complex pattern of group 2 includes 1,118 attacks from more than 126 IPs registered to Sharif University. The nodes are colored by IP address, showing clearly that there were two major groups of IPs (red and teal) and one smaller group (blue) of IPs involved in the attack.

Flares indicate sets of data that start with some commonality and then diverge — a series of events might start at roughly the same time from similar IP addresses using the same ports, but the ports on one set of IP addresses might increase over time while those of another set decrease.

Loops indicate cyclical data. The same general collection of ports used repeatedly over the course of many days or months, for example, could produce a loop. The shapes of the red and teal groups indicate cyclic but irregular patterns in the data. Some element of the events kept changing but with repetitions of some sort over time.

The common element binding these nodes appears to be that they all were directed against port 445, regardless of their source, target, or date. Port 445 has long been a target of malware and remains a potential vulnerability for poorly secured machines.

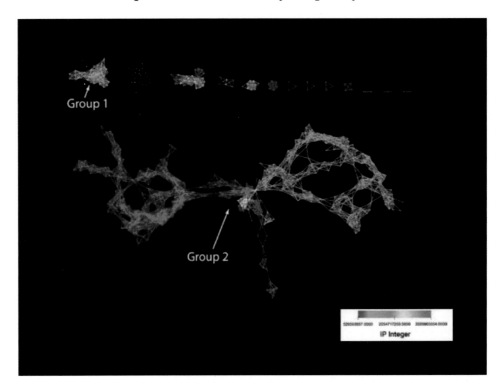

Figure CS4.1: Visualization of Sharif University Attacks on Norse System

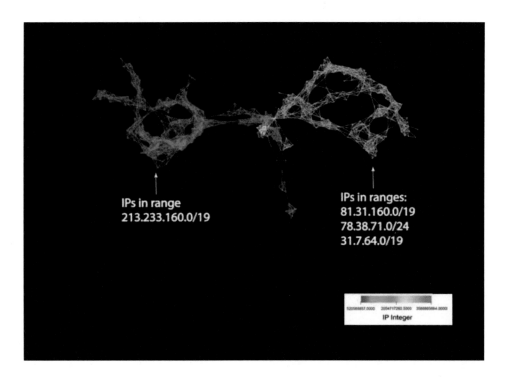

Figure CS4.2: IP Ranges from Sharif University Attacks

The Ayasdi tools have the ability to reshape the visualization by focusing on a particular element of the data, which it calls a "data lens™." When applied, a data lens focused on the source port of the events to produce a chart and colored it according to source port. Group 2 from the original chart is here, broken into three subgroups of very similar color patterns (yellow-green), showing that all of these IPs used a common selection of source ports ranging from 1037 to 4987 (with a handful of outliers).

The clusters themselves are distinguished from one another by the IP address ranges of the attacker. The visualizations clearly show multiple IP addresses from two different address ranges all using virtually the same set of source ports to attack the identical destination port. Closer examination of the data shows an additional pattern—in almost every case, the attacking IP hit its target from the same port twice within two to three seconds. In most cases, each IP conducted only one such paired attack. The attacks hit sensors on 56 different IPs in Australia, Bulgaria, Germany, France, Britain, Liechtenstein, Portugal, Russia, Thailand, Turkey, and the US.

The value of compromises using port 445 increases with the number of computers that can be effectively spoofed. It makes sense, then, that the attacks emanating from Sharif University hit so many different sensors. These attacks do not necessarily harm the target machine but, rather, represent an early-stage effort to develop a compromised cyber infrastructure from which to conduct future attacks of another variety. There is

Chapter 2

no way to know if the operation stopped because its controllers gave up on it, were caught somehow that has not made its way into the news, or simply obtained enough compromised systems to satisfy themselves. Considering the duration and breadth of the attacks, it is improbable to the point of nullity that they were unable to compromise any systems.

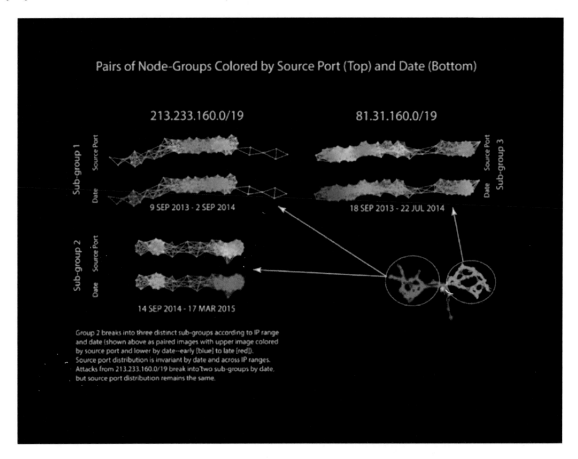

Figure CS4.3: IP Ranges from Sharif University, Colored by Source Port and Date

The application of visualization to large-scale cyber activity data offers the possibility of visualizing botnets and other complicated distributed cyber-reconnaissance and attack capabilities. The ability to color-wash by various fields facilitates the rapid identification of commonalities among seemingly-disparate threat nodes and behaviors. The ability to form geometrical patterns reflecting periodicity and inherent patterns within the data help separate signal from the enormous amount of noise inherent in cyber-event data. These capabilities together allow cyber-analysts to zoom in quickly on collections of IP addresses and patterns of cyber-reconnaissance or attack that adversaries intentionally seek to obfuscate. Further, analysis using visualization tools facilitates disaggregating the behaviors of individual reconnaissance- or attack-nodes into sub-groupings that may reflect the appearance or disappearance of individual actors or changes in underlying reconnaissance- or attack-algorithms. We anticipate that further work could begin to match algorithmic reconnaissance- or attack-patterns used by various actors against different targets to evaluate the spread of specific algorithms, as well as to surface questions about the relationships among apparently separate attackers. The ability to visualize patterns in large amounts of cyber-traffic data opens a new prospect in the field of strategic cyber-defense analysis.

Chapter 3: Data Cleaning: Organizing the Data Set

"Organizing is what you do before you do something, so that when you do it,
it is not all mixed up"
-Winnie the Pooh (AA Milne)

3.1 Chapter Preview

- The purpose of data cleaning and why it's important
- Data cleaning and its relationship to data quality
- Data cleaning and its relationship to data complexity
- Overview various data cleaning processes
- The challenges a data cleaner faces when dealing with complex healthcare data
- Streamlining the data cleaning process of healthcare data with data set standards: HL7 and FHIR.
- Case Studies
  - Case Study 5: Data Prep and Upload for Cardiac Surgery

3.2 Introduction

In the last chapter, we briefly introduced data cleaning. Given data cleaning is the most labor intensive aspect of data science and can represent 50%-80% of the effort, it's a topic worthy of a more complete discussion.

Data cleaning is the discipline within data science that improves organization of the initial data, by working on various attributes of data quality. In order to prepare the data set for predictive analysis and modeling, the data cleaning step is required. In this chapter the cleaning process is overviewed and discussed.

3.3 The Purpose of Data Cleaning

Data cleaning is a post-data collection process. The purpose of cleaning data is to improve the quality of the data set and thereby increase its predictive capabilities. Data cleaning concerns itself with removing redundancies, filling in missing values, correcting erroneous values, standardizing categories, determining similarity, filtering noise, removing irrelevant information and misleading patterns, within a data set. The end result of data cleaning is providing a training data set, of high predictive value to the researcher for analytic purposes.

The data cleaning procedures employed to clean the data depends on the nature of data. Data can be qualitative (categorical) or quantitative. Qualitative data generally has no natural order. Qualitative data is often described as discrete and finite.

Quantitative data is data consisting of numerical values. Quantitative data could be integers or floating point numbers that may consist of simple sets of numbers or complex arrays of numbers in multiple dimensions, captured over time. Quantitative data can be either discrete and finite or continuous and infinite.

- Examples of qualitative data: eye and hair color, social security numbers, postal addresses, etc.
- Examples of quantitative data: height, age, a continuum of location points across space-time, etc.
- Data exhibiting a natural order is considered ordinal data, whereas data not possessing a natural order is considered nominal data.

3.3.1 Data Cleaning Improves Data Quality

In the last chapter, we discussed dataset complexity and its components. Data complexity and data quality interact, but are indirectly related. Complexity is an informal notion depending on many intrinsic aspects of the dataset, including quality, though is not determined by any one characteristic of quality.[30]

Data quality relates to the relative prognostic character a data set possesses. Data complexity relates to the fundamental relationship between the data itself and the difficulty associated with interpreting it.

The dimensions of data quality are listed in the table below.

CHARACTERISTIC	DEFINITION
Accessibility	The degree to which the data is provided in a usable form. One million hand written entries on paper vs. data stored in a database is an example of accessibility.
Accuracy	The degree to which the data represents the real world they are attempting to predict. The correctness of the data. Incorrect spellings, digit inversions and misrepresentations, etc. are examples of inaccurate data. Accuracy is not precision.
Believability	Related to the veracity of the source of the data. Is the source reliable and trustworthy?
Completeness	The degree the data is all there, regarding missing values or values in an unusable state.
Conformity	The structure of the data. The degree to which it is presented in an expected format.
Consistency	The degree to which the data does not conflict with itself. The unambiguous nature of the data.
Duplication	The degree there are multiple or repetitive entries of the same object that add no new information and are irrelevant to the outcome.
Interpretability	The degree of difficulty to use the data for predictive purpose.
Precision	The consistency of measurements for the same instance. Precision is not accuracy.
Relevance	The data's importance to the stated problem being solved.
Timeliness	The data's relevance based on a time value. The relevance of the data over the time of study.

Table 3.1: Dimensions of Data Quality

3.3.2 Before Data Cleaning: Raw Data Quality

Given data cleaning's resource intensive nature, it's best to collect the highest quality data in order to avoid cleaning procedures as much possible. A little attention paid to the data quality of the gathering methods can go a long way in improving the efficiency of the cleaning of the data later.

The initial data set quality is often related to the collection methods employed and is a function of the organizational structure upon which the data is collected. The following are examples of some methods that improve quality[31]:

- Improving the human interface. Adding data type checks and bounding limits will help in avoiding key entry problems.
- Remove the human factor. Automated data collection processes often result in higher quality data as compared to human entered or human handled data collection. Also, the use of metadata to evaluate the correctness of data inputs is helpful in keeping a data set clean by filtering noise and culling out irrelevant data.
- Data Auditing. Maintain a feedback loop and regular examination of the data set over time to assure that problems are caught early and not compounded over time. This is particularly valuable for long term trials where data is collected over long periods of time.

3.4 Data Cleaning Procedures

Data cleaning isn't just one activity. It's a group of procedures employed to address deficiencies in one or more of the data quality dimensions. The goal of data cleaning is to provide the researcher a training data set of high quality. The data cleaning procedures are listed as follows:

1. Scrubbing
2. Integration
3. Transformation
4. Reduction
5. Feature Extraction and Selection
6. Discretization
7. Data Loading

Figure 3.1: Data Cleaning Cycle

3.4.1 Data Scrubbing

Data Scrubbing is the activity of filling in missing values, smoothing noisy data, identifying and removing outliers and resolving inconsistencies. The scrubbing is often a manual process, where one observes missing values or data elements of incorrect type and corrects or removes the data points. Another aspect of scrubbing is the removal of data elements that are of the correct type but are suspected of being erroneous because their values are very anomalous considering the distribution of the values of a particular feature. There are various methods for locating such values. Data points that are anomalous are often determined by a distance function on the data set, where points sufficiently far removed from the rest of the data set would be considered anomalous. This is frequently an ad hoc procedure, tailored to individual data sets.

3.4.2 Data Integration

Often the data resides within a number of different data sets. Integration is combining multiple data sets into one comprehensive data set. Data integration often precedes scrubbing because integration often leads to duplicate and conflicting data.

3.4.3 Data Transformation

Data transformation is the non-lossy process of converting data from one format into another. Normalization is one data transformation method. Data normalization scales data so that all the data falls within a manageable range.

3.4.4 Data Reduction

Data reduction is different from transformation. Where transformation may reformat or simplify the data set using a scaling method in a lossless manner, data reduction may or may not be lossy in its algorithmic method to simplify by removing data that is irrelevant or duplicated yet produces the same analytical result. Data compression and sampling are examples of data reduction. Data aggregation is a reduction method summarizing data with a simpler representative data set.

3.4.5 Feature Extraction and Selection

Often times a data set has data dimensions that do not support the prognostic topic of interest. Feature extraction creates new features from the data set and may reduce dimensionality of the data set in order to simplify it, making it more relevant to a specific task.

Feature selection is different from extraction. Feature selection does not create new features, rather reduces existing features that are unnecessary making the data set simpler and more directly applicable to a specific task.

3.4.6 Discretization

Discretization is the process of breaking data up into manageable pieces and analyzing the pieces individually, rather than as a single complex data set.

3.4.7 Data Loading

Data loading is formatting the training data set so that it is structured to meet some analytical need of the researcher. This could mean structuring the data set for use on a specific data base or a specific format to meet the requirements of a particular analytics tool.

3.5 Real-World Challenges in Using Complex Data Sets

Healthcare data produces complex data types. Electronic medical records include a great number of different kinds of information, such as administration of various pharmaceuticals, performance of various tests and clinical measurements, administration of immunizations, carrying out of various procedures, family medical records, healthcare provider information, healthcare payment plans, identifying specimens taken and results (some visible to the patient others not), recorded images and notes, surgeries performed, and numerous other information types. With the advent of consumer wearable devices and medical grade remote monitoring devices, the volume and variety of healthcare data brought to bear to understand the complete picture of individuals and populations is growing exponentially. When attempting to understand and manage the clinical, financial, socio-economic and genetic factors impacting health outcomes with the highest quality and most cost effective processes, one is faced with a plethora of variables and a rich interplay between various "sub-systems" of data.

Data of this type is not simple to put in a standard numerical spreadsheet format. If one had assigned unique identifiers to each kind of data element, one could perform counts of them, but would expect to find very sparse data, since many of the events would occur at most once, such that each patient's data record would include only a small number of a very large number of possible such events. Additionally, this kind of encoding does not include information about the timing of the events, which is critical in order to make best use of the data. For example, a patient might have had an X-ray examination performed twice, first in the context of a fracture, and later as part of a pre-surgery examination for chest surgery. The count of two X-ray examinations is not meaningful, but the information about the examination in each of the two different groups of events is. Once the data groups are obtained, there is still a question about how to encode them in the data set. Take for example trying to establish a standardized process of care for certain disease conditions. Suppose that a patient is regularly administered the cholesterol reducing medication simvastatin (brand name Zocor), but as part of an evolving cholesterol control regimen, the particular dosage is initially changed from 20mg to 80mg and subsequently the cholesterol reducing drug type is changed to Atorvastatin (brand name Lipitor) and dosage 40mg. Each of the different statin administrations is a distinct event, since they are encoded with different unique identifiers. However, from the standpoint of establishing an effective treatment path, the changes in specific statin type from Simvastatin to Atorvastatin may not be viewed as significant to the overall planned course of cholesterol reducing statins. It may just be important to know the timing, frequency and dosage of statins. What this suggests is that there is a need for a hierarchy structure on the events, roughly speaking dividing events into higher level *categories* in order to consider the different statin administrations as instances of the same type of medication. Expanding this example to various clinical, pharmaceutical and other concept hierarchies, it quickly becomes apparent that combining this kind of data can be a challenge. Topological Data Analysis (TDA) offers an elegant approach to considering the join interplay of a large plethora and variety of variables that work in concert to impact health outcomes. Fundamental to the TDA approach is the use of a quantitative similarity measure across all the variables under consideration. The design of such quantitative measures and their ability to encompass different encodings is an important modeling problem for this kind of data.

3.5.1 Standardizing Data Set Access: HL7 and FHIR

One of the biggest hurdles facing the analysis of data sets across any specific industry is the non-standard way data is stored. The analysis of any data set requires an initial data cleaning step to make it suitable for the method of analysis that is being used. For example, a hospital system database of employee records is in a spreadsheet format that has a fixed set of columns that are entered for each employee. For one hospital, it might include date of hire, age, salary, benefits selections, family status, etc, for another it may be the same data with a different order. For another hospital, more or less data may be kept. The decisions of what format to choose is an important one, because knowing what data to keep affects the way the analysis of the data is performed.

The data cleaning steps for analysis can be very time consuming, often taking much more time than the analysis itself. If one can foresee what kinds of analysis will be most prevalent, one can choose a method of data storage that will allow such analyses to be performed rapidly and simply. Of course, what happens is that different hospitals make different choices concerning the data format and structure, so if one wants to perform an analysis across multiple hospitals or a hospital wants to buy analytic tools, they (researcher or hospital) are confronted with a data transformation problem. One could imagine asking all hospitals to make identical choices for the format of the data, but such an approach is unlikely to be successful because most hospital systems are not willing to make a "one size fits all" choice. Even if they were willing to make a "one size fits all" choice, they would be dependent on the vendors of their IT systems to have designed their products around this standard.

A better approach is to develop a set of standards for the data, which describes the kind of information that can be extracted from the data, and how it is to be extracted. Once that is done, software can be designed for any internally chosen data structure which allows access to the data in a uniform way. This puts the onus on the individual systems to supply the needed transformations, as opposed to a situation where those building the analytic platforms are required to build "connectors" in each individual case. A benefit is that once the transformation to the standardized format is made, the data is then available to any analytic platform that works with the given standard, so the system need not make a single analytic choice once and for all.

Because of the complexity that is inherent in healthcare data, designing a set of uniform standards is not a simple task. Indeed, the process of developing interoperability standards has been ongoing for nearly thirty years. The so-called Health Level 7 (HL7) standards have developed over time. The initial versions (HL7 version 2.x) focused on establishing interoperability specifications for messaging of healthcare transactions between disparate health information systems. A typical HL7 v2 record of a message, as displayed below, utilizes an encoding syntax consisting of line segments and one character delimiters (typically vertical pipe delimiters).

```
MSH|^~\&|MegaReg|XYZHospC|SuperOE|XYZImgCtr|20060529090131-0500||ADT^A01^ADT_A01|01052901|P|2.5

EVN||200605290901|||||200605290900

PID|||56782445^^^UAReg^PI||KLEINSAMPLE^BARRY^Q^JR||19620910|M||2028-9^^HL70005^RA99113^^XYZ|260     GOODWIN     CREST

DRIVE^^BIRMINGHAM^AL^35209^^M-NICKELL'S PICKLES^10000 W 100TH AVE^BIRMINGHAM^AL^35200^^O||||||0105I30001^^^99DEF^AN

PV1||I|W^389^1^UABH^^^^3|||||12345^MORGAN^REX^J^^^MD^0010^UAMC^L||67890^GRAINGER^LUCY^X^^^MD^0010^UAMC^L|MED|||||A0||1

3579^POTTER^SHERMAN^T^^^MD^0010^UAMC^L||||||||||||||||||||||||||200605290900

OBX|1|NM|^Body Height||1.80|m^Meter^ISO+|||||F

OBX|2|NM|^Body Weight||79|kg^Kilogram^ISO+|||||F

AL1|1||^ASPIRIN

DG1|1||786.50^CHEST PAIN, UNSPECIFIED^I9|||A
```

Figure 3.2: HL7 Record

HL7 v2.x was widely adopted and continues to be the staple for interoperable transactional message exchanges such as Admission-Discharge-Transfer (ADT) messages. From an analytics perspective, the HL7 v2.x messaging format poses several challenges:

- The messaging format must be de-serialized and converted into structured representations to be presented for further analysis;
- Beyond the specified segment types HL7 v2.x imposes no structure on the messaging content. As a result, custom code must be written to extract structure from within the message segments. Such custom coding may be required for different types of analyses given that a potentially large amount of the messaging content may be irrelevant to a specific analysis.
- By virtue of the fact that HL7 v2.x messages are intended for communicating information on transactions, a large number of such messages must be assembled and reconciled to obtain the necessary clinical context of a patient or population for analysis
- The segment structure within HL7 v2.x messages cannot be manipulated independently as there may inherent dependencies in other segments in the message

The HL7 version 3 standards attempted to address these challenges by a placing records in an XML (extensible markup language) format that supported both messaging and the notion of more comprehensive clinical documents to share healthcare information. An example record in XML format looks like this:

```
<CareProvisionEvent classCode="PCPR" moodCode="EVN">
    <templateId root="2.16.840.1.113883.2.4.6.10.90.50"/>
        <id root="2.16.840.1.113883.2.4.99.23444.6" extension="cp16645"/>
        <statusCode code="active"/>
            <effectiveTime>
                    <low value="20130603"/>
            </effectiveTime>
    <subject typeCode="SBJ">
        <patient classCode="PAT">
        <!-- Item: 10 - SocialSecurityNumber -->
            <id root="2.16.840.1.113883.2.4.6.3" extension="100202020"/>
                <addr>
                    <postalCode>12008</postalCode>
                </addr>
                <statusCode code="active"/>
                <patientPerson classCode="PSN" determinerCode="INSTANCE">
                    <name use="L">
                        <given>Francesca</given>
                        <family qualifier="SP">Johnson</family>
                    </name>
                    <birthTime value="20110801"/>
                </patientPerson>
        </patient>
    </subject>
    <!--Item example - Highest diastolic blood pressure -->
    <pertinentInformation3 typeCode="PERT" contextConductionInd="true">
        <observation classCode="OBS" moodCode="EVN">
            <code code="X_IVDIASTPREG" codeSystem="2.16.840.1.113883.6.1"/>
                <value xsi:type="IVL_PQ">
                    <high value="95" unit="mm[Hg]"/>
                </value>
        </observation>
    </pertinentInformation3>
    <!-- rest of the message content starts here-->
    <!-- rest of the message content ends here-->
</CareProvisionEvent>
```

Figure 3.3: HL7 Code Snippet

This code actually specifies a semantic *data structure*. This means that there are now systematic methods for querying the record for particular data elements, and one is no longer required to write ad-hoc code to extract them from a message. The HL7 v3 Clinical Document Architecture (CDA) utilized the XML-based syntax to specify a standard structure for clinical documents such as discharge summaries, progress notes. With a strong emphasis on machine and human readability, CDA utilized both XML and embedded HTML syntaxes. Under the aegis of the CDA, several Standards Development Organization (SDOs) rallied to bring several commonly used clinical documents as a set of CDA templates under the Consolidated Clinical Document Architecture (C-CDA) umbrella. Government EHR "meaningful use" incentives introduced under the HITECH act of 2009 drove strong adoption of CCDA as a way of fulfilling the interoperability mandates of meaningful use.

While the HL7 v3.x CDA framework was a major step forward in achieving the portability and consumer access to health records, the focus on specific types of documents and in particular, clinical documents, greatly limited the ability to get to fundamental clinical and healthcare financial constructs. As such, the HL7 v3 messaging standards have failed to gain sufficient traction and HL7 v2.x continues to be the de facto messaging standard for healthcare transactional data exchange.

3.5.2 Fast Healthcare Interoperability Resources (FHIR)

FHIR (Fast Healthcare Interoperability Resources) is the rapidly emerging specification for the exchange of fundamental healthcare clinical and financial constructs by addressing the deficiencies of HL7 v3. Healthcare clinical and financial constructs can be retrieved and exchanged as messages or individual "resources" which can be built up into various kinds of "compositions" including but not restricted to documents such as the C-CDA class of clinical documents. FHIR supports the interoperability needs of all prior HL7 standards and more. In particular, analytics solutions can greatly benefit from the ability to retrieve and analyze longitudinal clinical and financial information about individual patients and populations across the continuum of care in a unified manner.

FHIR emphasizes deployment based on modern web standards such as XML, JSON, HTTP, RESTful architectures etc. FHIR solutions are based on manipulating a set of "Resources" which can be readily retrieved from Electronic Health Records (EHRs) and other health information systems. Instead of exchanging static clinical documents as defined by the C-CDA templates, FHIR solutions can retrieve a plethora of arbitrary clinical and financial constructs as necessary. A review of the list of FHIR resources in on the HL7 site[32] illustrates the rich and comprehensive set of clinical, operational and financial resources at various stages of maturity of development.

3.0 Resource Index ⊕

| Categorized | Alphabetical |

This page is provided to help find resources quickly. There is also a more detailed classification, ontology, and description.

Clinical

General:
- AllergyIntolerance 1
- Condition (Problem) 2
- Procedure 1
- ClinicalImpression 0
- FamilyMemberHistory 1
- RiskAssessment 0
- DetectedIssue 1

Care Provision:
- CarePlan 1
- Goal 1
- ReferralRequest 1
- ProcedureRequest 1
- NutritionOrder 1
- VisionPrescription 0

Medication & Immunization:
- Medication 1
- MedicationOrder 1
- MedicationAdministration 1
- MedicationDispense 1
- MedicationStatement 1
- Immunization 1
- ImmunizationRecommendation 1

Diagnostics:
- Observation 3
- DiagnosticReport 3
- DiagnosticOrder 1
- Specimen 1
- BodySite 0
- ImagingStudy 2
- ImagingObjectSelection 1

Identification

Individuals:
- Patient 3
- Practitioner 1
- RelatedPerson 1

Groups:
- Organization 1
- HealthcareService 1
- Group 1

Entities:
- Location 1
- Substance 1
- Person 1
- Contract 0

Devices:
- Device 1
- DeviceComponent 1
- DeviceMetric 1

Workflow

Patient Management:
- Encounter 1
- EpisodeOfCare 1
- Communication 1
- Flag 1

Scheduling:
- Appointment 1
- AppointmentResponse 1
- Schedule 1
- Slot 1

Workflow #1:
- Order 0
- OrderResponse 0
- CommunicationRequest 1
- DeviceUseRequest 0
- DeviceUseStatement 0

Workflow #2:
- ProcessRequest 0
- ProcessResponse 0
- SupplyRequest 0
- SupplyDelivery 0

Infrastructure

Information Tracking:
- Questionnaire 2
- QuestionnaireResponse 2
- Provenance 1
- AuditEvent 2

Documents & Lists:
- Composition 2
- DocumentManifest 1
- DocumentReference 2
- List 1

Structure:
- Media 1
- Binary 1
- Bundle 2
- Basic 1

Exchange:
- MessageHeader 2
- OperationOutcome 2
- Parameters 1
- Subscription 1

Conformance

Terminology:
- ValueSet 3
- ConceptMap 2
- NamingSystem 1

Content:
- StructureDefinition 2
- DataElement 1

Operations Control:
- Conformance 2
- OperationDefinition 1
- SearchParameter 1

Misc:
- ImplementationGuide 0
- TestScript 0

Financial

Support:
- Coverage 0
- EligibilityRequest 0
- EligibilityResponse 0
- EnrollmentRequest 0
- EnrollmentResponse 0

Billing:
- Claim 0
- ClaimResponse 0

Payment:
- PaymentNotice 0
- PaymentReconciliation 0

Other:
- ExplanationOfBenefit 0

Figure 3.4: FHIR DSTU 2 Resource List

Recognizing the need for flexibility and institution specific preferences, FHIR supports an extensibility framework to add resource level extensions.

A typical FHIR compliant JSON representation of a patient is illustrated below. (https://www.hl7.org/fhir/patient-example-a.json.html)

Patient-example-a.json

Raw JSON (canonical form)

Patient 1 for linking

```json
{
  "resourceType": "Patient",
  "id": "pat1",
  "text": {
    "status": "generated",
    "div": "<div>\n       \n        <p>Patient Donald DUCK @ Acme Healthcare, Inc. MR = 654 321</p>\n    \n  </div>"
  },
  "identifier": [
    {
      "use": "usual",
      "type": {
        "coding": [
          {
            "system": "http://hl7.org/fhir/v2/0203",
            "code": "MR"
          }
        ]
      },
      "system": "urn:oid:0.1.2.3.4.5.6.7",
      "value": "654321"
    }
  ],
  "active": true,
  "name": [
    {
      "use": "official",
      "family": [
        "Donald"
      ],
      "given": [
        "Duck"
      ]
    }
  ],
  "gender": "male",
  "photo": [
    {
      "contentType": "image/gif",
      "data": "R0lGODlhEwARAPcAAAAAAAA/+9aAO+1AP/WAP/eAP/eCP/eEP/eGP/nAP/nCP/nEP/nIf/nK f/nUv/nWv/vAP/vCP/vEP/vGP/vIf/vKf/vMf/vOf/vWv/vY//va//vjP/3c//3lP/3nP//tf//v
f
```
//

Figure 3.5: Sample FHIR Patient Resource (JSON Format)

Contemporary web solution developers will recognize the familiar JSON structure which is a staple of modern RESTful web and mobile application architectures. Similar to the patient resource, the FHIR specification identifies several resources corresponding to commonly used constructs in EHRs and other hospital information systems.

Only the data that is required for the transaction is retrieved rather than having to obtain a complete record for the patient. This enables a financial analyst to deal only with the account information, without having to deal with the imaging data that has no relevance to the analysis being performed. On the other hand, a physician that is interested in the information available in the imaging study would not need to obtain the account information which has no relevance to their task.

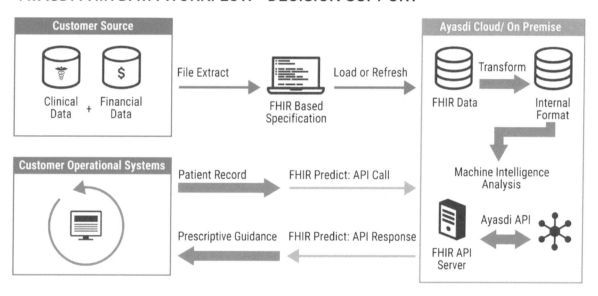

Figure 3.6: Ayasdi FHIR Data Workflow Diagram

Chapter 3

3.6 Case Study 5: Data Prep and Upload for Cardiac Surgery

3.6.1 Case Study Highlights

- Hospital data analysts performed data preparation and loading facilitated by use of the HL7 FHIR (Fast Healthcare Interoperability Resource) standard.
- Within a two-week period the health system data warehouse analyst completed the schema validation, data transformation and loading of 4,328 surgical cases to a Machine Intelligence platform.
- The Cardiac Surgery Quality Improvement Team selected clinically relevant parameters during the data interview process to efficiently include a large set of data elements previously unexplored at their hospital.

3.6.2 Introduction

A large regional cardiac surgery center sought to analyze their surgery cases for clinical variation across its group of (22) cardiac surgeons. The surgeons have used clinical pathways to establish protocols of care for patients undergoing coronary artery bypass graft (CABG) for more than 10 years and to perform analysis on basic aspects of performance related to the pathway guideline each year. Their annual report on CABG performance focuses on length of stay (LOS), blood transfusion practices, post-operative infections, hospital readmissions and 30-day mortality.

The data preparation process began with an interview of the cardiac surgery quality improvement team to understand their specific goals. They decided on the following:

- CABG surgery January 2009 – September 2015, n= 4,328 cases
- Include items costing >/= $100
- Compare patients with and without pre-operative arrhythmia
- Determine if there is variation across the 12 hospital operating rooms used

The data set for this analysis consisted of 620 columns/dimensions for each of the 4,328 patients. The hospital collected the data through the electronic health record which has system components from several best in breed commercial EHR systems and some home-grown components. During the time frame data collection (2009-2015) the health system used modules from both Cerner and Epic EHRs and moved all information to a central data warehouse.

Table CS5.1 shows the minimal data set with 52 mandatory columns of data. Figure CS5.2, shows the columns of data describing "procedures". In particular, start and end times for all procedures are included as well as location codes.

SUMMARY OF REQUIRED FILES	# MANDATORY COLUMNS	# OPTIONAL COLUMNS
patient	2	3
encounter	7	10
condition	7	2
procedure	15	4
medicationAdministration	11	5
diagnosticReport	10	5

Table CS5.1: Mandatory Data Required for Analysis

COLUMN FHIR RESOURCE	EXAMPLE	DATA TYPE	DESCRIPTION
Id	PROC1234	String or Integer	Logical id that distinguishes a procedure intervention.
encounter.id	ENC1234	String or Integer	Must match an id in the Encounters file. An encounter can match to multiple procedures.
performedPeriod.start	YYYY-MM-DDTHH:mm:ssZD	Date time	Period start when the procedure was performed (Used to determine the start time of a surgery, important for event calculations).
performedPeriod.end	YYYY-MM-DDTHH:mm:ssZD	Date time	Period end when the procedure was performed (Used to determine the end time of a surgery, important for event calculations).
performer.name	John Smith	String	Person who performed the procedure - name.
performer.id	NPI4567	String or Integer	Unique ID (e.g. NPI) of person who performed the procedure.
location.id	FAC156	String or Integer	Unique location ID of the encounter.
location.name	County Hospital	String	Location of the encounter.
category.coding.code	470	String	Category coding system (e.g. DRG, SnomedCT) for procedure category.
category.coding.system	MS-DRG	String	Coding system (eg. MS-DRG, Snomed-CT)
category.coding.version	2015	String or Integer	Category coding version for procedure.
category.coding.display	Major Joint Replacement	String	Description for code used in the procedure.
code.coding.system1	ICD	String	Coding system (e.g. ICD).
code.coding.version1	9-CM	String or Integer	Coding version (eg. 10-PCS).
code.coding.code1	81.54	String or Integer	Code for procedure.
cost.directTotalCost	3000	Double	Dollar amount associated with the direct total cost for this event.
cost.directVariableCost	2000	Double	Dollar amount associated with the direct variable cost for this event.
cost.directFixedCost	1000	Double	Dollar amount associated with the direct fixed cost for this event.

Table CS5.2: Detailed Data Fields Specifying "Procedures"

The data analysis process consists of the following steps:

1. Data Interview, where data dimensions for analysis are chosen.
2. Schema Validation, where data integrity is checked.

3. Data Transformation, where the data is configured to comply with the analysis tools.
4. Load the data for analysis.
5. Review Results.

3.6.2.1 Data Interview

Although the FHIR specification has details for virtually every aspect of the data including coding systems (e.g. ICD, CPT, SNOMED), data types and formats, it was necessary to make selection of specific fields from the hospital's data warehouse in order to insure compatibility with the analysis tools. The Cardiac Surgery Quality Improvement Team made decisions for several data types including the following:

- Since all the CABG surgeries were done at one hospital, the team chose to use location codes specifying the specific operating room for each procedure. In a future analysis of multiple hospitals in the health system they expect to use both operating room and hospital identifiers to enable comparison across hospitals.

- Medical and surgical equipment and lab testing with direct costs <$100 were deleted from the data set prior to data upload for their first analysis to enable them to focus on higher cost items. They planned for a future analysis including all the direct cost data for pattern analysis of lower cost items once they have completed the high cost variation analysis.

- The team decided to limit medications to just those administered and not include medication orders.

- The attending cardiac surgeon for each case was used for the "performer" name and ID. They are considering a separate analysis with anesthesiologist identifiers reasoning that many of the intra-operative medication and transfusion treatment decisions are driven by the anesthesiologist.

- Laboratory results with "critical values" were included and all others removed for the first analysis. For example, values of dangerously high potassium or anemia with very low hemoglobin became a focus for analysis.

3.6.2.2 Schema Validation

After the data has been prepared, it must pass a schema validation process.

The following attributes were checked during schema validation:

- TYPE: Date, time, double, string
- NULLS: No Nulls, no duplicates
- VALUES: Allowed values in column
- REFERENCES: Referential integrity e.g. foreign keys

3.6.2.3 Transformation

Following schema validation, the data is transformed into the analysis tool's internal syntax. This input format requires that all mandatory columns are available for patient encounter data, and that events have been captured per patient. The transformation process created a single "*procedure.tsv*" file for each episode of care to be loaded.

3.6.2.4 Load Data

The analyst then loaded the data. One week after the initial data load, the analyst did perform one refresh of the existing episodes of care using a standard "bumpup" operation. A bumpup is recommended to maintain previously developed carepaths. The analyst will perform future updates to enable tracking surgeon adherence on an ongoing basis. The quality improvement team requested a data update on a quarterly basis during the first year of use of the system.

3.7 Results

The hospital's data warehouse analyst was able to complete the data upload for the 4,328 CABG cases within 2 weeks of the start of the project. Due to excellent status of the hospital's data warehouse, the process went smoothly. The analyst was knowledgeable about the data quality and completeness of the data set and received prompt feedback from the QI team to make decisions about data selection. Over the following week the QI team completed their data analysis of the CABG data set and requested work to begin on the next group of major cardiac surgeries. Over a few more days the analyst proceeded to load large data sets for aortic valve replacement and mitral valve replacement surgeries. The data warehouse team had a very good experience with the FHIR specifications and is now planning new column headers and updates for large portions of the data warehouse based on the FHIR specifications since it is rapidly becoming the standard for data interchange and analysis across the country.

Chapter 4: Topological Data Modeling

"Topology is the science of fundamental pattern and structural relationships
of event constellations"
-R. Buckminister Fuller

4.1 Chapter Preview

- Discuss the shape of data and distance functions.
- Discuss various ways to measure distance and create distance functions.
- Provide an illustrated discussion on how TDA converts data into shape.
- Explore data subsets through data hotspots, what if queries and predictive models.
- Summarize this chapter with two examples of topological modeling in the context of building graphs representing a human hand and identification of different types among NBA basketball players.
- Case Studies
  - Case Study 6: Disease Tolerance
  - Case Study 7: Topological Data Analysis: A Promising Big Data Exploration Tool in Biology, Analytical Chemistry and Physical Chemistry

4.2 Introduction

Chapter 1 introduced the concept of a topological network as a mathematical construction that can represent shapes in a simple and compressed fashion. In this chapter, we will see that such networks can be constructed from data sets, and that the resulting shapes are very useful in the study of various kinds of data sets.

4.3 Data has Shape

Today, creating shape from data is a common method of analysis. In the 17th century, Rene Descartes and Pierre de Fermat, pioneers of analytic geometry, discovered that graphical representations of algebraic equations are a very effective way of understanding their meaning. Using graphical representations for empirical data was a practice made common throughout the 17th and 18th centuries, William Playfair made graphical representations into a methodology, arguing that visual representations of

Chapter 4

data are more efficient, publishing the first bar chart around 1786.[33] Playfair took incomplete data sets and inferred relationships by presenting the data in line, bar, area and pie charts. Figure 4.1 shows one example of Playfair's work[34]

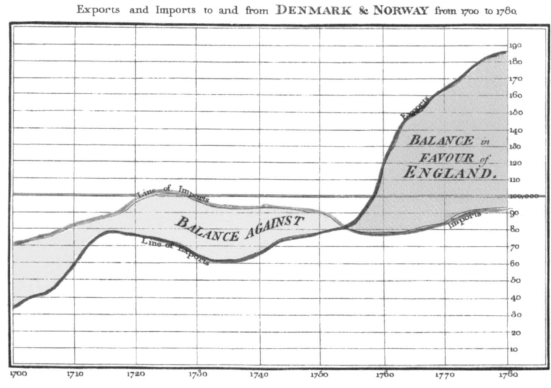

Exports and Imports to and from DENMARK & NORWAY from 1700 to 1780

Figure 4.1: Example of a Playfair Graph

A simple data shape commonly used is a curve that describes the graph as a function of the *x*-variable, or a scatter plot that can represent data in which there are two or possibly three dimensions (variables). Since the direct plotting of data is limited to the number of dimensions we are able to visualize, displaying multidimensional data can be challenging.

Modern data often has hundreds or thousands of dimensions which cannot be visualized well as a scatter plot. Although the number of dimensions in the data description can be very large, the actual data points are typically concentrated in small "regions" in the representing space. A way around this "sea of data poor dimensions" is to develop a notion of shape that is not simply obtained by a projection to two or three dimensions, but rather to use a *distance function* as an organizing principle.[35]

68

4.4 Distance Measure Backgrounder

This section provides a few basic definitions associated with distance functions to give the reader context for the rest of the chapter. A distance function on a set is defined as an assignment of a quantity d (p,q), called the distance, to each pair p,q of elements of a set. It is defined as an abstraction of the familiar notion of distance in the plane or in space, referred to as *Euclidean distance*. The following discussion briefly illustrates a few different distance functions. Often the word, "distance" and the word "metric" are used interchangeably in this context, i.e. Euclidean metric, instead of Euclidean distance, etc.

First, remember that the distance between two points in the plane or in space satisfies three natural properties. The first is that the distance never takes negative values, and that the distance between two points is equal to zero if and only if the two points are equal. The second is that the distance from p to q is the same as the distance from q to p. Finally, the third, called the *triangle inequality*, asserts that in any triangle, the sum of the lengths of any two distinct sides is always greater than or equal to the length of the third side. These properties translate to the following conditions.

- **d(x,y) ≥ 0, and d(x,y) = 0 if and only if x = y**
- **d(x,y) = d(y,x)**
- **d(x,y) + d(y,z) ≥ d(x,z), The significance of this condition is illustrated in the picture below.**

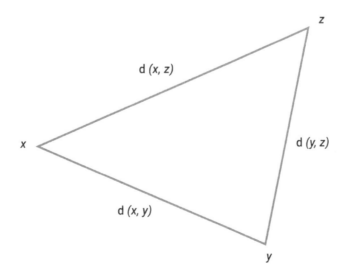

Figure 4.2: Triangle Inequality

Euclidean Distance: A distance function on a set is a function of pairs of points satisfying the three conditions above.

Taxicab or Manhattan distance: the distance between two points is the sum of the absolute differences of their Cartesian coordinates. The taxicab distance replaces a straight line path by the sums of distances projected on a grid. Consider the distance driven by a Manhattan taxi; New York City is laid out in a grid so the distance one travels on the grid between two points is longer than "as the crow flies". Taxicab distance is also called "rectilinear distance" and is translation invariant.

Orthodromic distance: Measuring the distance between two points on a sphere, where Euclidean straight lines are replaced by geodesics (great circle arcs), and distance is given by arc length.

Hamming distance: A measure of similarity between two strings of equal length defined to be minimum number of substitutions required to transform one string into another.

Vector distance: A vector consists of magnitude and direction. A vector can be broken up into component vectors along its dimensional axes. For example, an airplane flying may have 6 or more dimensional component vectors: three spacial, three positional (pitch, roll, yaw), one velocity, one acceleration, etc. The distance is computed by a formula that is a straightforward generalization of the formula applicable in two and three dimensions.

4.5 Modeling Data with Networks

Distance functions are typically difficult to understand as they are presented. In order to make use of the distance function, one must find a kind of model for distance functions that is easily interpretable by a human, and with which one can interact. The model we will work with is that of a *topological network* (sometimes also called a *graph*). The formal definition of a topological network consists of two elements, a set of nodes and a set of edges. The edges are unordered pairs of nodes, so if we lay out the set of nodes of a network, we can draw straight line segments between pairs of points which form edges. A simple example is given by choosing the set of nodes to be the set {A,B,C,D}, and the set of edges to be the set {AB,BC,CD,AD}. In this case, if we lay out the nodes at the corners of a square, we get the following representation.

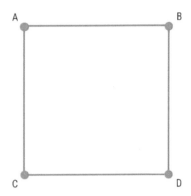

Figure 4.3: Layout of Topological Network

By laying networks out this way, we can obtain a shape. Here are two more examples of topological networks.

Figure 4.4: Polygon

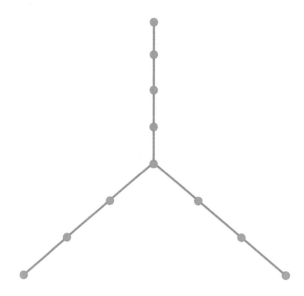

Figure 4.5: Y-junction

These two examples are simplified versions of phenomena that occur frequently in topological data analysis.

The goal of topological data analysis is to create topological networks from data sets equipped with a distance function, and by the layout process obtain a shape describing the data set. Our job is now to describe how to construct networks from data sets.

4.5.1 Network Nodes and Edges: How Data Becomes Shapes

Two properties completely describe how network shapes correspond to the data:

- Each node in a network corresponds to a *collection* of data points, not individual data points. The collections corresponding to different nodes may overlap.
- Two nodes whose corresponding collections of data points overlap are connected by an edge.

Figure 4.6 illustrates a data set and its corresponding network representation.

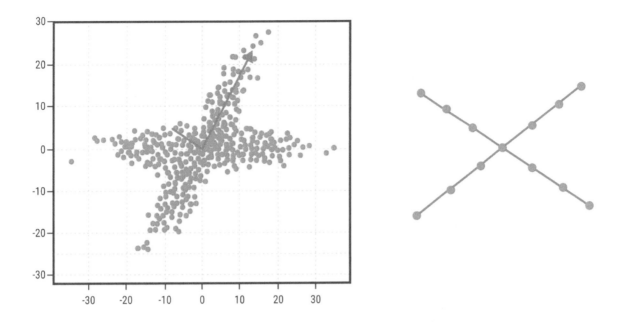

Figure 4.6: Scatter Graph vs. TDA Plot

Note both have the shape of a letter "X". Also note that the layout of the shape in the plane is **not well correlated with the positions of the points in the plane.** The model does not contain information about the exact positions of the data points in the plane, only their relative positions as encoded in the distances. If desired, the positions of the data points can be used to color the network model to give a representation which gives approximate positions for each of the nodes.

Briefly describing how the networks are built, a starting point is a projection from the data, by which we mean an assignment of one or more numbers to each data point. These numbers should carry meaning about the data. For example, they might be measures of density or centrality, or they might be coordinates in a principal component analysis. The situation is shown in the picture below.

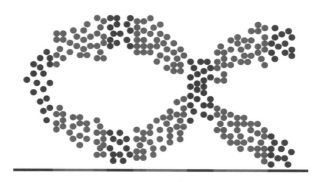

Figure 4.7: TDA Network Construction– Raw Data

The data points are projected onto the *x*-axis in this situation. The line on which the projection is made is broken into red and blue segments, with purple representing the regions of red and blue overlap. The points are colored by the segment they are projected onto with purple points projected to the purple overlap segments, etc. Effectively, the data is broken into red and blue overlapping *bins*, with the overlaps in the bins indicated by purple coloring on the points. The critical step is applying a clustering method (single linkage) to each of the bins, and creating a node for each such cluster.

Figure 4.8: TDA Network Construction– Node Construction

As it stands, there are only nodes, and no edges, so edges are created by connecting any two nodes whose corresponding clusters overlap. In this example, because the bins overlap, it is possible for a cluster in one bin to overlap a cluster in the overlapping bin. Here is the resulting network.

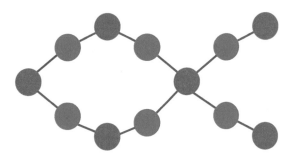

Figure 4.9: TDA Network Construction– Edge Construction

This collection of nodes and connecting edges are the model produced by TDA. The actual position of the nodes in the plane is not significant, as they are the result of a network layout algorithm. In fact, it would not be sensible to assign meaning to them, since the data set in general is defined with many more than two fields and therefore is not interpretable in two dimensions in a sensible way.

4.5.2 The Meaning of Shape

The networks constructed by the procedure in the previous section are often readily interpretable. For example, consider the following network.

Figure 4.10: Loopy network

The network above suggests that the data may have a shape similar to a loop. This kind of network frequently occurs when the data set **possesses** periodic or recurrent behavior. This could happen with the analysis of many time series with annual periodic behavior, or for example in the case of predator-prey models in mathematical biology. We will see an example of this kind of network in Case Study 6 below.

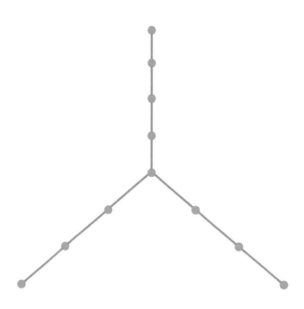

Figure 4.11: "Y"-shaped data

This network can arise from monitoring a complex process. For example, imagine that we have data from sensors from an airliner during a flight. We might identify four separate modes of behavior, namely flying at altitude in non-turbulent conditions, take off, landing, and flying at altitude in turbulent conditions. The first one will constitute normal behavior, and these points would lie in the central node. The others would be extreme behaviors, and would lie along the three branches or flares observed in the network.

Recognizing such geometric properties of geometric objects is one important aspect of human intelligence. By representing data sets via such geometric objects, we can use human intelligence for tasks that in their original form were not amenable to human analysis. This characterizes these methods as a prime example of Machine Intelligence.

4.5.3 Selecting Subsets of Interest

We have seen in the previous section that it is often possible to interpret properties of the network constructed in terms of properties of the data. In addition to interpretation, though one needs to have some methods for interacting with the data in order to make the method useful. One key capability present in topological models is the ability to easily select areas within the network using point and click methods like the "select" or "lasso selection" analogous to what is available in Adobe Photoshop™ or Adobe Illustrator™. The network is displayed on the screen via a layout algorithm, and then regions within the network are selected for further analysis. Regions are collections of nodes, which in turn correspond to groups or subpopulations within the data since each of the nodes is a collection of data points. This provides a quick method for interrogating the data set for significant regions in the network, which contain points that are similar to each other. For example, in the network below, it is natural to break it into three groups as indicated.

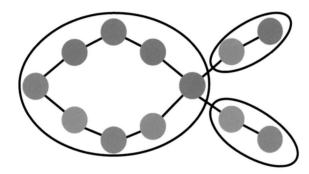

Figure 4.12: TDA Network Construction– Creating Groups

Note that coloring by the alternating red/blue method is no longer possible, because at this point the only structure that remains is the network structure, without information about the alternating bins. This is not a deterministic procedure for finding features of interest, rather it is a method to visually observing three gross features, namely the two flares on the right and the loop on the left. This kind of visual analysis is often a productive step in the analytical workflow. There are also ways of performing this kind of segmentation automatically.

4.5.4 Hot Spots and Data Exploration

Another criterion for selecting groups comes by coloring the network by an outcome variable of interest. This often results in "hot spots" within the network, where high or low values of the outcome variable are concentrated. For example, the following situation might occur in the network we are dealing with above.

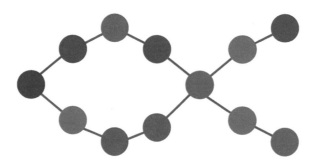

Figure 4.13: TDA Network Construction– Hot Spot Analysis

In this case, there are two red ("hot") regions, one at the tip of a flare and the other at the crossing point. For example, this network might be built from genetic data, and the outcome of interest might be length of survival from a particular condition. In this case, these two groups would then correspond to groups whose genetic profiles are internally consistent and for which the survival is elevated over the main part of the data set.

Discovery of such hot spots is an important capability for data analysis. When one is looking to understand the behavior of an outcome variable, it is a serious temptation to attempt, for example, to maximize the variable on the data set, obtaining a single maximum. Typically, though, one finds multiple "local maxima", with different values, and with different explanations. The ability to represent such a "landscape" is a very important feature. Another of the capabilities included in topological methods is the ability to find the variables which most effectively characterize a group in an appropriate statistical sense. Those variables will typically be different for different groups, and can, for example, result in different models describing the behavior around the hot spot.

4.6 "What if" Queries

An interesting application of topological modeling is investigating the effects of various strategies. For example, suppose one develops an investment strategy and is interested in understanding how it might affect return on investment. A key step is assessing how the strategy performs using retrospective data. A very useful approach is to apply the strategy to a set of data points that includes information about return on investment and color the nodes by the average value of what would have been the return on investment for the data points using this strategy. Typically, one can find some hot spots and some "cold spots". The outcome might then be a description of regions in which the strategy works well, and also of regions where it does not. One could then also begin to make estimates about how the return would be affected by adoption of the strategy. The revised strategy might very well include some classifiers for various regions in the data, together with a decision about what strategy should be adopted in each region.

4.7 Predictive models

Predictive models come in many forms. Regression models for various families of functions are common, but other methods include decision trees, randomized decision trees, and linear discriminant analysis. In all cases, when there is some ground truth, a topological model of the underlying data can be constructed and colored by the average value of model error, suitably defined.

In the case of linear regression, the error would be the magnitude of the numerical difference between the actual value of the output variable and the predicted value. One can then color by the average value of this numerical quantity. In the case of a binary classifier, one can color by the fraction of the data points in a node of the network that are misclassified. It can be done similarly, in the case of a decision tree, where there are typically more than two possible outcomes.

In the case of regression models, since they are based on some rather straightforward optimization strategies, there are automatic ways to create some new features and actually improve the overall error. The idea is to locate groups enriched for model error and build features which permit localization of features to such groups. Adding these features is guaranteed to improve the overall error. However, as in all prediction schemes, overfitting results from adding too many new features. Overfitting describes a situation in which the mathematical model has had too many features adjoined, such that while the fit is excellent on existing data, the predictor greatly underperforms on new data points on which the predictor is being applied. A way to mitigate this is to break up the existing data into two groups, a training set and a test set. The training set is used to construct a model, and this method is tested against the test set. One can perform such tests within topological modeling, and find localized regions of overfitting.

4.8 TDA and the Real World[36]

The fundamental take away from this chapter is that topological methods are a geometric approach to pattern recognition within data. Recognizing patterns in data is critical to discovering insights in the data and identifying meaningful sub-groups. In the referenced paper above[37], an analysis was done on a data set obtained from all National Basketball Association players in the 2010-2011 seasons. It illustrates the use of topological network models in understanding the different profiles of these players.

Distinguishing players based only on physical characteristics such as height or speed is somewhat arbitrary and outdated. One can then ask if there is a more informative stratification of player types based on their in-game performance. To answer this question, performance profiles for each of the 452 players in the NBA by using data from the 2010–2011 NBA season were constructed.

Using rates (per minute played) of rebounds, assists, turnovers, steals, blocked shots, personal fouls, and points scored, we identified more playing styles than the traditional five. Positions in basketball are traditionally classified as guards, forwards, and centers. Over time, this classification has been refined further into five distinct positions, namely *point guard, shooting guard, small forward, power forward, and center.* These positions represent a spectrum of players from short, fast, and playing outside the key to tall, slow, and playing inside the key.

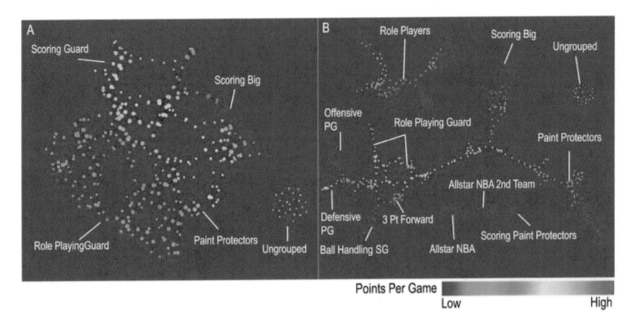

Figure 4.14: TDA for NBA Players

Description of Figure 4.12: A) Low resolution map at 20 intervals for each filter B) High resolution map at 30 intervals for each filter. Each interval overlaps with half of the adjacent intervals, the graphs are colored by points per game, and a variance normalized Euclidean distance metric is applied. Metric: Variance Normalized Euclidean; Lens: Principal SVD Value (Resolution 20, Gain 2.0x, Equalized) and Secondary SVD Value (Resolution 20, Gain 2.0x, Equalized). Color: red: high values, blue: low values.

From the networks, one obtains a much finer structure than five distinct categories. This structure represents groups of players based on their in-game performance statistics. For example, the left side of the main network reveals a finer stratification of guards into three groups, namely offensive point guards, defensive point guards, and ball handling shooting guards. We also see three smaller structures in the lower central part of the map that we labeled "Allstar NBA" and "Allstar NBA 2nd team". The "Allstar NBA" network consists of the NBA's most exceptional players and the second team consists of players who are also all-around excellent players but perhaps not as top-performing as the "Allstar NBA" players. Within "Allstar NBA" group are all-star players like LeBron James and Kobe Bryant. Interestingly, there are some less well-known players in the "All NBA" network such as Brook Lopez, suggesting that they are potential up and coming stars. It is of note that the "Allstar NBA" and "Allstar NBA 2nd team" networks are well separated from the large network, indicating that their in-game statistics are very different from the main body of NBA players. To illustrate the capability to perform multi-resolution analyses simultaneously on the same dataset and how that kind of analysis is important, we compared the high-resolution network (Figure 4.12, right panel) to the lower resolution network (Figure 4.12, left panel). The right panel shows

81

that at a lower resolution, these players form 4 categories, which are scoring big men, paint protectors, scoring guards, and ball handling guards. In summary, this topological network suggests a much finer stratification of players into thirteen positions rather than the traditional division into five positions.

The three key concepts of topological methods coordinate freeness, invariance to deformation and compressed representations of shapes are of particular value for applications to data analysis. Coordinate free analysis means that the representation is independent of the particular way in which the data set is given coordinates, but rather depends only on the similarity of the points as reflected in the distance function. Coordinate free representations are vital when one is studying data collected with different technologies or from different labs when the methodologies cannot be standardized. The invariance to deformation provides some robustness to noise. Compressed representations are obviously important when one is dealing with very large data sets, but even for moderate size data sets they provide more succinct and understandable representations than most standard methods.

4.9 Case Study 6: Disease Tolerance

Title: Tracking Resilience to Infections by Mapping Disease Space[38] & How Many Parameters Does It Take to Describe Disease Tolerance?[39]

4.9.1 Contributors:

Dr. David Schneider, Professor, Stanford Microbiology and Immunology

Drs. Brenda Torres and Alexander Louie are graduate students in Dr. David Schneider's lab

4.9.2 Case Study Highlights

- Examined are two case studies discussing the use of TDA in analyzing the course of disease as it relates to outcome and intensity.
- Shows how to create disease maps that track the arc of an illness.
- Explores how to create symptom intensity diagrams at different stages of illness.

4.9.3 Introduction

Tracking Resilience to Infections by Mapping Disease Space

"When we get sick, we long for recovery; thus, a major goal of medicine is to promote resilience—the ability of a host to return to its original health following an infection. While in the laboratory we can study the response to infection with precise knowledge of inoculation time and dose, sick patients in the clinic do not have this information. This creates a problem because we can't easily differentiate between patients who are early in the stages of infection that will develop severe disease from more disease-tolerant patients who present later in the infection. The distinction between these two types of patients is important, as the less disease-tolerant patient would require a more aggressive treatment regime. To determine where patients lie along the infection timeline, we charted "disease maps" that trace a patient's route through "disease space." We select symptoms that produce looping graphs as patients grow sick and recover. Using a mouse–malaria model, we demonstrate that less resilient individuals take wider loops through this space, representing a longer infection time with more severe symptoms. We find this looping behavior also applies to humans and suggest that people carrying the sickle cell trait are more resilient to malaria infections."

4.9.3.1 How Many Parameters Does It Take to Describe Disease Tolerance?

"It is an intuitive assumption that the severity of symptoms suffered during an infection must be linked to pathogen loads. However, the dose–response relationship explaining how health varies with respect to pathogen load is non-linear and can be described as a "disease tolerance curve;" this relationship can vary in response to the genetic properties of the host or pathogen as well as environmental conditions. We studied what changes in the shape of this curve can teach us about the underlying circuitry of the immune response. Using a model system in which we infected fruit flies with the bacterial pathogen Listeria monocytogenes, we observed an S-shaped disease tolerance curve. This type of curve can be described by three or four parameters in a standard manner, which allowed us to develop a simple mathematical model to explain how the curve is expected to change shape as the immune response changes. After observing the variation in curve shape due to host and pathogen genetic variation, we conclude that the damage caused by Listeria infection does not result from an over-exuberant immune response but rather is caused more directly by the pathogen."

4.9.4 Results

4.9.4.1 Outcome

- Developed methods for visualizing disease maps from cross-sectional data.
- In both papers, TDA was used to map the way hosts loop through the disease space in an unsupervised fashion.

4.9.4.2 Summary Findings

- Applied TDA to cluster data without imposing a connection structure such as a hierarchical pattern or least branching tree
    - Topological networks provide a striking representation of the health space that resembles the disease maps in which distinct regions of the networks correspond to distinct parts of the disease: comfort, sickness, and recovery - both the mouse and human data sets form looping structures.
    - Mapped the intensity of parameters such as parasites, RBCs, granulocytes, or reticulocytes – found that the mouse and human infections are collinear in many respects, having the same order of events.
- Network models separated the living and dying mice into two different paths and then determined how gene expression differed between the two groups.
    - Demonstrated that RBCs and reticulocytes differed in their representation in living and dying mice as their paths through disease space separated.
- Visualized the "disease space" traversed by infected flies and identified the different states of the infection process.
    - Resilient systems should not be fit by a tree and are better described by loops.
    - Network models are sensitive to the topology of the data and will not arbitrarily linearize a loop and then force it to fit a tree. Instead, the analysis simply clusters related data points, represented as nodes on a network graph, and the shape of that graph reveals the connections between the time points. In the case of a resilient system, such as flies recovering from an infection, this graph forms a loop.

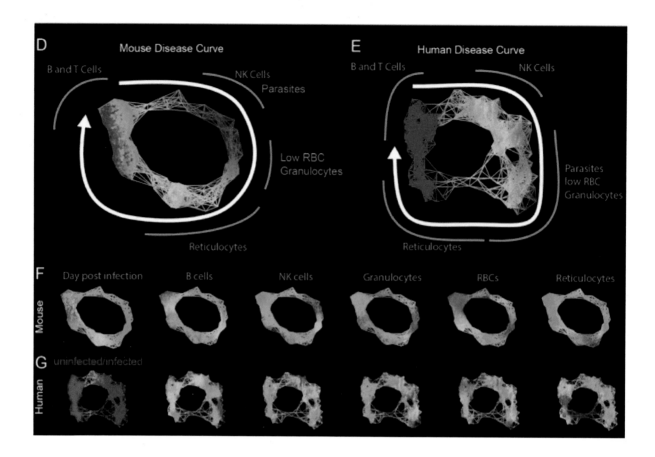

Figure CS6.1: Topological Models of Mice and Humans Suffering from Malaria.

Figure CS6.1 Discussion: Topological network maps of mice (D) and humans (E) suffering from malaria. The known timeline in the mice runs clockwise as marked by the white arrow. The inferred human timeline is marked similarly. The color scheme in (D) and (E) marks parasite density, where blue represents low values while red represents high values. Segments of the map are marked in grey to show transcript or cell counts reporting the relative abundance of marked cell types. Red blood cells were counted directly using flow cytometry. The markers for B cells, granulocytes, NK cells, and reticulocytes are: Faim3, Lcn2, Nkg7, Trim10 for both mice and humans. (F,G) show mouse and human malaria maps reporting different parameters. Colors mark the progression of time or the relative abundance of marked parameters. Ranges for (D–G) and parameters for deriving the graphs are listed in S6 Table.

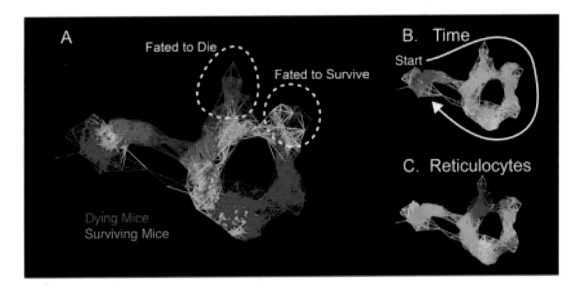

Figure CS6.2: Disease Maps of Mice with Warped Disease Spaces.

Figure CS6.2 Discussion: (A) A topological network map for malaria infected mice following the mice for a maximum of 26 d post infection. The surviving mice are marked in blue (n = 3), while those who died are marked in red (n = 4); other colors show overlap in the map. (B–C) show the same disease map as in (A), but colored according to (B) time or (C) reticulocytes (Ferrochelatase).

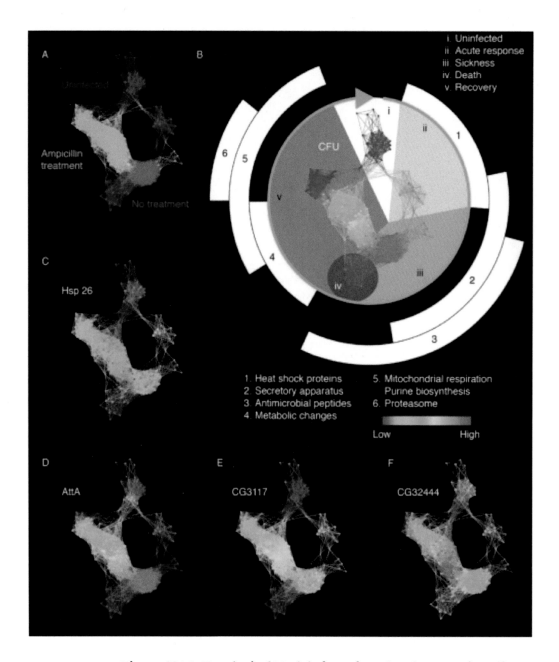

Figure CS6.3: Topological Models for Infected and Recovering Flies.

Figure CS6.3 Discussion: (A) Infection map colored by treatment groups. The network was built using Ayasdi Core. Samples with similar expression patterns are binned together. Nodes are bins of individual samples. Bins containing the same sample are connected by edges. Cyan is the overlap of uninfected and no treatment groups, and orange is the overlap of ampicillin treatment and no treatment groups. (B) Infection map colored by CFU. The green arrow marks disease progression. Pathways of upregulated genes are numbered. Phases of infection are indicated by Roman numerals. (C) Infection map colored by heat shock protein 26. (D) Infection map colored by Attacin A. (E) Infection map colored by CG3117 (peptidase and death gene). (F) Infection map colored by CG32444 (aldose-1 epimerase and recovery gene)

4.10 Case Study 7: Topological Data Analysis: A Promising Big Data Exploration Tool in Biology, Analytical Chemistry and Physical Chemistry

4.10.1   Contributors:

Dr. Ludovic Duponchel, Professor, University of Lille, France

This case study is largely reproduced from its original publication: Marc Offroy, L. Duponchel, "Topological Data Analysis: A Promising Big Data Exploration Tool in Biology, Analytical Chemistry, and Physical Chemistry," Analytica Chimica Acta, Vol. 910, 3March 2016, P. 1-11

4.10.2   Case Study Highlights:

- An example application of TDA to air biomonitoring illustrates how it can be used in this area of chemistry.
- In the example, an effectiveness comparison is made between TDA and other data analysis methodologies.
- TDA is shown to be able to "retrieve valuable information from different data structures with very low signal to noise ratio, variable shifts and missing data."

4.10.3   Example of TDA Method Applied to Air Biomonitoring

Analysis of single bacteria is a hot topic particularly in the framework of air biomonitoring. This is largely due to the need to develop new spectroscopic instrumentations capable of detecting agents in real time for civil and military applications. In this context, four bacteria strains were prepared in this work i.e. Staphylococcus epidermidis (a Gram-positive bacterium), Pseudomonas fluorescens (a Gram-negative bacterium), Pseudomonas syringae and Escherichia coli (a Gram-negative bacterium). Bacteria were first aerosolized and deposited on a CaF2 window for Raman analysis. This method was necessary to have a good dispersion and insure single bacteria Raman analysis described below.

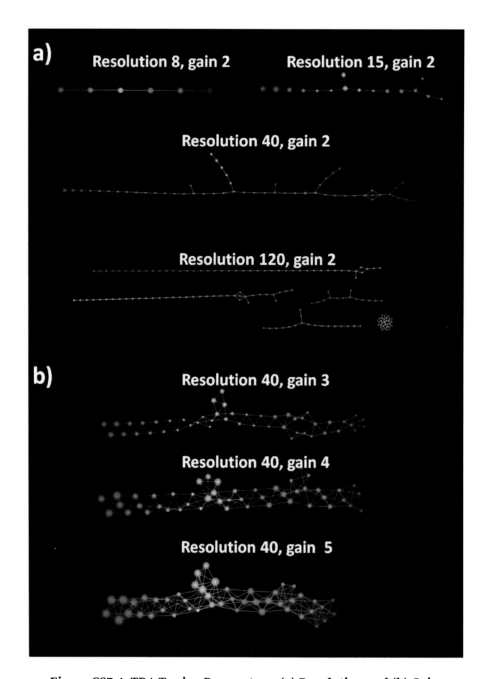

Figure CS7.4: TDA Tuning Parameters: (a) Resolution and (b) Gain

4.10.4   Comparison of TDA to Other Data Methods and Results of Example

The main aim of this part is to observe the behavior of common data analysis tools vs. TDA when exposed to different data structures induced by different experimental conditions. First when working with spectroscopic data sets, it is almost compulsory to apply a spectral pretreatment in order to suppress artifacts or unwanted variances. Because finding a good preprocessing algorithm or a combination of several ones is not always a trivial task, it is interesting to see if raw data can be analyzed directly with TDA. Figure CS7.5a shows Raman spectra of the 4000 single bacteria acquired in 1 min each. An important baseline shift is observed due to fluorescence. PCA analysis of the data set is shown in Figure CS7.5b where the four strains are retrieved with a strong overlap (S. epidermidis in red, P. fluorescens in dark green, P. syringae in dark blue and Escherichia coli in light blue). As observed, PCA is unable to retrieve four distinct clusters. It is mainly due to the fact that directions of main variances (i.e. fluorescence) are not correlated to strain type for this data set. Moreover, this overlap is observed whatever the selected PCA hyperplane. Unfortunately, chemical variance, the more interesting information, is really smaller than fluorescence in this case. HCA results in Figure CS7.5c reveal the same trend. Figure CS7.5d were generated by performing Topological Data Analysis on the same data set. Nodes in the network represent clusters of bacteria and edges connect nodes that contain samples (i.e. single bacteria) in common. In the first representation nodes are colored by the total number of bacteria while the four others are colored in order to indicate the presence of a particular bacteria strain. On its part, TDA extracts distinct groups for the four strains. Sub-groups or sub-populations of bacteria are even observed particularly for S. epidermidis and E. coli which are not present in PCA nor HCA. Considering now the same data set corrected by a first derivative and SNV normalization, PCA scatterplot (Figure CS7.6b) shows a better clustering with a persistent overlap between S. epidermidis (in red) and P. fluorescens (in green).

Chapter 4

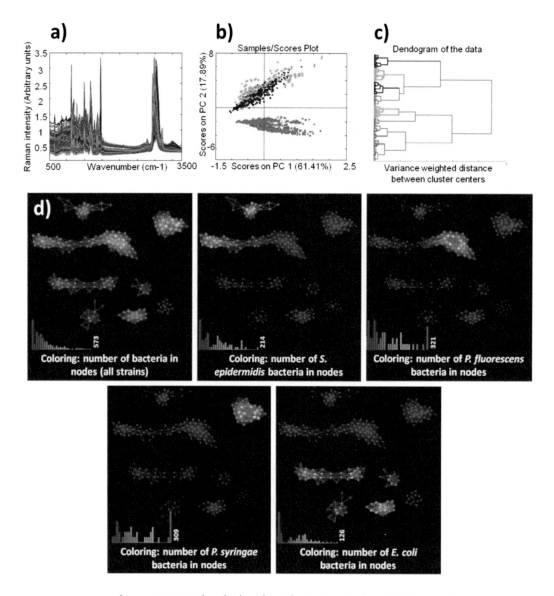

Figure CS7.5: Discriminating Single Bacteria with Raman Spectroscopy.

Figure CS7.5 Discussion: (a) Raw data, (b) PCA score plot, (c) HCA dendogram. PCA and HCA coloring: Staphylococcus epidermidis in red, Pseudomonas fluorescens in dark green, Pseudomonas syringae in dark blue and Escherichia coli in light blue. (d) TDA network (metric: Euclidean distance, Neighborhood lens, resolution = 30 and gain = 3). (For interpretation of the references to colour in this figure legend, the reader is referred to the web version of this article.)

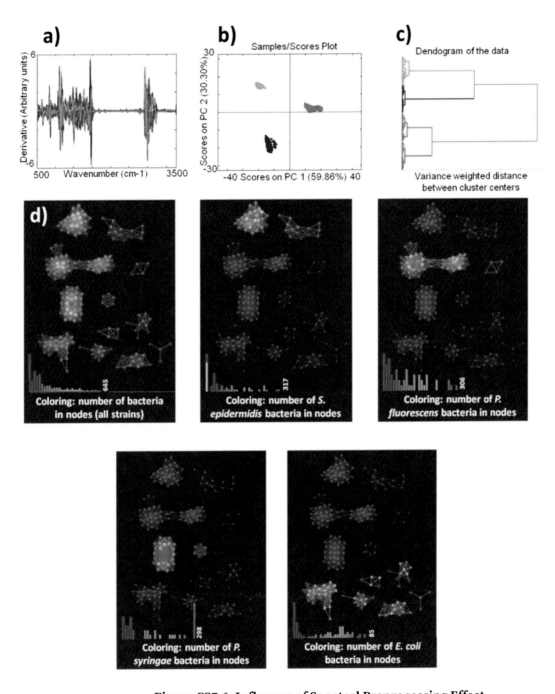

Figure CS7.6: Influence of Spectral Preprocessing Effect

Figure CS7.6 Discussion (a) First derivative and SNV normalized spectra, (b) PCA score plot, (c) HCA dendogram (d) TDA network (metric: Eucledian distance, Neighborhood lens, resolution = 30 and gain = 3). (For interpretation of the references to colour in this figure legend, the reader is referred to the web version of this article.) Clustering with a persistent overlap between S. epidermidis (in red) and P. fluorescens (in green). HCA result in Figure CS7.6c is good, but what is the more interesting is that strains and sub-populations are always observed with TDA. With this first part, it is observed that TDA can be invariant to deformation which is observed in spectroscopy when a preprocessing method is not applied. Another problem we often face in spectroscopy is the weakness of the signal to noise ratio. It happens when the observed physical effect (scattering, absorption ...) is weak or when acquisition time is low. Thus it is proposed here to study the same bacteria with an acquisition of 60 ms instead of 1 min Figure CS7.7a shows preprocessed spectra (first derivative, SNV) of the 4000 single bacteria considering this new acquisition time. One can observe an extremely low signal to noise ratio. Indeed it is very difficult to retrieve spectral features previously observed on Figure CS7.6a. The noise level is so high in these conditions that a maximum overlap is observed of the four strains in the PCA scatterplot. Indeed the high variance coming from noise is now expressed by the first principal components. It should be noted that HCA cannot retrieve the fours strains for the same reason (Figure CS7.7c). Topological data analysis provides interesting results as specific parts of the network are dedicated to specific strains despite the very low signal to noise ratio (Figure CS7.7d). In particular, P. syringae and E. coli bacteria are strictly separated whereas they completely overlap with PCA. Topological data analysis shows here the ability to handle noisy data which will be an important issue for the exploration of our next big data set.

4.10.5   Merged Experiments

From another point of view, when we look at big data sets a little closer, they often consist of merged experiments and even sometimes acquired with different methodologies or platforms. Thus, the idea of the next part is to try to analyze such data structures. Because modern Raman spectrometers have very good wavelength reproducibility, a wavelength shift is artificially introduced on the data set in order to simulate two different instruments. It is important to look at this issue because it is apparent for other spectroscopic techniques or even sometimes when matrix effect is observed. Given the initial data set with 1 min acquisition time (corrected with first derivative and SNV normalization), an offset of 8 cm^1 is introduced (i.e. 4 spectral variables) on half of the spectra for each strain. However, both the total number of spectral variables (i.e. 1501) and the spectral resolution (i.e. 2 cm^1) are kept. Figure CS7.8a and b present PCA and HCA results respectively. One can observe the shift effect introducing new variances in the data set. Consequently, in addition to the four strains (S. epidermidis in red, P. fluorescens in dark green, P. syringae in dark blue and E. coli in light blue) new clusters corresponding to their shifted spectra are observed ("shifted" S. epidermidis in pink, "shifted" P. fluorescens in light green, "shifted" P. syringae in purple and "shifted" E. coli in black). TDA does not fall into the trap because a dedicated part of the network is observed for each strain whatever the spectral shift applied or not (Figure CS7.8c). This feature is particularly important because developing a spectral alignment procedure is never a trivial task. Moreover, considering big data sets, it is never easy to know if such spectral shifts are present.

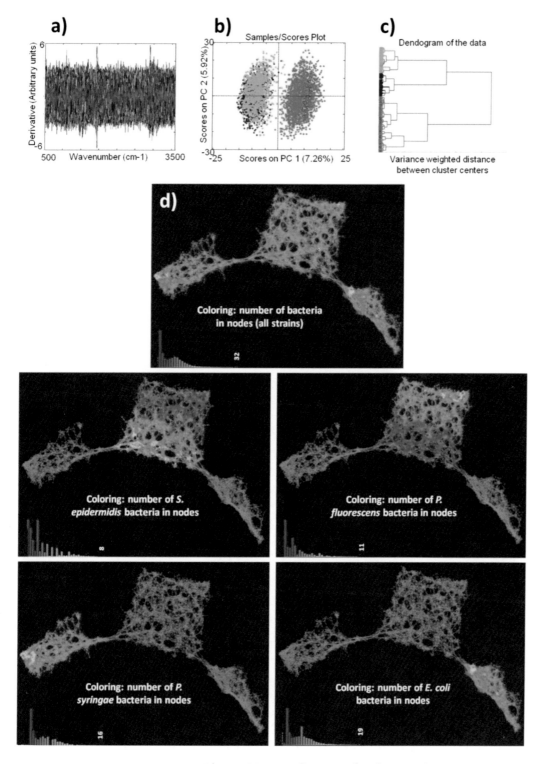

Figure CS7.7: Influence of Noise Level

Figure CS7.7 Discussion: (a) Noisy derivative and SNV normalized spectra, (b) PCA score plot, (c) HCA dendogram. PCA and HCA coloring: Staphylococcus epidermidis in red, Pseudomonas fluorescens in dark green, Pseudomonas syringae in dark blue and Escherichia coli in light blue. (d) Topological model (metric: Norm correlation, lens: MDS scores, resolution = 30 and gain= 3).

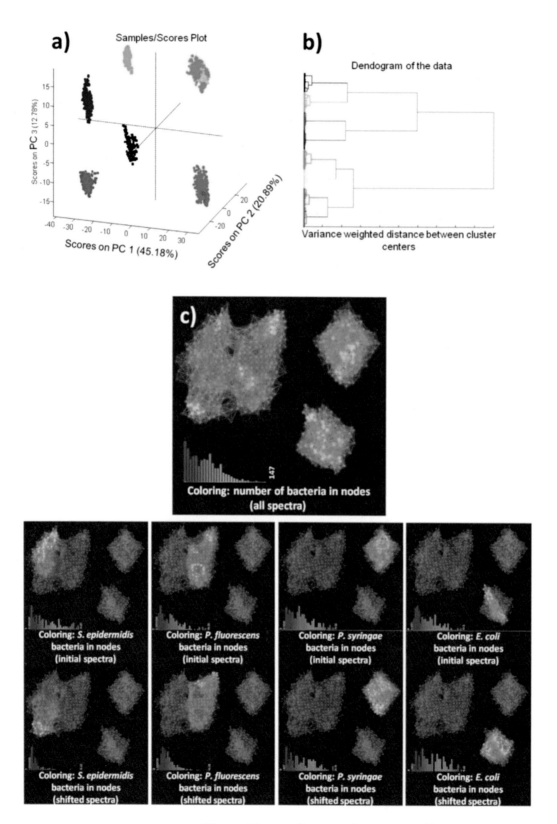

Figure CS7.8: Influence of Spectral Shift.

Figure CS7.8 Discussion: (a) PCA score plot, (b) HCA dendogram. PCA and HCA coloring: S. epidermidis in red, P. fluorescens in dark green, P. syringae in dark blue, E. coli in light blue, "shifted" S. epidermidis in pink, "shifted" P. fluorescens in light green, "shifted" P. syringae in purple and "shifted" E. coli in black. (c) TDA network (metric: Variance normalized Euclidean distance, lens: PCA scores, resolution = 40 and gain = 3).

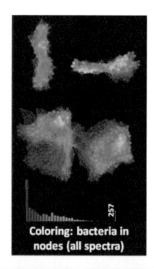

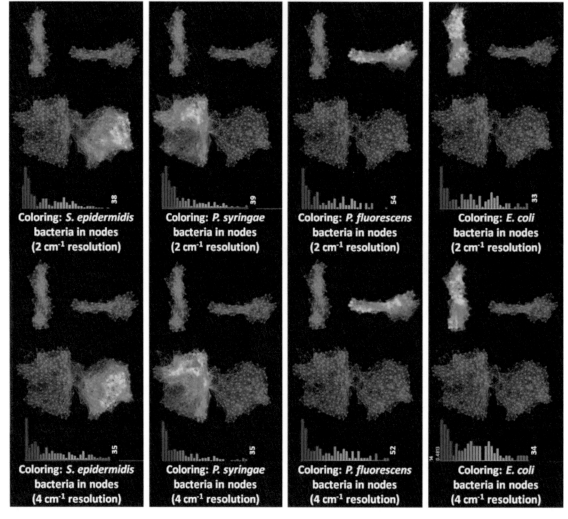

Figure CS7.9: Influence of Spectral Resolution

Figure CS7.9 Discussion: The TDA network with missing data (metric: Norm correlation, lens: MDS scores, resolution = 30 and gain = 3).

Because data sets can be acquired with different spectrometers with potentially different spectral resolutions, it is interesting in the last part of this work to see if TDA is able to manage this situation for a simultaneous exploration of all spectra. In order to reproduce this conditions, given the initial data set with 1 min acquisition time (corrected with first derivative and SNV normalization), one in two wave numbers have been deleted on half of the spectra for each strain. In this way, it is possible to observe 500 bacteria for each strain with two different spectral resolutions i.e. 2 cm^{1} and 4 cm^{1}. However, the total number of spectral variables (i.e. 1501) is kept leading to a missing data structure on half of the spectra. Figure CS7.9 shows impressive results since four specific parts of the TDA network are dedicated to the different strains whatever the spectral resolution. However selected metric and lens must be able to manage such missing data structure. In this example norm correlation and MDS scores were respectively used. They handle null values by first projecting the pair of rows to the intersection of their non-null columns. This TDA feature is very important because it is often difficult and even sometimes impossible to manage missing values with conventional data analysis tools. Nevertheless, even if TDA calculations are rather fast, we must spend time in finding a good metric/lens combination for the observation of clusters or subpopulations.

4.10.6   Conclusion

The main objective of the work was to compare topological data analysis with a conventional chemometric tools. This allowed us to highlight nice properties of the method. Indeed TDA was able retrieve valuable information from different data structures with very low signal to noise ratio, variable shifts and missing data. As a consequence, it might be regarded as a very robust and promising method to cope with such situations. From a general point of view, it is difficult to say that this 4000 spectra example is huge for the big data community but for us and at the present time it can be. However, we are convinced that Topological Data Analysis which is very scalable will be one of the best exploration tools for our future big data sets with several hundred thousand or even millions of rows (not only spectra). Deep learning in biology, analytical chemistry and physical chemistry is not so far away.

Chapter 5: Machine Learning and Machine Intelligence

"I'm sorry, Dave. I'm afraid I can't do that."
-HAL9000[40]

(Author's note: A book about Machine Learning must have at least one reference to HAL. It's a rule.)

5.1 Chapter Preview

- Define Machine Learning.
- Explain the difference between Machine Learning, Artificial Intelligence, deep intelligence and Machine Intelligence.
- Provide a Machine Learning process diagram and explain each block's function.
- A research backgrounder is provided with some key definitions.
- Distinguish between supervised and unsupervised learning highlighting a few ML algorithms.
- Introduce the concepts of exploratory data analysis contrasting it to confirmatory data analysis.
- Discuss topological data analysis in the context of Machine Learning.
- Explain the benefits of TDA over some common ML algorithms using real world examples.
- Case Studies
  - Case Study 8: Application of Principal Component Analysis to the Analysis of Microarrays
  - Case Study 9: TDA Microbiome Analysis

5.2 What is Machine Learning?

Machine Learning (ML) is a collection of mathematical and computer science techniques for extracting information from large data sets, and the use of these techniques for the construction of automated solutions to classification, prediction, and estimation problems.

ML is not the same thing as Artificial Intelligence (AI). For our purposes, AI and ML are different techniques to create machine cognition. AI depends on human experts to create *heuristic rule sets* that explain the world for an AI machine to refer to in order to make decisions about a problem. AI's ability to solve a problem is dependent on having a human anticipate the problem in advance.

Machine Learning uses stochastic methods to analyze a data set to create its own rule set, in order to predict correct solutions to problems based on interpretations of data, as well as modify the data set as new information is learned. ML's ability to solve a problem is dependent on its ability to infer a solution from a data set, such that a ML system is not limited to problems pre-anticipated by the developer. In fact, ML is simply an attempt to substitute for human experience in an AI problem where humans do not know what the rules are, and therefore need to be determined from data.

5.2.1 Machine Learning Example

The following is a very simplistic and highly idealized example to distinguish ML from AI. Assume there is a market for a machine that can answer questions about Christmas. In an AI machine, a human trainer would input into the data set relationships about Christmas:

- Santa Claus is an imaginary human associated with Christmas
- Christmas lights are decorations associated with Christmas
- Scrooge is a fictitious human associated with Christmas
- Wreaths are decorations associated with Christmas

When asked the question, "who is the most famous human associated with Christmas?" The above AI system would reply nothing/either/both Scrooge or Santa, since the information isn't available to make a distinction of popularity, and not consider Jesus Christ, since the human trainer didn't consider it. If you asked about reindeer, the AI machine would be at a loss because the human trainer hasn't provided the AI system a relationship associated with reindeer. The human trainer would now go back, realizing that the system is missing information, and add information about Christ, reindeer and popularity statistics. If asked again the same question, it would make a response based on the popularity data input by the trainer, but if asked about fruitcake, it would be at a loss again until the human trainer input that information into the data set. An AI system adapts over time as the human trainer allows it to adapt.

For the ML machine in our example, a researcher loads a data set with the book "A Christmas Carol"[41] , "The Old Farmer's Almanac[42]", a year's worth of New York Times and the book "Ho Ho Ho, The Complete Book of Christmas Words"[43] . Having been programmed with a model to analyze written language and a statistical predictive model, the ML machine provides answers to questions based on the use context and likelihood of correctness. It might relate that Santa or Christ are more popular than Scrooge because there are more references, and tangentially might mention Maulana Karenga the creator of Kwanzaa, someone the questioner or the researcher never considered, but was often mentioned in the New York Times with Christmas. Regardless of the question, the ML Christmas machine will attempt to answer any question asked, whether it was related to Christmas or not. If you asked a question about jack-o-lanterns, it might just relate that jack-o-lanterns are not a part of Christmas because it can't find a contextual reference related to Christmas, or given the season, the holiday and the availability of pumpkins may suggest pumpkin pie as an alternative to pudding at Christmas dinner, because a jack-o-lantern in the context of Christmas is a wasteful use of pumpkins.

An AI machine is only as good as the human who creates its rules and the logic that model the world, whereas a ML machine is only as good as the algorithm developed to improve its knowledge base and infer solutions about the world from its data set. Another important distinction between AI and ML is that ML generally uses a great deal of processing power, lots of data, and bigger and more complex algorithms.

5.2.2 A Little ML History

The term "Artificial Intelligence" was coined in 1955 by John McCarthy at Dartmouth University. Prior to that, Alan Turing in 1950, released a paper describing the "Imitation Game", later renamed, "Turing Test" in his honor. The Turing Test is a test for intelligence in a computer, requiring that a human being should be unable to distinguish the machine from another human being by using the replies to questions put to both.[44] At the time, though attempts were made to define a thinking machine[45], over time the technical limitations made this goal appear unlikely, so research dollars evaporated.

AI grew up at a time when data storage and processing power were very limited and expensive. The branch of computer science AI ultimately took was "expert systems" targeted at lower processing power and small memory systems that assist humans in making decisions. ML was exiled from being an AI method in 1980, because expert systems were considered a more practical solution. Further, researchers at the time were more concerned with applying knowledge to problems, regardless of the knowledge source, rather than creating learning capabilities in machines.[46] Although ideas in the direction of ML appeared as early as the 1950's, the ML field didn't begin to flourish as a separate field until the 1990's, where huge leaps in memory size and processing power began to take place. Research in ML has been rapidly expanding ever since.

To recap, AI typically deals with human trained, rule based systems, without a stochastic or statistical component. ML explicitly includes statistical notions in most tasks it undertakes, and therefore is able to deal with many real-world situations that are not accessible to AI in its current form.

5.2.3 Machine Intelligence

Machine Intelligence (MI) can be viewed as an extension of ML and AI. ML may be considered a "black box" decision tool that attempts to provide the user with the "best" solution possible given environmental input. MI on the other hand, given the same environmental input as a ML tool, would often provide the user with an array of solutions. An MI opens up the decision process for observation, allowing the user to observe the strong as well as the weak conclusions. MI is about aiding the decision process, rather than just providing an answer, as ML or AI stresses. The following are a number of distinctions to be noted about MI:

- MI provides analyses that permit human interpretation and interaction, allowing iteration between machine and human analysis. It goes beyond the "black box" nature of Machine Learning solutions.
- MI offers output that captures the full complexity of phenomena, rather than reducing to a single optimal answer.
- MI permits the detection of phenomena with "weak signal", which is often drowned out by the "strong signal" in standard Machine Learning analyses.
- MI provides explanations of the results of analyses for human consumption.

Since MI uses ML techniques to provide an array of solutions, studying ML is a key step in understanding MI.

5.3 How Machine Learning Systems Work

Machine Learning is a collection of mathematical and statistical methods for extracting knowledge, preferably actionable knowledge, from data sets of all kinds. ML encompasses tools whose goal is to obtain an understanding of the data, to formulating and designing automatic mathematical methods for prediction and classification for new data points. The term "Machine Learning" refers to the automatization of learning. Learning, defined as the process of obtaining understanding and building on that understanding to obtain useful criteria for informing actions based on data. ML often consists of methods for optimizing parameters in a family of parametric models, and these models can take various forms.

MACHINE LEARNING MODEL

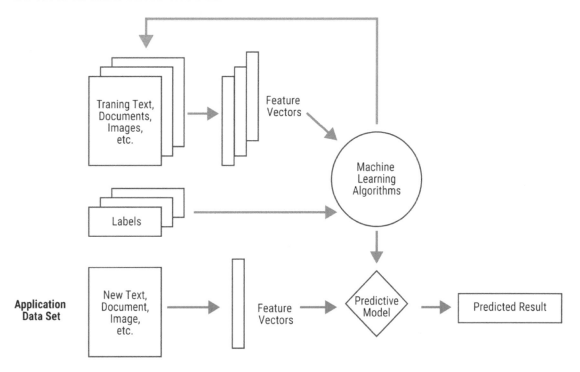

Figure 5.1: The Components of a Machine Learning System

Note: the model selection and training process is an iterative activity comprised of the components training data set, feature vectors and Machine Learning algorithm.

5.3.1 ML Component Description

5.3.1.1 Decomposing the Data Set

In considering a supervised data analysis problem, where the ultimate goal is to perform some kind of prediction of an outcome variable, one needs to be aware that various kinds of prediction procedures are vulnerable to the problem of *overfitting*. Overfitting occurs, for example, when one enlarges the number of variables or features to the point where it is possible to fit the model almost perfectly no matter what the data set is. In this situation, one will find that although the model gives excellent results on the data on which the model was trained, it will fail miserably when applied to new data. One way to mitigate this problem is through a collection of validation procedures known as *cross-validation*. The idea is to train the model on a subset of the data, and then assess how well it performs on the remainder of the data. This process typically involves three data sets:

1. The training data set is used to train the model by pairing the input with the expected output.
2. The validation data set provides a feedback loop in developing the model. The model is tested on the validation data set, and if it does not perform well on it, one may retrain it on the training set.
3. The testing data set is used to measure accuracy of the model. It provides the ultimate assessment of the final model, and one does not further tune the parameters based on the outcome on the testing set.

Generally, the testing data set is larger than the training data set, but the actual size ratio between the three phases is a decision for the researcher.

5.3.1.2 Feature Vectors

Feature vectors are the numerical representation of the data's features. Their entries are also called "variables" of "dimensions". Categorical and non-numeric information must be converted into numeric representations, so statistical models can be used. In this step qualitative data is assigned a numeric representation and quantitative data might be normalized or transformed, so that ML algorithms are applicable. For example, if a data set consists of a collection of text documents, and is therefore non-numerical, one may assign to each word in the English language the count of the number of occurrences of that word in the document. In this way, each document is assigned a "vector" with numerical entries, one entry for each word in the English language.

5.3.1.3 Machine Learning Algorithms

Below is a graph displaying and categorizing various types of Machine Learning algorithms. The choice of which algorithms to use depend on the data type and the type of result desired.

Machine Learning algorithms are broadly classified as supervised or unsupervised. Determining whether to use a supervised learning or unsupervised learning method is determined by the purpose of the solution. In supervised learning, given a number of traits of the new specimen under examination, the goal is to predict the value of some kind of outcome variable. If the variable is discrete it's called classification. If the variable is continuous it's called regression. In supervised learning, a ML algorithm is trained with known outcomes.

The result of an unsupervised learning algorithm may be a clustering or a dimensionality reduction. In either case, the analysis does not provide prediction of an outcome variable but instead produces a representation which yields additional understanding of the data set. Of course, this understanding can ultimately lead to the construction of classifiers and predictors, but that requires the application of supervised algorithms with inputs based on the understanding acquired via the unsupervised analysis.

After components of Machine Learning are introduced, some examples of supervised and unsupervised learning algorithms will be shown. Figure 5.2 shows some of the various types of Machine Learning algorithms.

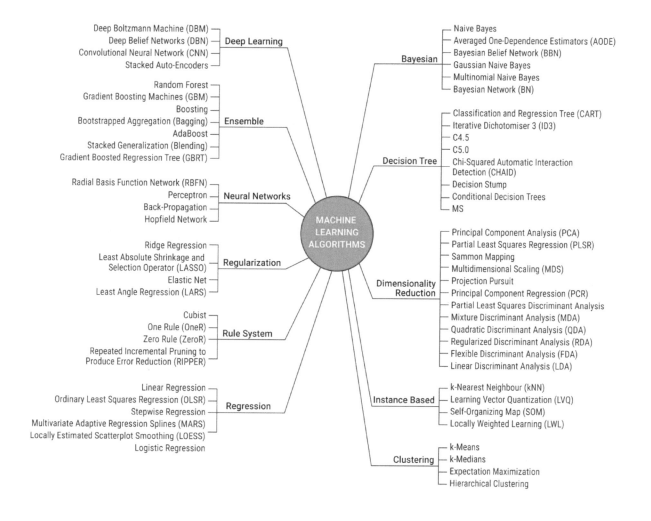

Figure 5.2: Machine Learning Algorithms[47]

5.4 Research Backgrounder

This section provides a few basic definitions associated with research to give the reader context for the rest of the chapter.

Non-experimental research is the study of pre-existing data, where a researcher cannot control or manipulate the predictor variables, but instead, relies on interpretation and observation of the data to come to a conclusion. "Control" in this context means ability to exclude influence of outside variables, not under consideration. An example is a clinical study attempting to determine whether a human trait predicts success, suitably defined. Humans live lives that generally can't be controlled, even when they are subjects of research.

Experimental research is a study where a researcher can modify inputs (independent variables) to observe their effect on outputs (dependent variables). An example is a clinical study where dose size of a new drug is modified to determine efficacy.

Null Hypothesis refers to a default position that there is no relationship between two measured phenomena, or no association among groups.[48] The goal of determining a relationship between members of a data set relies on disproving the null hypothesis. For example, in a study to determine whether or not smoking and lung cancer are correlated, the null hypothesis might be that they are not correlated, and disproving the null hypothesis would show that they are indeed correlated.

The table below provides different types of variables used in experimental and non-experimental research.

VARIABLE	DESCRIPTION
Binary Variable	Observations (i.e., dependent variables) that occur in one of two possible states, often labelled zero and one. E.g., "improved/not improved" and "completed task/failed to complete task."
Categorical Variable	Usually an independent or predictor variable that contains values indicating membership in one of several possible categories. E.g., gender (male or female), marital status (married, single, divorced, widowed). The categories are often assigned numerical values for nominal variable used as labels, e.g., 0 = male; 1 = female.
Dependent Variable	The presumed effect in an experimental study. The values of the dependent variable depend upon another variable, the independent variable. Strictly speaking, "dependent variable" should not be used when writing about non-experimental designs.
Discrete Variable	Variable having only integer values. For example, number of trials need by a student to learn a memorization task.
Independent Variable	The presumed cause in an experimental study. All other variables that may impact the dependent variable are controlled. The values of the independent variable are under experimenter control. Strictly speaking, "independent variable" should not be used when writing about nonexperimental designs, but are often used instead of predictor variable.
Outcome Variable	The presumed effect in a nonexperimental study. Synonym for criterion variable.
Predictor Variable	The presumed "cause" on a nonexperimental study. Often used in correlational studies. For example, SAT scores predict first semester GPA. The SAT score is the predictor variable.

Table 5.1: Short List of Variable Types

5.5 Selected Machine Learning Algorithms Illustrated

This section summarizes a number of methodologies used in ML. A high level description of the various methods is shown, describing the task each one attempts to address, and a description of how the task is carried out.

5.5.1 Supervised Machine Learning Algorithm Types

5.5.1.1 Linear Regression

This method applies when one has a data set consisting of numerical variables, and one or more of the variables are labeled as dependent variables. The variables that are not among the dependent variables are called independent variables. The goal is to find linear algebraic formulas in the independent variables which predict the dependent variables, in an optimal way. This is a relatively simple mathematical problem to solve, and frequently gives very useful information.

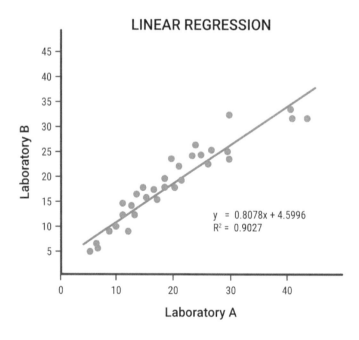

Figure 5.3: Linear Regression

The example shows a line of best fit to the set of data points, together with the formula relating y to x. From the example above, y is the dependent variable and x is the independent variable. The method can be adapted to multiple linear regression, where more than one category of independent variables describe the dependent variable, fitting by best curves or surfaces of higher degrees, or by graphs of other families of functions.

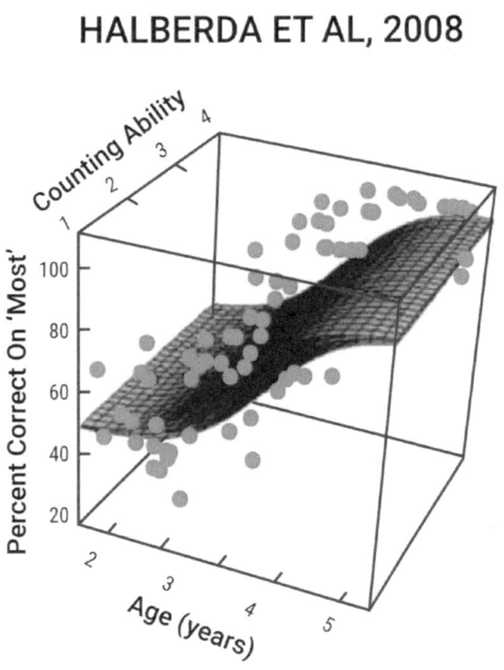

HALBERDA ET AL, 2008

Figure 5.4: 3-d Linear Regression

When it works, this is an excellent method for understanding data as well as providing predictions and actionable knowledge from it. As we saw in Chapter 2, data sets do not always fit along such algebraic surfaces.

5.5.1.2 Logistic Regression

Predicting an outcome that is not numerical but is categorical or binary is often desirable. For example, predicting whether or not a subject in healthcare study will survive, the outcome might be coded as 0 for death and 1 for survival. In this case, one could attempt to simply treat the 0/1-values as a numerical variable and apply linear regression. Unfortunately, experience shows that this approach does not work very well for many 0/1-valued outcome variables. However, it is possible to use another family of functions to perform the regression.

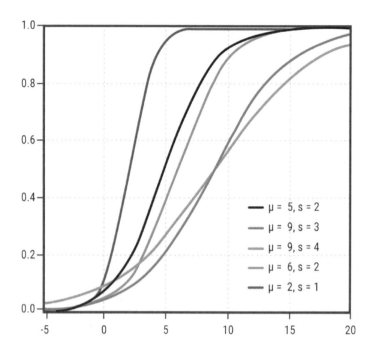

Figure 5.5: Logistic Regression

The family is shown in the picture above, and it is called the family of generalized logistic functions. Fitting such a family of functions typically does much better at classification than the linear strategy alluded to above.

5.5.1.3 Decision Trees

Decision trees are collections of rules based on the values of coordinates (numerical or categorical) that can often do well when one is trying to classify a data point or more generally to make a decision on an incoming data point. A sample decision tree might look like this.

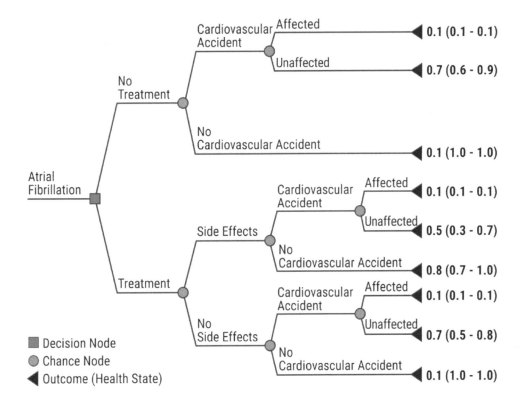

Figure 5.6: Decision Tree

This particular decision tree takes patients who have experienced atrial fibrillation, and assigns a utility score for each path through the tree. The idea is to determine whether the patient should undergo treatment, and each patient will be assigned a utility score (seen at the right) for each of the two branches "Treatment" and "No treatment". Such decision trees can be constructed by a number of methods.

5.5.2 Unsupervised Machine Learning Algorithm Types

Unsupervised methods are generally useful in providing and overall understanding of a data set. From such analyses, one may ultimately build operational models based on the understanding obtained in the unsupervised analysis. They are also useful in problems of anomaly detection, and can be useful in the data cleaning process.

5.5.2.1 Discriminant Analysis and Support Vector Machines

Discriminant analysis attempts to classify data points by drawing a "decision boundary" in the space in which the data points reside and then classify them according to which side of the boundary they're on. The decision boundary can be a line, a plane or higher dimensional analogue, a curve, a surface or a higher dimensional analogue. When there is a classification involving more than two alternatives, it is possible to build multiple decision boundaries so that there are multiple regions in the classification.

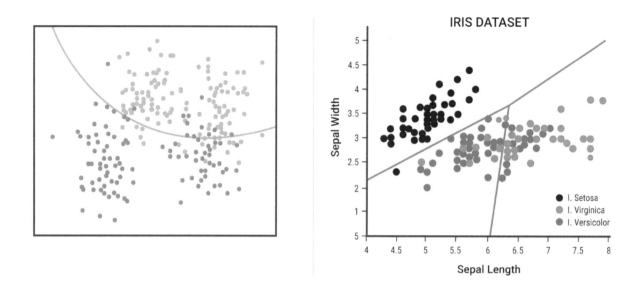

Figure 5.7: Discriminate Analysis

5.5.2.2 Cluster Analysis

Cluster analysis is a collection of methodologies for breaking data sets up into groups, ideally with the property that data points within a cluster are more similar to each other than they are to members of another cluster. There are many mathematical approaches to this problem.

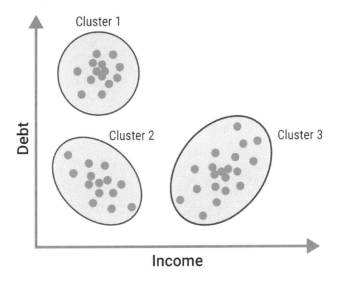

Figure 5.8: Cluster Analysis

Although most of the algorithms that perform this task produce a single cluster decomposition, there are some which produce a "multiscale" cluster decomposition. In this case, the output, rather than being one decomposition, is a dendrogram that represents a family of decompositions parametrized by a numerical parameter so that the decomposition becomes increasingly coarse as the parameter increases. At the zero value of the parameter, the cluster decomposition consists entirely of singleton groups, while for large enough values it consists of a single cluster, which coincides with the entire data set.

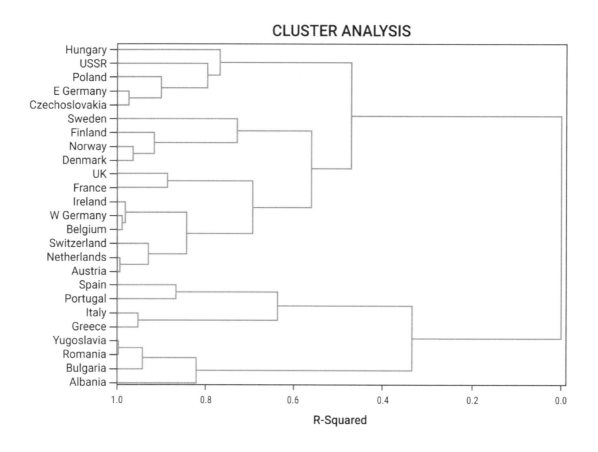

Figure 5.9: Hierarchal Cluster Analysis

In the example above, the finest clusters consist of single countries, whereas at the next to the highest level a rough decomposition of the countries into northern Europe vs. southern Europe is found.

5.5.2.3 Dimensionality reduction/PCA/MDS

Principal component analysis (PCA) and multidimensional scaling (MDS) are methods that produce a scatter plot (in 2 or 3 dimensions), with each point in the scatter plot corresponding to exactly one data point in the original set.

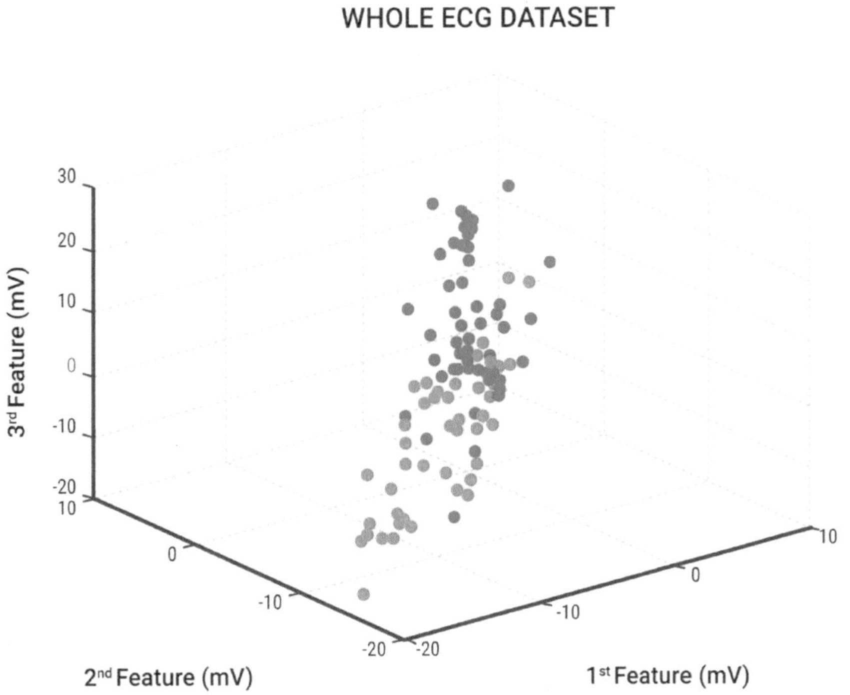

WHOLE ECG DATASET

Figure 5.10: Principal Component Analysis

Both are matrix based. In the case of PCA, the input is a data matrix, with rows corresponding to data points and columns corresponding to fields or features of the data. In the case of MDS, the starting point is a distance measure that is computable on pairs of data points. The distance measure might be given as a formula computable on pairs of data points, or it might be given as a distance matrix, where rows and columns both correspond to data points, and the distance between a pair of points is the corresponding entry in the matrix.

In addition to constructing a scatter plot, the actual structure of the projection to 2 or 3 dimensional space can be quite useful. The coordinates of the points in the scatter plot are very informative, and can be viewed as new features. One can also consider projections to dimensions greater than 3. They cannot be visualized, but they provide a very useful dimensionality reduction for the data set. For example, when text data is viewed as a matrix by using word counts for all the words in an English dictionary, it is very useful and effective to perform PCA to get a projection that has only 30 or 40 features, rather than a million or so features, corresponding to the entries in the dictionary. Each of the coordinates (called principal components) is a weighted sum of the features (in this case words) of the original data set. The weighting features are very useful to understand.

5.5.2.4 Topological Data Analysis

One can view Machine Learning as producing models that make the data more understandable. We have seen models whose output is an algebraic equation (regression models), a tree with nodes labeled by questions or probabilities of outcomes, a binary classifier, or a scatter plot of the data. The scatter plot example fits under the heading of unsupervised analysis, since it simply presents a view of the data which can make it more understandable, and can suggest properties of the data such as breaking into clusters or fitting along lines or planes.

TDA provides a very useful alternative to scatter plots, producing models of data sets that permit both quicker and more accurate understanding of them, as well as the production of operational models which automate tasks based on the outcomes of the data analysis. TDA's output is a topological network. The network is laid out on the screen, where a user can interact with it in ways similar to the methods used in Adobe Photoshop™ and Illustrator™. It retains rough geometric features of the data that are often obscured in two or three dimensional scatter plots. Also possible is interacting with the model in a very useful way, which is more difficult in scatter plots. These capabilities are extremely useful for the process of extracting information from the data, in particular for determining segmentations of the data into coherent regions or categories. There are also methods for performing and improving various kinds of supervised analysis based on the network. For example, given a regression problem, it is possible to improve its overall error by introducing features created from properties of the network. Similarly, for any classification method, it is possible to find "regions" within the data that define systematic ways in which the classifier fails, and then append new features coming from the topological model to improve performance in the local regions.

5.6 Machine Intelligence and Traditional Statistical Analysis

Statistical analysis can be divided into two types, confirmatory data analysis (CDA) and exploratory data analysis (EDA). Both are key components in Machine Intelligence. The goal of CDA is to determine whether a perceived result is in fact "real", in the sense that it is very improbable that it occurred simply as the result of random variation. EDA permits the exploration of a data set to determine useful features and suggest likely hypotheses concerning the data. Both of these tasks are properties that are important in human cognition, and therefore are a part of Machine Intelligence.

5.6.1 Confirmatory Data Analysis

Confirmatory data analysis develops methods to determine whether or not an observed phenomenon could have appeared at random, or stated more technically, whether or not the null hypothesis is supported or rejected. Consider a coin tossing experiment consisting of tossing a coin a large number of times. If heads appeared many more times than tails, one might suspect that the coin is biased. Given the null hypothesis presumes the coin is unbiased, the expected observation is seeing neither side of the coin more often than the other. In order to quantify the expected observation and prove that the hypothesis is indeed valid, a researcher models the experiment with probabilistic methods by estimating the probability that an unbiased coin would produce a given number of heads greater than or equal to the number actually witnessed. If this estimated probability is sufficiently small thereby disproving the null hypothesis, and in so doing convincing the researcher that the coin is highly likely to be biased.

This kind of analysis is very important. Humans often have a sense that they are seeing a systematic phenomenon, when in fact their observations are consistent with what is observed under random behavior. Confirmatory analysis is used to show that an observation is very unlikely to have occurred by chance, and therefore confirm our impression is "real".

5.6.2 Exploratory Data Analysis (EDA)

Confirmatory data analysis usually requires a formulation step, in which one creates a family of hypotheses, one of which is the null hypothesis. These hypotheses are then turned into mathematical models, for which one can perform analyses like the one in the example of the coin above, to permit one to reject the null hypothesis and conclude that there must some explanation for the outcome separate from the null hypothesis.

Exploratory Data Analysis (EDA) addresses the problem of creating the hypotheses in the first place. This is a very important problem to deal with. Although in the early days of data analysis (Galileo, Newton) the nature of the hypotheses was often not too difficult to discern, it is certainly the case that for most of the large and complex data we are dealing with, it is by no means clear what hypotheses are likely to be accurate. Further, because of the large number of features, the collection of possible hypotheses is now very much larger than has been the case previously, so hypothesis generation is now of paramount importance.

The statistician John Tukey, considered the father of EDA, felt that too much time was being spent on sophisticated analysis with too little emphasis on the formulation of hypotheses and models. Tukey wrote:[49]

"Far better an approximate answer to the right question, which is often vague, than an exact answer to the wrong question, which can always be made precise."

In Tukey's groundbreaking book, "Exploratory Data Analysis"[50], he proposes a variety of techniques, mostly visual, for studying data without the need to create hypothetical models as a basis to study the data. He echoed Playfair's view that many insights about a data set are easier to understand when visually presented. For Tukey, mathematical models left much to be desired when trying to understand data, as he describes:

*"Consistent with this view, we believe, is a clear demand that pictures based on exploration of data should **force** their messages upon us. Pictures that emphasize what we already know --" security blankets" to reassure us--are frequently not worth the space they take. Pictures that have to be gone over with a reading glass to see the main point are wasteful of time and inadequate of effect. The greatest value of a picture is when it forces us to notice what we never expected to see."*

Tukey didn't mean that EDA is superior to CDA, but rather is a first step in the process of understanding the data. Tukey felt that EDA could improve the understanding of the data prior to modeling, so that the researcher would create a more informed CDA, avoiding the trap of becoming distracted and/or overly enamored with a very elegant incorrect algebraic model; more bluntly put, all parents love their children beyond reason, even ugly ones.

5.6.3 TDA as an EDA Method

Topological data analysis does not require explicit modeling and doesn't depend on the formulation of hypotheses, but rather starts from a quantitative measure of the similarity between data points. To be sure, one could generate different similarity measures for a given data set, but they are comprised of much more primitive information about the data and involve less room for the insertion of bias into the analysis. By contrast, with TDA one isn't limited to a single similarity measure, TDA permits the comparison between two or more choices of similarity measures, so that one can understand what is being emphasized and de-emphasized in each of the choices. The TDA models also support interaction, rather than simply constructing a model for visual inspection. It then follows that they can often be used in the same way as one uses algebraic models, but taking advantage of additional flexibility, thus permitting the discovery of the unexpected.

Emphasizing that TDA works in concert with confirmatory analysis, the TDA model is not by itself proof of significance or validity; it suggests hypotheses that ultimately need to be validated using standard statistical technique.

One of the standard forms of hypotheses generated by a TDA network is the discovery of groups or subpopulations with distinct behavior, often with enrichment of an outcome variable. TDA provides an excellent way to interrogate data sets for coherent subpopulations, and standard statistics is very well equipped to confirm and quantify that the groups are effectively distinguishable by several of the variables, and that it is extremely unlikely that they would have appeared from simple random models.

5.6.4 Topological Modeling Compared to Principal Component Analysis and Multidimensional Scaling

Earlier in this chapter, we briefly discussed other Machine Learning techniques, including Principal Component Analysis (PCA), Multidimensional Scaling (MDS), and Hierarchical clustering (HCA). The first two methods produce the same kind of output, a *scatter plot*, while the third produces a dendrogram, and all can be regarded as methods for exploratory data analysis (EDA). A scatter plot is simply a collection of points in the plane or in space, which can be visualized by a scatter plot diagram.

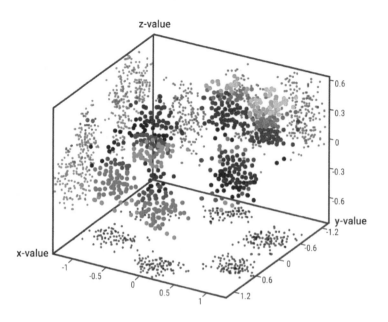

Figure 5.11: Scatter Plot

Describing the relationship between these constructions and the TDA models, there are two key features about both PCA and MDS which are important to understand.

- Each point in the scatter plot diagram corresponds to a single data point. If there are very many data points, then there will be very many points in the scatter plot.
- Both methods are produced using algebraic methods.

A topological model is a network consisting of nodes and edges, which can then be laid out in the plane or in space using standard graph layout methods. Each node of the network thus corresponds to a point in the plane or in space, and can therefore be thought of as a scatter plot. However, each node in the network generally corresponds to groups of data points, often large groups, which mean that the number of points in this scatter plot is much smaller than that produced by PCA or MDS. Additionally, each node corresponds to a family of points which are regarded as similar by the similarity measure we have used in order to create the model. So, in a sense, **the nodes correspond to families of similar behaviors in the data.** Secondly, the topological model is more than a scatter plot, in that it also has **information about edges (node interconnects) encoded in it**, and these are displayed. In this way, one gets a representation of the collection of all pair wise similarities between families of closely correlated data points.

This kind of representation is very powerful, and allows for the implementation of various modeling methods in a way which is intrinsic to the data.

The production of the TDA network often uses information from a PCA or MDS representation. This is one of the reasons that we consider TDA to be an extension of existing ML technique, rather than a competitor of it. Suppose we construct a network from a distance function and a PCA or MDS projection. It turns out that by performing this construction and applying a force directed layout algorithm for visual display, one obtains a visual representation that captures more information than the scatter plot representations. Compare the following two plots:

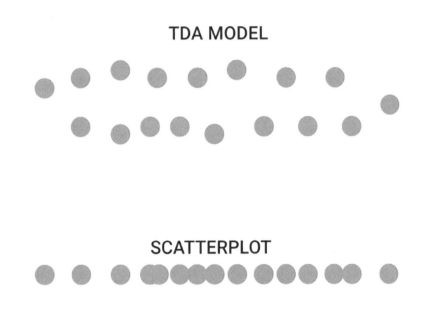

Figure 5.12: TDA vs. Scatter Plot

The TDA model can be viewed as a very flat loop, while the scatter plot does not reflect that, because the distances between points projecting to the same point in the scatter plot are much smaller than the scale in the scatter plot. The following pictures illustrate what the consequences are for a particular data set.

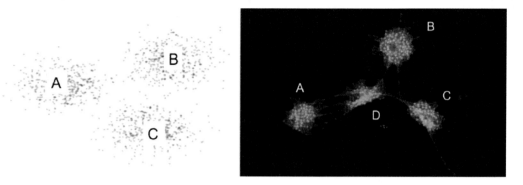

Figure 5.13: TDA vs. Cluster Analysis

The two sides represent scatter plot and TDA representations of the same data set. In the PCA scatter plot on the left, the data divides into three distinct clusters. In the TDA representation, one sees four clusters. In the scatter plot two of the clusters were lying over each other and appeared as the same cluster, so the distinction between them was missed. However, all four clusters in the TDA model were meaningful and recognizable as distinct from each other.

Another example[51], concerning spectroscopic analysis of bacterial strains, the data consisted of Raman spectra of 4000 single bacteria, and containing 4 distinct strains, *S. epidermidis, P. fluorescens, P. syringae,* and *Escherichia coli.* The analysis was done on the *raw data,* with no preprocessing. In the image below, a) represents the actual raw data represented graphically, b) shows a PCA analysis of the data, c) shows the dendrogram obtained by hierarchical clustering, and the images in d) show the TDA network colored by various quantities. The nodes in the first (upper left) network areis colored by the number of data points corresponding to a given node, and then the remaining four are colored by the number of data points that belong to each of the strains, in order *S. Epidermis, P.fluorescens, P. syringae,* and *E. coli.* PCA does not obtain good separation of the four groups, and neither does the dendrogram but TDA clearly segments species within the network.

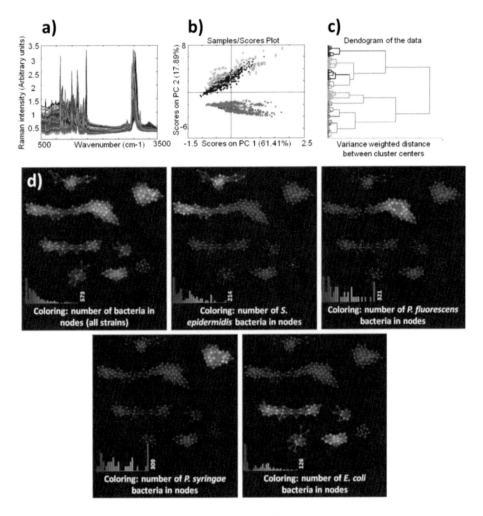

Figure 5.14: TDA vs. Principle Component Analysis

This example was discussed in more detail in Chapter 4, Case Study 7.

5.6.5 TDA and Linear Regression

Linear Regression is another modeling mechanism for data, where the variables are divided into a set of independent variables and a single dependent variable. As we have seen in earlier in this chapter, it consists of approximating the data by the graph of a linear equation. When this approximation is a good one, the linear regression model permits us to predict the outcome variable based on the independent variables. The linear regression methodology uses a simple optimization method for the overall model error, and measures performance relative to the overall model error. There are some TDA procedures which can yield more understanding of the failure of the approximation, and also suggest modified procedures that can yield improved prediction of the dependent variable.

To see how this works, consider this data set with associated regression line.

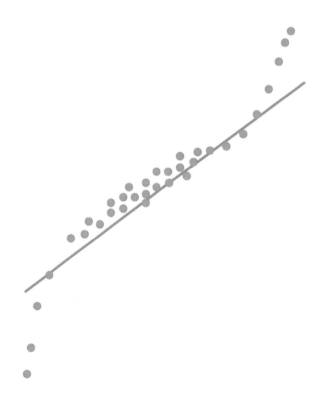

Figure 5.15: Error in Linear Regression

There is substantial failure in the approximation, but it is concentrated at the two ends. The regression model only deals with overall error. By understanding where the failure is concentrated, the recognition of the regions where the prediction is better than the overall error rate would suggest becomes apparent. Having new data points which are close to points in such a region, can assign better confidence in the prediction. In this case, the TDA model (colored by the average model error in the node) looks like this.

Figure 5.16: TDA Version of Error in Linear Regression

One can see that the model error is red (high) at the ends and more blue (low) in the central region. Given a new data point, if one finds that it lies closest to points in the central region, one will have more confidence in the prediction result, and can also find ways to make that certainty more quantifiable. Here is another example.

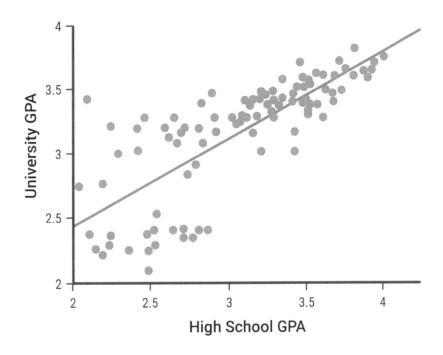

Figure 5.17: Scatter Plot and Linear Regression

This is a data set is attempting to predict a student's university grade point average using his/her grade point average from high school. In this case, it is clear that the error in the prediction will be much greater in the lower GPA range. So in this case, the topological model, colored by regression error, would look like this.

Figure 5.18: Topological Model of Linear Regression

The red node on the end would demonstrate the increased model error on the left side, gradually improving as one moves to the right.

In general, the network will be considerably more complicated for data with more independent variables, and the elevated error regions would appear in a way which is not obvious from pictures of the regression situation. For regression problems, there are also systematic methods for modifying the regression problem based on the network so as to improve the overall error rate in the prediction. This involves producing new "features" or coordinates in the regression in a systematic way based on the network.

5.7 Topological Modeling for Combined Cohort Study Analysis

Cohort studies are a method attempting to understand correlations between particular attributes of a subject and an outcome. For example, one might be interested in understanding whether or not the attribute of being a smoker is correlated with contracting lung cancer later in life. A cohort study for this situation would be constructed by choosing a sample population, dividing it into the two cohorts consisting of smokers and non-smokers, and studying the difference in the cancer rates of the two cohorts.

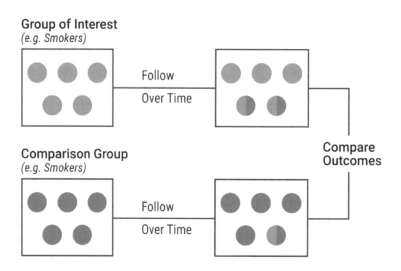

Figure 5.19: Smokers Cohort Diagram

Cohort studies are clearly a part of confirmatory analysis, since they involve an a priori choice of model or hypothesis which asks whether or not smoking is involved, and only attempts to verify that single hypothesis. There might be many other factors involved in lung cancer, which would not be uncovered by this procedure. A more topological approach to the study of lung cancer might proceed as follows. First, construct a single cohort, and record many features, including smoking/non-smoking but also various other factors, perhaps including genomic information. Then construct a network model of the different participants, summarizing the similarity relations among the patients. Once that's done, one can color each node of the network by the percentage of members of that node who contracted lung cancer. A typical outcome of this analysis is several hot spot regions in which the fraction of lung cancer patients is substantially elevated over the average for the whole data set. What such an analysis shows is that there are several distinct profiles for patients who are likely to contract lung cancer. It is likely that some of these profiles include mostly smokers, but there might be other groups who are non-smokers but are likely to contract lung cancer for other reasons. There might even be regions in the network consisting mostly of smokers whose likelihood of contracting lung cancer is not elevated. Each group needs its own explanation and that can be provided by examining the explanatory variables, i.e. the ones whose distribution in the group is most differentiated from its distribution on the entire data set.

Here is an example of how this might work. Suppose the cohort study goal is to determine the correlation of sugar consumption with the occurrence of diabetes. Obtaining a population of mice and feeding one population a very low sugar diet and the other a high sugar diet, and then observing the occurrence of diabetes after a period of time. In a **typical** cohort study, we might make the two diets very uniform between subjects, so that each low sugar mouse is fed the same low sugar diet, and each high sugar mouse the same high sugar diet. The standard cohort methodology would then determine the different rates of diabetes occurrence between the two cohorts. Another approach would be to vary the higher sugar diets, for example by feeding some mice soft drinks, others ice cream, and yet others sugary bread products. Carrying out the same procedure by comparing the diabetes rates for the two cohorts, more information is obtained because the rates for the different types of sugary diets might be different. Collecting the data concerning the mice and the diets, and constructing a TDA network model for this study might look as follows.

Chapter 5

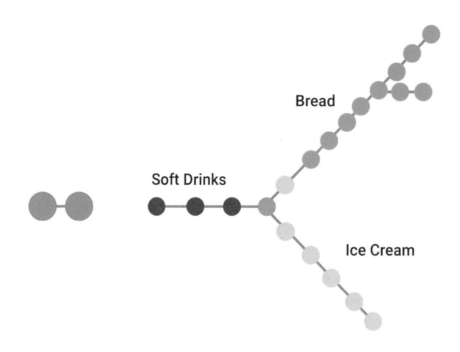

Figure 5.20: TDA of Sugary Food

The network is colored by occurrence of diabetes. The two cohorts are represented in the two connected structures. The blue structure on the left represents all the mice receiving low sugar diets. The coloring is blue because they have low occurrence of diabetes. The structure on the right contains all the mice receiving high sugar diets. Notice that there are three distinct regions of structures or flares, each corresponding to the different kinds of high sugar diets. Each of these diets has a different rate of occurrence of diabetes, and this is reflected in the coloring of the network. Notice the network with coloring has more information than a straightforward cohort analysis would provide, since it is able to distinguish more effectively between different types of diets. This kind of analysis is very useful, since it can be extended to observational studies where it's not possible to plan diets or other properties of the subjects.

5.8 Practical Examples of Unsupervised and Supervised Machine Learning

5.8.1 Unsupervised Learning

As we have defined it, unsupervised learning refers to the study of data without the direct objective of optimizing an outcome, but instead with the goal of obtaining an overall understanding of the data. The expectation is that such an understanding will be useful in the solution of many problems concerning the data. TDA, cluster analysis, PCA and

MDS, can all be used in an unsupervised manner. The scatter plots obtained through PCA and MDS in 2 and 3 dimensions can be used as useful visualizations of the data from which interesting structural information about the data can be obtained. Cluster analysis is almost by its definition an unsupervised method, since clustering techniques are not designed to deal with a particular outcome variable but instead give an overall taxonomy of the data, each one of the groups constituting one taxon. Figure 5.21 is a diagram that demonstrates the use of cluster analysis in the study of gene expression.[52] The picture below is a picture of a microarray, where both the rows and the columns have been clustered. The colors denote expression levels. There is a dendrogram for the genes on the right-hand side of the array and a similar dendrogram on the top of the array for the samples in the analysis.

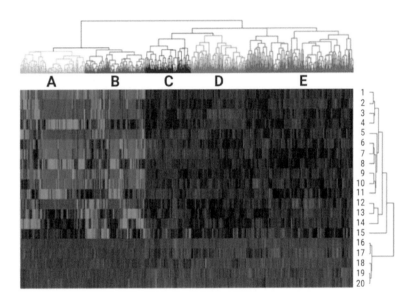

Figure 5.21: Dendrograms for Microarrays

Understanding the clusters in the samples is very interesting in that it provides a taxonomy of the samples in the study. The clustering of the genes gives a very useful overall view of the correlations (as measured by their expression levels) among the genes.

An interesting example of the use of MDS for unsupervised analysis is illustrated in the image below. What is shown is a three dimensional scatter plot, with the data points corresponding to genetic pathways. The distance matrix is constructed using correlation information between them, observed in a genome-wide association study consisting of patients suffering from psychiatric disorders.

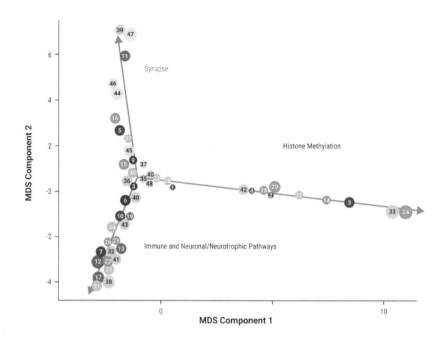

Figure 5.22: MDS Graph

The family of pathways lies along axes that have been labeled with larger scale groups of pathways, i.e. histone methylation, synapse, and immune and neuronal/neurotrophic pathways. In this case, there is a very clear decomposition of the data into pieces corresponding to the various groups, although a clustering method would not be likely to distinguish between the synapse and immune/neuronal/neurotrophic groups since they both have members near the origin.

5.8.2 Supervised Learning

In supervised learning, we have noted that the goal is to optimize an objective function, predict an outcome, or classify an incoming data point based on data one already has. The goal is generally to provide a recommendation for action of some kind. Regression, decision trees, and discriminant analysis from the list of methods are applicable to this family of problems. Supervised methods require some kind of model, such as the selection of an objective function, a model giving categories to which a data point might belong, or an outcome (categorical or numeric) to be predicted. In the example below, the data set consists of breast tumors, and the desired result is a prediction of whether or not the tumor is malignant. One has information concerning the perimeter and smoothness of the tumor. The outcome variable is binary (malignant/benign), and a natural approach is therefore logistic regression. Figure 5.23 below shows the plot of a two variable logistic regression model for classifying the tumor based on the two continuous variables that are part of the data.

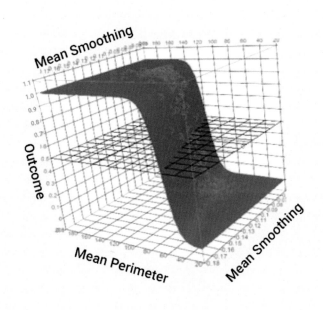

Figure 5.23: 3-d Graph of Tumors

Another classification problem might concern the passengers on the Titanic. The goal is to classify according to whether the passenger survived or not, depending on certain properties of the passenger, namely his/her gender, his/her age, and whether or not the passenger had siblings on board.

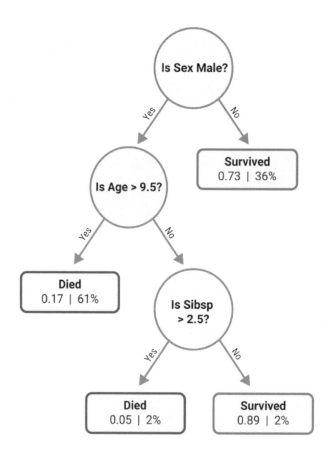

Figure 5.24: Flow Chart of Titanic Passengers

The numbers below each node indicate the likelihood of survival of passengers in the node and the percentage of passengers who belong to each one.

5.9 Case Study 8: Application of Principal Component Analysis to the Analysis of Microarrays[53]

5.9.1 Case Study Highlights

- Using Machine Learning Technique, PCA, to order a dataset by weighted combinations of samples and genes
- Discovered through ML classification of eigensamples that they correspond to different portions of the cell cycle.

5.9.2 Introduction

The goal of microarray technology is to use the study of various products of cellular biological processes to understand function within a tissue sample. The products include various categories, including messenger RNA, proteins, peptides, antibodies, and many others. In the particular case of messenger RNA, one is able to identify numerical quantities attached to particular genes, called *expression levels*. The relative expression levels for various genes are very useful indicators of function, and are characteristic of various disorders, including cancer. They are used in diagnostic tests, and also contribute the personalization of treatments for diseases.

Microarray studies are applied to a collection of tissue samples, obtained from patients or the subjects of an experiment. The output of an mRNA based microarray study can be thought of as a spreadsheet, with one column for each gene in a preselected collection of genes, one row for each microarray or sample, and a numerical value, the expression level, for each row and column. So, the (i,j) entry in the spreadsheet is the expression level of the j-th gene in the i-th sample. The number of columns is frequently in the thousands, while the number of rows can vary a great deal. The fact that the number of columns is quite large makes the direct interpretation of the outputs difficult, and suggests the possibility that one should attempt to reduce the dimensionality to a much smaller number of significant variables. These variables need not be individual genes, but can be numerically weighted combinations of genes. One approach to this kind of data is principal component analysis.

The spreadsheet can be thought of as an r×c matrix, where r is the number of samples and c is the number of genes. As such, one can apply principal component analysis to it to obtain a new matrix, where the rows and columns are no longer attached to individual samples and genes, but rather to what one might call *eigensamples* and *eigengenes*, respectively. These appear in ordered lists, ordered by a mathematical notion of significance. The eigensamples and eigengenes are actually weighted combinations of the samples and genes, but can usefully be thought of as collections of samples and genes. Thus, the eigensamples can be thought of as subpopulations of the collection of all samples, and eigengenes can be thought of as collection of genes all contributing to a particular biological process. In addition, some of the eigengenes may be interpreted as coming from noise in the system.

5.9.3 Result

The method described above was introduced in the paper[54], where it was applied to a microarray study of yeast cells, where there were 5981 genes and 14 samples. The authors were able to determine that the first (and most significant) eigengene represented expression levels that were nearly constant during the course of the cell cycle, and that third one represented expression levels that oscillate through the cell cycle. The second and fourth eigengenes are interpreted as initial increase and decrease in expression in response to elutriation, which is a processing step imposed on the cells in the construction of the study. The eigensamples turn out to correspond to different portions of the cell cycle.

Principal component analysis is a powerful method for the analysis of large data matrices. It can be used to create scatterplots for visualization, but is also an important tool for dimensionality reduction. These reductions often have useful interpretations, which can then be used to create simplified models for the processes being studied.

5.10 Case Study 9: TDA Microbiome Analysis[55]

5.10.1 Contributors:

Larry Smarr, Harry E. Gruber Professor, and Mehrdad Yazdani, Research Scientist, University of California, San Diego

5.10.2 Case Study Highlights

- Shows that TDA as a ML technique is more effective than PCA or MDS in correctly categorizing six unique microbial clusters
- Topological methods proved to be more robust to data noise and scale.
- Topological methods were shown to be an improvement over PCA or MDS in visualizing this high dimensional data.

5.10.3 Introduction

TDA can be used as a general framework for unsupervised learning to embed high dimensional datasets into graph-based representation. This case study compares Topological Data Analysis (TDA) to two other unsupervised analysis methods, Principle Component Analysis (PCA) and Multidimensional Scaling (MDS), in their ability to correctly categorize a set of six unique microbial clusters. Body site samples of stool, skin and saliva for male and female subjects are analyzed. The results show that TDA more completely identifies the six total microbial communities, where PCA and MDS identify only three total microbial communities, having problems clearly distinguishing between male and female membership. In this study, TDA appears better suited to identify clusters that other methods may otherwise miss.

This study illustrates that TDA can use an arbitrary number of projections to embed in a graph and uses the method of persistent homology so that the analysis is robust against noise and scale of data. It also highlights the limitations of PCA and MDS in visualizing high dimensional data given that visualization is limited typical to two or three dimensions.

5.10.4   Results

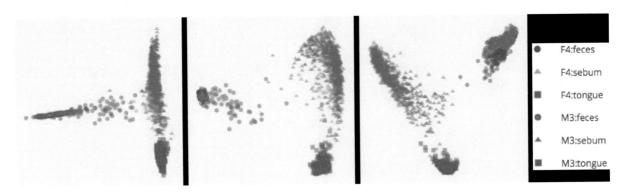

Figure CS9.1: Comparison of Three Unsupervised Methods

Description of Figure CS9.1: Left panel shows the PCA using of the family relative abundances of our data set. Middle panel shows the MDS of using the Bray-Curtis distance and the right panel is MDS using the UniFrac distance. From this analysis it appears that the samples from the male and female are not significantly different within body sites.

Figure CS9.2 shows the results when applying TDA. For each panel, the color of the nodes in the graph represent the proportion of samples that belong to a subject and body site (red corresponds to higher proportion of samples). Note that in TDA each node in the graph corresponds to several samples and edges drawn based on overlap of samples between nodes.

Notice that shifting every subject and body site, the central density of the nodes in the graph changes accordingly. In Figures CS9.2 (a) and (b), corresponding to the female and male stool samples respectively, the most dramatic shift occurs, as the majority of nodes in the graph consist of two separate connected components. These two separate connected components fit as natural candidates of being distinct groups (labels in the data, distinguish two different subjects). Figures CS9.2 (c) and (d), corresponding to the saliva samples, also show a separation between the female and male subjects as the shift in color in the heat map indicates. Finally, in Figures CS9.2 (e) and (f) corresponding to skin samples the separation is not as strong as the other body sites.

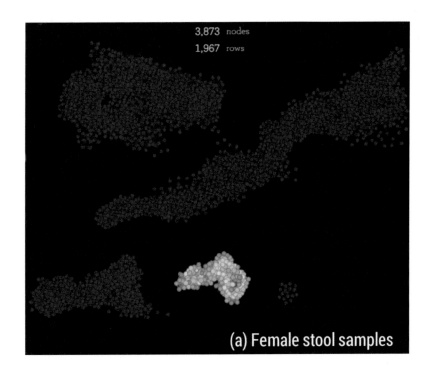

(a) Female stool samples

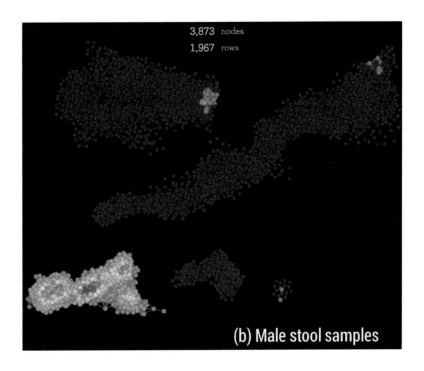

(b) Male stool samples

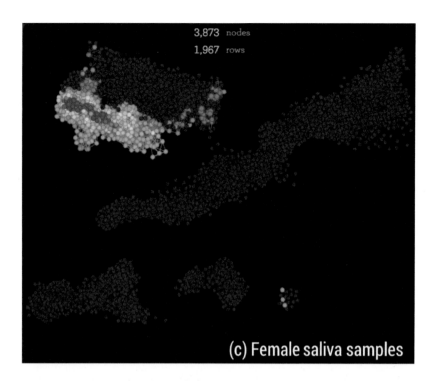

(c) Female saliva samples

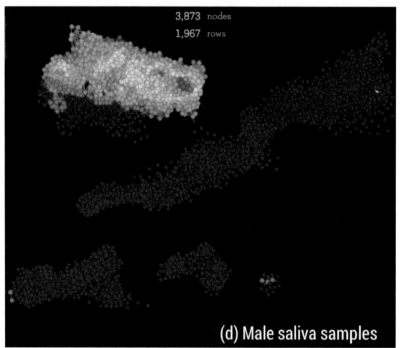

(d) Male saliva samples

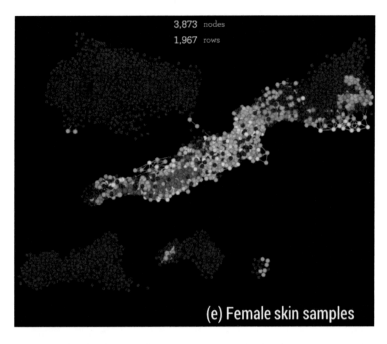

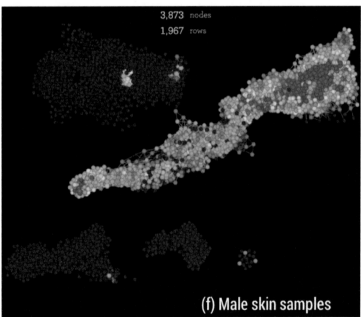

Figure CS9.2: TDA of Subject Sample Data (Plates a-f)

Description of Figure CS9.2: Unsupervised Topological Data Analysis (TDA, computed using Ayasdi [1]): the color of nodes indicates the proportion of data samples corresponding to the specific subject and body site (red means higher). In (a) and (b) there are two connected components corresponding to female and male stool samples. In (c) and (d) there is little overlap in the samples corresponding to the female and male saliva samples. In (e) and (f), the significant proportions of samples between female and male samples are in shifted in the graph.

Chapter 5

Chapter 6: The Learning Healthcare System

"Isn't it a bit unnerving that doctors call what they do 'practice'?"
-George Carlin

6.1 Chapter Preview

- Introduced the IOM's Learning Healthcare System
- Discussed various aspects of Precision Medicine
- Discussed implementation science as it relates to healthcare
- Examined the mechanism of innovation dispersion for healthcare
- Provided a comparison of the fee-for-service and value based model of healthcare financing.
- Case Studies
  - Case Study 10: Breast Cancer BRCA Analysis
  - Case Study 11: TDA for Discovery in Preclinical Spinal Cord Injury and Traumatic Brain Injury

6.2 Introduction

In the previous chapters, the technologies of TDA and Machine Learning were introduced as methods to add cognitive capabilities to machines. Going forward, the rest of the book will discuss the intersection of computer science and medical science. This chapter starts the discussion by offering various frameworks for information age medicine called "the Learning Healthcare System", "Precision Medicine", "Implementation Science" and "Value Based Medicine", which are laying the groundwork for the formal integration of Machine Learning technologies into routine medical practice.

6.3 A Call for Change

Ever since Hippocrates promoted a systematic approach to the treatment of disease, healthcare delivery has largely depended on a lone clinician ministering to a sick patient face to face; the patient's outcome depending largely on a single clinician's experience and knowledge. This venerable healthcare delivery model has remained un-changed for thousands of years. Statistics suggest the model needs improvement.

- In 2000, an IOM study estimated that between 44,000 and 98,000 Americans die annually due to medical errors.[56]

- In 2016, a study performed at Johns Hopkins Medicine reported about 250,000 Americans die of medical errors annually, ranking medical errors as the third leading cause of death in the United States.[57]

- *"The US spending on medical care has been on an unrelenting upward path for a number of decades. In 1960, aggregate health expenditures in the U.S. totaled $27 billion; in 2003, the figure stood at nearly $1.7 trillion a 63-fold rise, In contrast, the U.S. population grew by only 51 percent." "...The overall economic dimensions of the growth have been equally impressive, with the share of the economy devoted to healthcare tripling over the period, rising from approximately 5 percent of gross domestic product (GDP) in 1960 to over 15 percent in 2003 and the rise continues."*[58]

- National healthcare expenditures for 2014 grew 5.3% to $3.0 trillion. This represents an expenditure of $9,523 per person accounting for 17.5% of Gross Domestic Product (GDP). CMS projects health spending for the period 2015-25 to grow 5.8% per year.[59] *"Health spending is projected to grow 1.3 percentage points faster than Gross Domestic Product (GDP) per year over this period; as a result, the health share of GDP is expected to rise from 17.5 percent in 2014 to 20.1 percent by 2025."*[60]

- Regarding the delivery of medical services, in 2010, it is calculated that approximately 30%[3] of all medical spending is wasted. Medical care systematic waste is broken down as follows: $210B unnecessary services, $130B inefficient service delivery, $190B in excess administrative costs, $105B in price overcharges, $55B missed prevention opportunities and $75B in fraud, representing $765B in unnecessary medical expense.[61]

- As of 2009, over 2.5 million new scientific papers were being published every year and there were at least 28,100 active scholarly peer-reviewed journals.[62] In 2010, approximately 750,000 medical journal articles were published, which is over three times the number published in 1970 and the number is accelerating.[63]

- Global scientific output is doubling approximately every 8-9 years.[64]

The implications of these statistics for the US healthcare system are that an individual physician or a doctor's group, even large hospital systems, may be missing out on the benefits of technological advancements, due simply to the lack of integration of the

---

[3] 2010 US GDP $14.96T @ 17%=$2.54T US Health Expenditure, $765B/$2.54T=30%

latest information. Sociologists point out their concern with a lack of innovation diffusion in many fields, due to information overload, budget limitations, time limitations as well as lack of social contact with knowledgeable sources. The consequences of inefficient innovation diffusion for the US healthcare system are that the overall advancement of modern medicine in the US for a large part is left to the randomness of casual contact.[65]

To be considered successful, the goal of any macro-improvements to the healthcare system must address a more efficient method of innovation diffusion. Without which, the goals of improving patient outcomes and taming the unsustainable medical cost spiral is at best problematic.

6.4 What is the Learning Healthcare System (LHS)?

The learning healthcare system encompasses a number of key components committed to a collaborative sharing of data and ideas across institutions and sectors of the healthcare and scientific communities. The goal is to achieve safer, more effective and higher value healthcare and health outcomes for society. A core feature is the widespread adoption and linkage of electronic health records (EHR). New tools for data analysis and novel research methods will be employed to create the knowledgebase and clinically relevant insight to foster practice change.

The Institute of Medicine (IOM)[4] is a non-governmental organization, congressionally chartered under the National Academy of Sciences. The IOM is tasked to improve healthcare in the US by providing unbiased, evidence-based, and authoritative information concerning health and science policy. Through what the IOM calls the "learning healthcare system" knowledge and medical research is promoted to physicians so that routine clinical care benefits from the latest advancements in medical research at the point of care.[66]

The learning healthcare system is an initiative promoted by the IOM's "Roundtable on Evidence-Based Medicine." The purpose of the initiative is to help improve the way evidence is generated and applied to improve healthcare.

"The participants of the roundtable defined evidence-based medicine as the notion that 'to the greatest extent possible, the decisions that shape the health and healthcare of

---

[4] Author's note: The name "Institute of Medicine" has been changed to "National Academy of Medicine", but so much of the work on the Learning Healthcare System is categorized under the IOM, it would be confusing at this point to use the current name.

Americans—by patients, providers, payers, and policy makers alike—will be grounded on a reliable evidence base, will account appropriately for individual variation in patient needs, and will support the generation of new insights on clinical effectiveness."
"...Roundtable members specified a goal that by 2020, 90 percent of all clinical decisions will be supported by accurate, timely, and up-to-date clinical information and will reflect the best available evidence."[67]

The IOM's call for change was rooted in its earlier work identifying the scope of medical error and patient injury in our healthcare system detailed in 2000 in their publication, *To Err Is Human: Building a Safer Health System*.[68] Their findings were shocking to many, estimating that 44,000 to 98,000 Americans may die annually due to medical errors, making medical errors the tenth leading cause of death in the country. Shortly after that the IOM Committee on the Quality of Healthcare in America called for systematic redesign of the system in their report, *Crossing the Quality Chasm*.[69] Since that time, most of the policy, incentives and financing changes from both the private sector and the Centers for Medicare and Medicaid have moved to support these concepts of redesign to achieve improved safety, effectiveness, patient centeredness, timeliness, efficiency, and equity. Having already seen dramatic changes since that prescient call for the learning healthcare system, this call to action brought about CMS incentive program for EHR adoption ("Meaningful Use Program" 2011-2016) and the rapid changes to healthcare reimbursement now referred to as "value based purchasing" regulated by the sweeping legislation known as MACRA (Medicare Access & CHIP Reauthorization Act of 2015).[70]

6.4.1 Characteristics of a Learning Healthcare System

Given the pace by which scientific research and advancement is accelerating, the present model of "casual" or "word of mouth" innovation diffusion is not serving the patient, evidenced by the dismal statistics on medical efficacy. What the LHS model builds into the healthcare delivery system is a notion that knowledge is cumulative. It is a system that learns from past medical outcomes as a course of routine procedure, where results are continuously fed back into the system to inform and improve future patient outcomes over time.

Quoting directly from the IOM Workshop Summary[71], the following are the key elements of a learning healthcare system:

- **Continuous improvement in the value delivered.** A learning health-care system is one that maintains a constant focus on the health and economic value returned by care delivered and continuously improves in its performance.

- **Learning in healthcare as a partnership enterprise.** Broad culture change is needed to enable the evolution of the learning environment as a common partnership of patients, providers, and researchers alike.

- **Developing the point of care as the knowledge engine.** Given the rate at which new interventions are developed, along with new insights about individual variation in response to interventions, the point of care must be the central focus for the continuous learning process.

- **Full application of information technology.** The rate of learning—both the application and the development of evidence—will depend on the full and strategic application of information technology, including electronic health records central to long-term change.

- **Database linkage and use.** The emergence of large, electronically based datasets offers important new sources for quality improvement and evidence development. Progress requires fostering interoperable platforms, linking analyses, establishing networks, and developing new approaches for ongoing searching of the databases for patterns and clinical insights.

- **Advancing clinical data as a public utility.** Meeting the potential for using new datasets as central sources of evidence on the effectiveness and efficiency of medical care will require recognition of their qualities as a public good, including assessing issues related to their ownership, availability, and use for real-time clinical insights.

- **Building innovative clinical effectiveness research into practice.** Improving the speed and reliability of evidence development requires fostering development of a new clinical research paradigm—one that deploys careful criteria for trial conduct, draws clinical research more closely to the experience of clinical practice, advances new study methodologies adapted to the practice environment, and engages cultural incentives to foster more rapid learning.

- **Patient engagement in the evidence process.** Accelerating the potential for better development and application of evidence requires improved communication between patients and healthcare professionals about the nature of the evidence base, and the need for partnership in its development and use.

- **Development of a trusted scientific intermediary.** Greater synchrony, consistency, and coordination in the priority setting, development, interpretation, and application of clinical evidence require a trusted scientific intermediary to broker the perspectives of different parties.

- **Leadership that stems from every quarter.** Strong, visible, multi-faceted leadership from all involved sectors is necessary to marshal the vision, nurture the strategy, and motivate the actions necessary to create the learning healthcare system we need.

Quoting directly from the IOM study[72], the resulting improvements to the healthcare delivery by implementing the above elements will be:

- Real-time access to knowledge—A learning healthcare system that continuously and reliably captures, curates, and delivers the best available evidence to guide, support, tailor, and improve clinical decision making and care safety and quality.
- Digital capture of the care experience—A learning healthcare system that captures the care experience on digital platforms for real-time generation and application of knowledge for care improvement.
- Engaged, empowered patients—A learning healthcare system that is anchored on patient needs and perspectives and promotes the inclusion of patients, families, and other caregivers as vital members of the continuously learning care team.
- Incentives aligned for value—In a learning healthcare system, incentives are actively aligned to encourage continuous improvement, identify and reduce waste, and reward high-value care.
- Full transparency—A learning healthcare system systematically monitors the safety, quality, processes, prices, costs, and outcomes of care, and makes information available for care improvement and informed choices and decision making by clinicians, patients and their families.
- Leadership-instilled culture of learning—A learning healthcare system is stewarded by leadership committed to a culture of teamwork, collaboration, and adaptability in support of continuous learning as a core aim.
- Supportive system competencies—In a learning healthcare system, complex care operations and processes are constantly refined through ongoing team training and skill building, systems analysis and information development, and creation of the feedback loops for continuous learning and system improvement.

6.5 The Birth of Precision Medicine

During the same timeframe as the promotion and adoption of the LHS, scientific progress in genetics, proteomics and nano-materials have accelerated, bringing the promise of "precision medicine." Precision medicine,[5] as defined by the National Academy of Sciences (NAS), is *"the use of genomic, epigenomic exposure and other data to define individual patterns of disease, potentially leading to better individual treatment."*[73] Precision medicine presupposes a day when genetic markers will classify personally the most effective treatment for each individual, for example, help select the best medication to treat, a patient's high blood pressure, depression or rheumatoid arthritis, where the number of treatment options is extensive.

The selection of medication and other therapies throughout history have for the most part been administered on a trial and error basis for both acute and chronic conditions;[74] the fallout is measured in poorly controlled disease, medication side effects, low treatment adherence and discouraged patients. Figure 6.1 below shows the large gap in treatment described as the percentage of patients for whom medication treatment is ineffective for numerous common conditions.

Modern cancer care treatment is the poster child for the benefits precision medicine offers. For example, tumor-specific genetics, receptor proteins and other biomarkers are now routinely used in the selection of specific chemotherapy, growth factors, hormonal therapies and to help establish prognosis. For lung cancer treatment, tumor markers help guide the selection of tyrosine kinase inhibitors. In breast cancer, presence or absence of estrogen, progesterone and HER receptors help guide therapy. Genetic markers such as the BRCA gene locus are now regularly used to assist family members of patients with breast cancer to formulate a personalized strategy for early detection and prevention of breast and ovarian cancer. Gene mapping, cell surface proteins and other biomarkers are having profound impact on cancer and other diseases including changes in the definitions of staging of cancers and the naming of cancers and immune-mediated diseases.

---

[5] Some would argue "precision medicine" is synonymous with "personalized medicine"

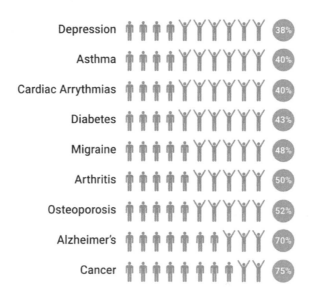

Figure 6.1: Percentage of Patients for Whom Drugs are Ineffective[75]

As gene-sequencing becomes more cost effective, the storage of genetic testing results will become increasingly available alongside more traditional clinical data in EHRs. These vast data sets along with insurance and pharmacy claims data are now becoming available for research. Turning these data stores into useful insight is challenging researchers and clinicians alike.

Traditionally, the randomized controlled trial has been and continues to be the gold standard for generating evidence for scientific and clinical research. But increasingly we find that very large randomized trials are quite expensive and often too slow in generating insight. In its seminal work on the effectiveness of care in 2001, the IOM raised the issue of whether or not the randomized control trial should still be considered the "gold standard" of evidence. Their purpose was to shake up the status quo and open doors for the big data studies which are now coming to reality. Change is coming soon. In 2016 the U.S. Congress passed the "21st Century Cures Act" which calls for numerous changes to accelerate the discovery and adoption of precision medicine. Among these are directives to the FDA to "issue guidance that addresses using alternative statistical methods in clinical trials and in the development and review of drugs." Additionally, they state that "To support approval of a drug for a new indication, the FDA must evaluate the use of evidence from clinical experience (in place of evidence from clinical trials) and establish a streamlined data review process."[76]

Clinical scientists are now pursuing innovative research strategies to investigate important issues related to the effectiveness of drugs, devices and new surgical techniques. The "randomized registry trial" is a concept capitalizing on the success of large national registries in cardiovascular and stroke care.[77] Research design is evolving to take advantage of large data sets now growing in health system data warehouses due to widespread EHR adoption. Studies covering multiple clinics and health systems have increased the use of cluster randomized trials. Inherently, observational studies are hampered by confounding variables which may not be controlled due to the lack of randomization. There is increasing opportunity to pair large observational studies with other research methods to draw conclusions faster. A powerful hybrid design pairs a retrospective observational study with smaller prospective experimental studies designed around the findings from the retrospective study.

New study designs often demand more innovative analytic approaches. Researchers are now using sensitivity analysis, propensity scores and instrumental variables to help work with the effects of confounding variables. [78] [79] [80] The sheer size and complexity of data sets requires new analytic paradigms. Machine Learning algorithms, topological data analysis and Machine Intelligence software are well positioned to enable researchers and clinicians to unlock the insight we know is present in these data stores.

6.6 Implementation Science for Healthcare Delivery

Implementation science is the practice of turning science driven medical evidence into every day clinical practice. The volume of new knowledge in clinical science continues to accelerate. Medical students are now instructed that many of the treatments they learn to be standard of care will become outdated within a decade. Implementation science is exploring ways to use technologies such as Machine Learning to aid the healthcare field in staying on top of the explosion of new medical advances.

Bench research and epidemiological studies continue to explain fundamental mechanisms of disease and the effects of our treatments, though these methods are prevalent in moving medical science forward, it often results in a "two steps forward, one step back" paradigm of advancement. Take for example, in the 1980s, the discovery that the vast majority of gastric ulcers were actually caused by the Helicobacter Pylori bacterial infection in the lining of the stomach. With the development of antibiotic protocols and powerful medications (H2 blockers and proton pump inhibitors) to reduce stomach acid production, the treatment of ulcer disease moved from a surgical disease to a medical condition. Now, years later, it's becoming apparent that the long term benefits and potentially harmful effects of proton pump inhibitors such as omeprazole and pantoprazole on the body, need more exploration. Another example, after years of routinely prescribing estrogens to post menopausal women to alleviate hot flashes, improve bone health and possibly reduce cardiovascular risk, large population studies published between 2002 and 2008 discovered that estrogen treatments may be causing more harm than good in terms of excess breast cancer risk.[81] Invasive procedures and surgery are also subject to continuous learning. After initial enthusiasm for the use of bone marrow transplantation for women with metastatic breast cancer in the late 1990s, it became apparent that longer term outcomes were not so favorable and has now been replaced by more promising treatments.[82] Similarly, the early published reports of the use of lung volume reduction surgery for patients with chronic obstructive pulmonary disease (COPD) led to early adoption of the procedure. Fortunately, a national comparative effectiveness research trial was launched and the now the procedure is made available to only a relatively narrow set of patients with the best chance for improvement.[83]

Some innovations seem to fall into a category of "sleeper technologies", whose benefits take many years to gain appropriate widespread adoption. Good examples include hand hygiene,[6][84] beta blockers, aspirin for patients with coronary artery disease, and influenza vaccine among healthcare workers. Some of these are decidedly "low tech" and do not gain early visibility or recognized champions for their cause.

In medicine, new technologies are under continuous scrutiny to identify ones that work and ones that don't. Clinicians are constantly seeking to understand if specific treatments "do more good than harm" through formal research as well as through trial and error. Rigorous application of learning health system methods and implementation science promise the best opportunity to efficiently determine the optimal use of new technologies and disseminate their widespread use to maximize effectiveness.

6.6.1 The Mechanism of Innovation Dispersion for Healthcare and the Need for Data Analytics

As defined by the Institute of Medicine, clinical practice guidelines are *"systematically developed statements to assist practitioner and patient decisions about appropriate healthcare for specific clinical circumstances."*[85] They may offer concise instructions on

---

[6] After 190 years of knowledge regarding the effectiveness of hand hygiene in stopping the spread of diseases, according to a 2002 CDC report, healthcare worker compliance to hand hygiene standards averages are at 40 percent.

which diagnostic or screening tests to order, how to provide medical or surgical services, how long patients should stay in hospital, or other details of clinical practice.

Physicians, in part, rely on national and international professional societies to produce clinical guidelines. But keeping pace with the medical science is very challenging. Each guideline typically requires convening an expert panel of clinicians and scientists, careful review of the primary medical literature and review of meta-analyses when available. The American Heart Association and American College of Cardiology have teamed up to jointly formulate guidelines on the treatment of heart failure, acute coronary syndrome and stroke. The American Thoracic Society maintains guidelines on the management of asthma and chronic obstructive pulmonary disease. Some medical associations have created national registries to enable hospitals and medical practices to compare performance measures on the processes and outcomes of care to help accelerate adoption of best practices. The American Heart Association's "Get with the Guidelines" program has over 1800 hospitals logging data on stroke patients and the Cystic Fibrosis Foundation has over 120 certified care centers participating in its nationwide registry. These methods have been incredibly successful over the years, and will continue to be an important source of clinical practice research. However, the overhead cost of national registries is quite substantial, making it difficult to establish registries for all of the disease conditions and procedures deserving study. New methods of data analytics at the hospital, health system and national levels are needed to achieve the widespread adoption of best practices envisioned by the IOM for the learning healthcare system.

In a January 2016, in a JAMA[7] viewpoint article, Drs. Fisher, Shortell and Savitz call for systemic use of "implementation science" to drive the data analytics transformation.[86] They noted that not every change is an improvement and encourage use of implementation science to understand how change takes place at the organizational level. Fundamental to successful change is an understanding of the forces which lead to the adoption and to the purging of clinical practices.

Damschroder and colleagues describe four factors at the root of these changing behaviors:

1. The external environment (e.g. payment systems)
2. The structure of the organization (e.g. hospital systems and medical groups)
3. The characteristics of innovation (e.g. the strength of the evidence supporting it)

---

[7] The Journal of the American Medical Association

4. The process used (e.g. top down authoritative vs bottoms up grass roots approach).

Additional insight comes from understanding the multiple levels at which innovation is occurring - biomedical innovations, care-delivery innovations and patient-engagement innovations. Each has separate but overlapping stakeholders. At the health system or enterprise level, it becomes apparent that a disciplined application of data analysis is needed to drive informed decision making and avoid haphazard and counterproductive change.

Advanced analytics can help leverage systematic improvements in clinical practice in several pivotal areas. These include development of hospital clinical pathways, the monitoring of pathway adherence across a physician group, population risk stratification and predictive analytics for chronic disease. Most hospitals have implemented clinical pathways or care models for specific procedures and diagnoses over the past 20 years. It is common for hospitals to try to manage dozens of clinical pathways such as total knee replacement, coronary bypass surgery, stroke and community acquired pneumonia. Typically, each hospital appoints a multidisciplinary committee of physicians, nurses, pharmacists, physical therapists, case managers and others to review the medical literature, evaluate current practice and create all of the necessary support materials. They develop physician order sets, daily progress note templates, nursing protocols, wound care instructions, recommended diets, therapies, consultation requests, pain management routines and patient education materials. It is an expensive undertaking, in terms of personnel hours and information assets. Unfortunately, most institutions are underequipped with data analytic capability, personnel, statistical software, data visualization and reporting tools. It is common for pathways to be created but not be implemented fully. Most institutions lack sustained follow through to measure the compliance to pathway recommendations or impact on patient care. Trade offs are routinely made on the distribution of effort for maintenance of existing pathways and creation of new ones. Commonly, resources are lacking to measure the cost impact of care pathway implementation, even though in many instances, cost control is a key factor in selecting diagnoses for pathway development. As health systems grow larger, they seek to drive quality improvements through pathway development and adoption across multiple hospitals. The promise for the largest systems is the ability to identify best practices already in their midst and amplify it to become standard care across their organization.

The recognition of the need for more sophisticated analytic tools to efficiently consume the most recent clinical practice data, achieve insight into evolving best practices as well as anomalous behaviors are the unifying conclusion among leading health systems. The result is the adoption of sophisticated quality improvement departments with innovation centers and well-equipped data analysis groups. Increasingly, larger health systems are applying Machine Learning and topological data analysis techniques in support of the development of more effective clinical pathways. Mercy Health System (St. Louis, MO) and Intermountain Health (Salt Lake City, UT) are exemplary in this area.

6.7 Transition from Fee-for-service to Value Based Healthcare Model

For most of medical history the payment of medical services has been a fee-for-service model. It is what it sounds like, for every procedure performed, a fee is charged. In a fee-for service model the amount of payment has little to do with the most important outcome, whether the patients' health improves. Given the stubborn 6% compounding grow rate of healthcare costs over decades, this fee-for-service model is giving way, in favor of a value based care model.

In a value based healthcare model, doctors and hospitals are paid for helping keep people healthy and for improving the health of those who have chronic conditions in an evidence-based, cost-effective way.

6.7.1 A Value Based Healthcare System

Most agree that the rapidly advancing transition from fee-for-service based reimbursement to value-based reimbursement is now the greatest driver of behavior change for providers, payers and patients alike. Beginning in the 1980s, the creation of health maintenance organizations (HMO), the implementation of managed care, rise of the Health Employer Data Information Set (HEDIS), and adoption of diagnosis related groups (DRGs) spawned new models of care. But none of these forces have adequately reduced the relentless rise in cost of care as measured by the percentage of GDP expended for healthcare in the U.S.

Starting in 2011, the Centers for Medicare and Medicaid Services (CMS) began a series of payment reforms which are attempting to address the upward cost spiral. CMS is instituting a strategy of payment reforms to force healthcare providers to become responsible for both the quality and the cost of care. Measuring and improving quality of care explicitly and driving down the cost of care at the population level will lead to the improvement in the value of healthcare across the system. CMS selected its first (22) Pioneer Accountable Care Organizations (ACOs) to become the pilots of this grand experiment. After substantial re-working of the rules through several iterations, there were only (11) Pioneer ACOs still in operation as of January 2016. However refined models of "Medicare Shared Savings" have led to the creation of over 700 ACOs which now are poised to continue expansion. CMS is launching pilot programs to determine the feasibility of paying for "episodes of care." Under the shared savings model, provider organizations are responsible for a specified group of Medicare patients. At the end of the year, if the cost of care to that group of patients is delivered below a specified total cost, then the ACO provider organization shares in the cost savings with CMS. Whether the provider receives the shared savings bonus payment is predicated on reporting specific quality outcome measures and achieving quality targets across the population.

The Comprehensive Care for Joint Replacement Model will test the effectiveness of bundled payments to improve the value of care. CMS named over 800 hospitals which began receiving payment for episodes of care for total knee and total hip replacement including the hospital phase of care and extending through 90 days of recovery.[87] The program started in 2016. CMS reports that average Medicare expenditure for surgery, hospitalization, and recovery ranges from $16,500 to $33,000 across geographic areas. Hospitals and providers in the test group will be reimbursed a fixed amount (around $25,000) for each knee or hip surgery, and are responsible for any costs that exceed the reimbursed amount. It is clear that health systems will need new tools to keep pace with the change ahead.

The transition to value based care has reached a tipping point for the provider community. The rapid pace of change is truly remarkable. CMS initiated the Physician Quality Reporting System in 2007, a voluntary program allowing physicians to receive small (1-2%) bonus payments for reporting quality codes to CMS. The EHR Incentive ("Meaningful Use") Program started in 2011 to provide payments to physicians and hospitals to adopt electronic health records and substantially automate the reporting of quality measures to CMS. Through the combination of quality incentives and value based payment CMS reports that lower cost of care is indeed being achieved. HHS estimates that the Pioneer and Shared Savings ACO programs have reduced Medicare spending by $417 million in its first three years. They reported that these efforts, along with specific payment penalties for hospital readmissions, led to a reduction in readmissions by 8% in 2012 and 2013.[88] This resulted in 150,000 fewer hospitalizations for Medicare patients. By 2014, CMS transitioned 20% of the Medicare population to value based payment models. In 2015, CMS announced its intention to further accelerate the transition to Shared Savings programs and population based payments. The stated goal is to achieve value based purchasing for 50% or more of Medicare patients by the end of 2018.[89] Besides public sector insurance programs, the commercial health insurance market is simultaneously pursuing value based contracting with providers.

The combination of electronic health record adoption and payment reform has fueled unprecedented consolidation of medical groups and hospital systems to achieve the scale and sophistication needed to compete and be successful in this new world. New organizational structures, roles and responsibilities are taking shape to enable the efficient use of clinical and business data to create the information needed to manage care across the continuum for large populations of patients. We see close collaboration between existing insurers and health systems. In some instances, traditional insurers are purchasing or developing their own provider networks. At the same time, some health systems are launching their own insurance programs including plans for their own employees as well as sponsoring Medicare Advantage plans for seniors. Some of the larger health systems are even offering direct contracting to large employers. Large employers such as The Boeing Company, Wal-Mart Stores, Inc. and Intel Corporation are embracing direct contracting to make health expenditures more predictable and raise standards of quality and service for their employees as a strategic advantage.[90]

Advanced analytics are rapidly becoming a necessity for providers and payers alike. Timely understanding of technology adoption, cost of treatment, the prediction of population needs and the assessment of variation in practice are now becoming the keys to success.

6.8 Case Study 10: Breast Cancer Genetic Marker Analysis

6.8.1 Case Study Highlights

- Using topological methods and microarray technology, breast cancer survivors are correctly identified by expression levels of their genes.
- Patients with tumors expressing the c-MYB+ tumors had excellent survival compared to other breast cancer patients making this a clinically useful genetic marker for the care of patients.
- A topological model of gene expressions is compared to a dendrogram of a standard hierarchical cluster analysis for the same gene expressions, illustrating the benefits of TDA.

6.8.2 Introduction

Microarray technology is one of the most striking developments in biotechnology over the last 30 years. Some of the development occurred as early as the late 1970's, and it was turned into a usable technology in the 1980's and 90's. It is able to measure so-called *expression levels* of various genes, or collections of genes, from a sample of an organism, and these expression levels are often useful indicators of function in the organism. For example, one strategy in the study of various cancers is to perform microarray analysis of samples from tumors and attempt to understand how expression levels of various genes or collections of genes differ in the tumor samples as compared with the normal tissue. Another strategy is to study the expression levels in tumor tissue, and attempt to find expression levels that correlate with improved outcomes.

6.8.3 Results

The output of the microarray technology can be thought of as a spreadsheet with one column for each gene or collection of genes that is being studied, and a row for each sample. For each column and sample, there is a number entered in the corresponding cell which is the expression value for the given gene (or collection of genes) in the given sample. The standard method for analyzing such data sets is through hierarchical clustering, whose output is a dendrogram. Hierarchical clustering is a standard method within Machine Learning. One important data set analyzed with these methods is the so-called *NKI data set*. It was constructed at the Netherlands Cancer Institute, and consists of slightly under 300 samples. An early topological analysis (see [1]) of this data set produced the following topological model.

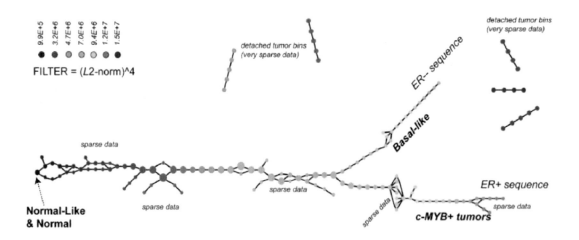

Figure CS 10.1: Topological Model of Gene Expressions

The data set includes information about which sample came from patients who survived the full length of the study, and which ones came from non-survivors. It turns out that the group in the lower right flare, labeled *c-MYB+ tumors* all survived the full length of the study. It consists of roughly 8% of all the samples, and it should be noted that *no* survival or clinical information was used in the construction of the model. Only expression information was used. On the other hand, a standard hierarchical clustering analysis of the same data set yields this dendrogram.

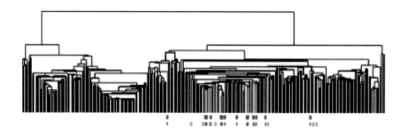

Figure CS 10.2: Dendrogram of a Standard Hierarchical Cluster Analysis of Gene Expressions

The members of the high survival group from the topological analysis are labeled in red. One observes that they all belong to one of the two high level groups specified by the dendrogram, but below that level, they are spread out rather widely. This analysis demonstrates the strength of the topological method, since it is able to identify a coherent group that is not concentrated or localized in the dendrogram. Philosophically, the reason is that clustering algorithms operate by splitting data sets apart. When a data set does not naturally split, one will rapidly begin to separate data points that belong together.

The Machine Learning software with TDA enabled the unbiased analysis of this dataset including biomarker data and clinical data including survival. The TDA software facilitated data visualization by the use of coloring (for survival) and identified this important correlation of the *c-MYB+* genetic marker with improved survival. Routine use of this Machine Learning approach using clinical data sets shows promise to accelerate knowledge which can be applied for the benefit of patients.

6.9 Case Study 11: TDA for Discovery in Preclinical Spinal Cord Injury and Traumatic Brain Injury[91]

6.9.1 Contributors:

Dr. Jessica L. Nielson, Postdoctoral Fellow, Assistant Professional Researcher and Principal Investigator, Brain and Spinal Injury Center (BASIC), Department of Neurological Surgery, University of California, San Francisco (UCSF)

Dr. Adam R. Ferguson, Associate Professor and Principal Investigator, Brain and Spinal Injury Center (BASIC), Department of Neurological Surgery, University of California, San Francisco (UCSF), Principal Investigator, San Francisco VA Medical Center

6.9.2 Case Study Highlights

- TDA analysis of experimental preclinical trials demonstrates a previously unreported correlation between elevated blood pressure just prior to surgery and poorer long term neurological outcomes for treatment of spinal cord injury and traumatic brain injury.
- Shows that using new data analytic techniques, such as TDA, one can extend the definition of precision medicine by converting "dark-data", from expensive past research studies, into relevant new results, at a relatively low cost.
- Demonstrates the value of TDA in formulating hypotheses from complex, heterogeneous data sets from experimental studies and implications for clinical practice.

6.9.3 Introduction

Using data sets from multiple older and smaller studies of spinal cord injuries, biomedical researchers have recently discovered a previously unknown relationship between the long-term recovery from spinal cord injury (SCI) victims and high blood pressure during their initial surgeries. The re-use of data from prior, older studies is sometimes referred to as "dark data." Researchers at UCSF used data sets from the Visualized Syndromic Information and Outcomes for Neurotrauma-SCI (VISION-SCI) repository. This included the reconstruction of data from multiple studies including some from the Multicenter Animal Spinal Cord Injury Study conducted at Ohio State University in the mid-1990s. The original research studies cost over $60 million.

Employing TDA tools, researchers search for patterns without human supervision (or bias) before rendering the results as a network diagram of variables for further analysis.

6.9.4 Results

This series of analyses using individual as some combined data sets uncovered a number of important findings including the location-specific impact of SCI and TBI polytrauma on recovery of forelimb function and differential sensitivity of forelimb measures and locomotion measures in cervical SCI. The analysis revealed irreproducible efficacy of methylprednisolone (MP) and minocycline treatment between cervical and thoracic SCI. Most important was the novel discovery that perioperative hypertension predicts worse neurological recovery following thoracic SCI in preclinical trials.

The concept of precision medicine is expanded to include the application of TDA to preclinical translational discovery. Traditionally, studies begin with a hypothesis that the study is attempting to prove or disprove. What this study shows, *"TDA can apply PCA through singular value decomposition (SVD) to reveal the complex multivariate relationship of all predictor and outcome variables simultaneously as a network diagram. Similar individuals are clustered into nodes, and clusters that share one or more individuals are joined by an edge. The full syndromic topological map provides a platform for rapid and intuitive exploration of the data set in an unbiased, data-driven manner. Once the network is generated, the shape of the data set can be investigated to understand the relationship of each variable across the topological syndromic space to identify groups of clustered individuals that can be further probed for specific relationships among outcomes, validation and targeted hypothesis testing."*

Dr. Ferguson commented, "We could never have found this correlation with hypertension using traditional tools, because with thousands of variables to test, it would have never occurred to us. Spinal cord injuries are enormously complex and thus still poorly understood compared to other systems. Efforts to isolate simple causal mechanisms have proven elusive and that's a real threat to discovering new therapies."

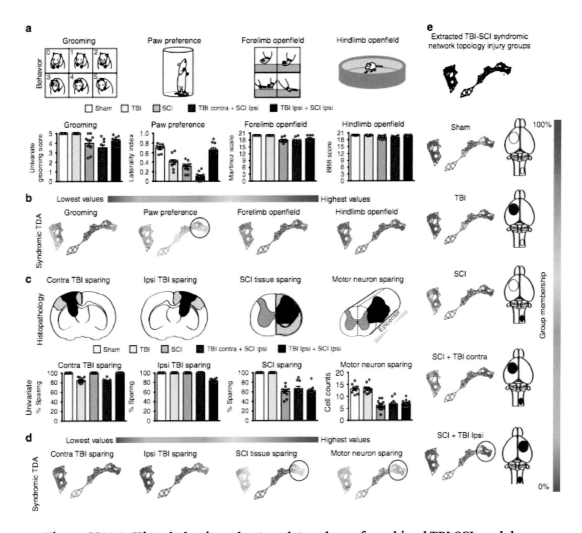

Figure CS11.1: Histo-behavioural network topology of combined TBI-SCI model.

Figure CS11.1 Description: (a,b) Behavioral outcomes of forelimb function and (c,d) histopathology were mapped onto the topological network using TDA. Data from this model shows a distinct recovery pattern depending on whether the combined TBI is contralateral (contra) or ipsilateral (ipsi) to the SCI. (e) Each injury group occupies a distinct region of the network topology, highlighted as red nodes for 100% enrichment (heat map) for each particular injury model. Sham controls (n = 9) and TBI-only (n = 10) subjects are located in the right cluster. SCI-only (n = 10) and SCI+TBI contra (n = 10) are both located in the left cluster. SCI+TBI ipsi (n = 10) interestingly are grouped next to the sham subjects in the right cluster (circled part of the network), due to a syndromic functional recovery similar to shams (a), despite showing no difference in pathology compared with subjects with SCI alone or SCI+TBI contra (c).

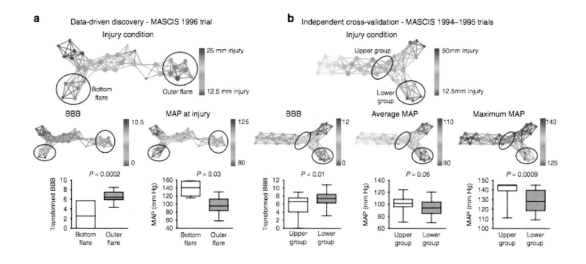

Figure CS11.2: Perioperative hypertension predicts worse recovery after thoracic SCI.

Figure CS11.2 Description: (a) Exploration of the TDA network from the MASCIS OSU 1996 methylprednisolone trial (N = 72) revealed a cluster of subjects in the network given the same targeted injury (circled bottom and outer flares) that showed very significant differences in walking function, measured by the BBB scale (P < 0.0002). A query of variables with significant differences based on KS test results between these two groups uncovered subjects with significant hypertension during SCI surgery (P < 0.03) clustering in the groups with poorer functional recovery. (b) Crossvalidation of these relationships between perioperative blood pressure and functional recovery was performed in a separate group of test subjects from the same 3-year drug trial (MASCIS 1994–1995, N < 154) with matching outcome measures and subject grouping. Visually guided identification of subjects in the network given the same injury condition (circled upper and lower groups) but showing poorer functional recovery on the BBB scale (P < 0.01) uncovered the same significant detrimental effect of hypertension during SCI surgery on recovery (P < 0.06), specifically when assessing peak MAP values recorded during surgery (P < 0.0009). Box and whisker plots show mean and minimum/maximum range of values. P values obtained using student t-test for significant differences between groups.

Chapter 7: Clinical Variation and Hospital Clinical Pathways

"Intelligence is not the ability to store information, but to know where to find it."
-Albert Einstein

7.1 Chapter Preview

- Discuss DRG classification and how it relates to clinical pathways.
- Provide an overview of what clinical pathways are and how they are created.
- Demonstrate how EHR gather data and point out some of their weaknesses.
- Introduce how the Meaningful Use of EHR program is promoting medical record standards, such as ICD10 and RxNorm, as methods to improve data interchange across the industry.
- Provide examples of applying Machine Learning to clinical pathway creation and practitioner monitoring and reporting.
- Case Studies
    - Case Study 12: Total Knee Replacement
    - Case Study 13: Colectomy Surgery

7.2 Introduction

Clinical pathways also known as care process models, care pathways or care maps, are a tool used in clinical practice that reduces variability in the approach to treatment by standardizing methods of practice. Clinical pathways have been shown to improve patient outcomes[92] and Machine Learning is now being shown to improve pathway quality.

Given the fact that medical data is very complex and multi-dimensional in nature makes it an ideal candidate for Machine Learning. Machine Learning can assist hospital staff in creating and improving the quality of clinical pathways. In some health systems a challenge remains with incompatibilities across EHRs and other clinical data sources. As we've been discussing in previous chapters, creating a high-quality data set is fundamental in the application of Machine Learning.

In the not too distant past, medical records were characterized as hand scrawled paper binders sitting in filing cabinets in the doctor's office or hospital basement. Identifying s across patient groups or across physician practices was next to impossible. Due to the efforts of CMS and other healthcare organizations, the standardization of electronic medical records for data exchange and interoperability is being promoted and shown to improve healthcare outcomes and reduce costs. This standardization process is providing a secondary benefit in the structuring of healthcare data so it is accessible to clinicians and researchers for analysis, and rapidly banishing forever the hand scrawled file from medicine. At leading health systems larger and more complex datasets including clinical results, physician orders, patient demographics, surgical supplies, nursing services, medical claims and other sources are now accessible for advanced analysis.

7.3 Clinical Pathways (CP) and Diagnosis-Related Groups (DRG): The Introduction of Qualitative Classification of Diagnoses and Treatment

7.3.1 DRGs: Classification for Payment

A Diagnosis-Related Group (DRG) is a method to standardize classification of diagnoses into product groups for billing hospital inpatient care. It was first introduced in the 1980s, by the Medicare program and has since spread to most Medicaid and private health insurance plans. In 2007, the DRG system used by CMS was modified into the MS-DRG (Medical Severity Diagnosis Related Groups) to include new classification vectors.

"A Diagnosis-Related Group (DRG) is a statistical system of classifying any inpatient stay into groups for the purposes of payment. The DRG classification system divides possible diagnoses into more than 20 major body systems and subdivides them into almost 500 groups for the purpose of Medicare reimbursement. Factors used to determine the DRG payment amount include the diagnosis involved as well as the hospital resources necessary to treat the condition. Also used by a few states for all payers and by many private health plans (usually non-HMO) for contracting purpose. Hospitals are paid a fixed rate for inpatient services corresponding to the DRG group assigned to a given patient."[93]

As you may remember from Chapter 3, creating classification vectors is a primary step in data analysis. What makes the DRG system important to Machine Learning is it is creating classification vectors for medical diagnoses. Though far from perfect, and thanks to CMS, the DRG is providing a uniform system of structuring medical data that

Pathways

is being widely deployed. We will discuss later how EHR data standards are being deployed to improve data quality.

DESCRIPTION	COMPLICATING CONDITION (CC) PRESENT	MAJOR COMPLICATING CONDITION (MCC) PRESENT	MD-DRG
Simple Pneumonia and Pleurisy		yes	193
	yes		194
	no		195
Major Chest Trauma		yes	183
	yes		184
	no		185
Gastrointestinal Hemorrhage		yes	377
	yes		378
	no		379
Allogeneic Bone Marrow Transplant	(n/a)	(n/a)	014
Pancreas Transplant	(n/a)	(n/a)	010
Major Joint Replacement or Reattachment of the Lower Extremity		yes	469
		no	470

Table 7.1: Example Medical Severity Diagnosis Related Groups (MS-DRGs)[94]

7.4 Clinical Pathways: Organizing Care

Clinical pathways (CP) are standardized plans of care for common diagnoses or procedures typically performed in a hospital. In 1982, when the Medicare program began paying hospitals on a per episode basis defined by DRGs, hospitals became motivated to develop CPs to streamline hospital practice and avoid unnecessary variation in care. In the 1980s, the Joint Commission[95] began requiring hospitals to report performance measures on common diagnoses such as acute myocardial infarction, community acquired pneumonia and congestive heart failure. This built upon important findings in the medical literature about management of these conditions according to new treatment guidelines. The Joint Commission, American Hospital Association and professional societies set goals to make these improvements in care widespread. When properly implemented, CPs can help reduce costs of providing healthcare and in many cases improve patient outcomes.[96] [97] [98]

7.4.1 How Clinical Pathways are Created

Clinical pathways are typically created by a hospital's sponsored multidisciplinary committee, tasked to review the medical literature, select the best practices and create the specific content and workflow of care within their facility. Physicians, nurses, pharmacists, physical therapists, nutritionists, and other team members usually receive performance reports on a periodic basis and are responsible for updating the pathways. The condition or procedure-specific pathways include a number of supporting materials including a clinical guideline, physician order sets, diagnostic and decision algorithms, documentation templates, nursing protocols and patient education materials. Materials should be tailored for the workflow and patient population served by the hospital. Commonly there is great enthusiasm at the time of pathway creation and launch within the hospital. However, it takes significant resources to maintenance a successful clinical pathways program, and many hospitals find it challenging to do so.

When clinical science advances, new drugs are developed, surgical procedures modified or new patient risks identified, these support materials, staff training and patient education need to be updated. Achieving adoption within the hospital community, among physicians and nurses requires a sustained effort bolstered by relevant and timely reporting. Some hospitals have made their pathways available to colleagues and patients on their public web sites as a demonstration of their commitment to high standards of care. Intermountain Healthcare maintains a very complete set of materials for their "care process models" for over 60 inpatient and ambulatory care diagnoses for use by physicians across the country as well as patient education materials.[99] The Children's Hospital of Philadelphia has exemplary detailed clinical pathway and related decision making algorithms available to all.[100] This commitment to standardized care takes enormous effort and resources to maintain. The vast majority of hospitals are usually able to initiate and maintain only a fraction of the clinical pathways they aspire to implement. Even when health systems have created pathways, keeping them up-to-date is challenging. Measuring performance of individual hospitals and physicians against the guideline standards is even more time and resource intensive. Physicians are interested in receiving a combination of utilization, cost and clinical outcomes of their care with relevant comparisons to peers. However, most health systems just are not able to produce this breadth of reporting using traditional business intelligence software and find it challenging to hire the analytic staff needed to maintain such a learning cycle for improvement. Properly deployed Machine Learning now offers the opportunity to efficiently perform this large volume of calculation and automate the creation of insight needed to unlock the best practices within each hospital system.

See Table 7.1 below for an example clinical pathway for surgical repair of pectus excavatum, a congenital birth defect of the chest wall, from the Hospital for Sick Children, Toronto, Canada. This shows just one portion of the pathway detailing the activity, diet, medications, and patient/family teaching expected during the pre-operative and hospital phase of care leading to hospital discharge. The web-based version includes links to further guidelines relating to selection of intravenous fluids, pain management and other important aspects of clinical decision making.

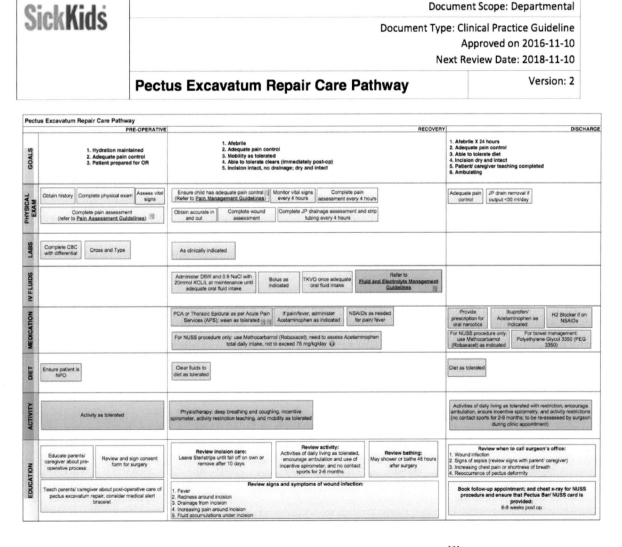

Figure 7.1: Pes Excavatum Repair Care Pathway[101]

Professional organizations such as the American Heart Association, American College of Cardiology, American Society of Thoracic Surgeons, American Society of Clinical Oncology, and many others, began convening national guideline committees and established detailed numerator and denominator definitions of both process and outcome measures.

In 1999, the National Quality Forum, an independent, multi-stakeholder membership organization, was established to take on the role of organizing and curating the hundreds of quality measures across the healthcare delivery spectrum.[102] CMS committed to promoting and incentivizing the use of quality measures vetted through NQF. Examples of NQF programs are the Physician Quality Reporting Service, which began in 2007, the EHR Incentive (Meaningful Use) program, in 2011, and in the Merit-Based Incentive Payment System (MIPS) and the Advanced Alternative Payment Models (APM), launched in 2016.

7.5 Creating Medical Data Sets: EHR and Inpatient Clinical Data Sources

The process for developing clinical pathways is time and resource intensive. One of the most important, but often most challenging steps in developing CPs is identifying and analyzing current practice patterns within the hospital or hospital system.

Tables 7.2 and 7.3 below illustrate typical questions asked to aid in analyzing current practice patterns.

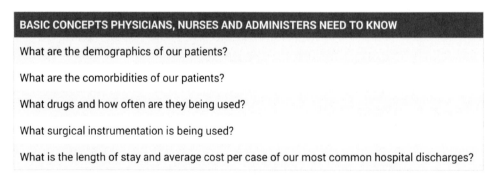

BASIC CONCEPTS PHYSICIANS, NURSES AND ADMINISTERS NEED TO KNOW
What are the demographics of our patients?
What are the comorbidities of our patients?
What drugs and how often are they being used?
What surgical instrumentation is being used?
What is the length of stay and average cost per case of our most common hospital discharges?

Table 7.2: Basic Concepts for Quality Improvement

ADVANCED CONCEPTS FOR VALUE BASED CARE IMPROVEMENTS
What are the most cost-effective treatments for acute injuries, chronic diseases, patients requiring surgery?
What is the timeliness of our care for medication administration, medical imaging, consultations, etc.?
What is the most efficient diagnostic strategy for patients presenting with specific signs or symptoms?
Which physicians and which hospitals are most progressive in adopting the best practices recommended in our pathways?
What are the long term outcomes for our patients?
Which patients are most likely to experience surgical wound complications, sepsis, require transfusions unexpectedly, have drug reactions, return for unplanned readmission within thirty days, die unexpectedly?

Table 7.3: Advanced Concepts for Value Care Improvements

Answers to these questions and many others though fundamental for improving care, don't become useful until sophisticated data management and reporting capabilities are employed making the data accessible for use. Data must come from many subsystems within the hospital environment including electronic health records (EHRs), pharmacy systems, operating room management systems, laboratory systems and billing and accounting systems. Within EHRs it is important that electronic order sets, drug dosing routines, diagnosis and procedure code selection lists, referral request templates, adverse reaction flags, and other subsystems be maintained to allow ease of use and facilitate good care decision making and documentation. At the database level, data completeness and data quality can be challenging when attempting to compare care across hospitals, particularly when those hospitals have disparate EHRs.

7.6 Standards for the Reporting of Medical Data

In order to use clinical data across institutions for quality improvement or clinical research, it is critically important to establish consistent data taxonomy and ensure data quality. This is true for comparing clinical practice among hospitals, such as the goal of improving timeliness of coronary artery stenting for acute myocardial infarction. It is equally true if one is pooling data across communities for research in rare diseases such as analysis of treatments to improve survival in cystic fibrosis. Attention to data standards is particularly important when applying Machine Learning methods to healthcare data. Traditionally, hospitals and medical groups unknowingly created their own "islands" of medical data. This is despite the use of national standard codes sets for diagnosis and procedures. Due to the use of locally-defined terms such as location codes or laboratory-hospital interface systems, it became very challenging to compare data to outside organizations without substantial (and costly) efforts for data mapping and clean up.

Fortunately, strong standards for healthcare data are emerging from a combination of market forces and regulation. The HL7 (Health Level Seven) organization has helped foster practical standards for healthcare data to serve the needs of clinicians, researchers, insurers, imaging equipment manufacturers, pharmaceutical companies, government regulators and other stakeholders for many years.

From HL7 website,

"HL7 is a non-profit, ANSI accredited standards development organization dedicated to providing a comprehensive framework and related standards for the exchange, integration, sharing, and retrieval of electronic health information that supports clinical practice and the management, delivery and evaluation of health services."[103]

HL7 helps address issues of data interchange among information subsystems and across provider organizations. Major advances in standardization have been made since 2011, with the onset of the EHR Incentive Program by CMS. The program, which is commonly referred to as the "Meaningful Use Program" included the adoption of HL7 and other data standards for use in EHRs.[104] See Table 7.4 below for a list examples of HL7 approved data standards required by the Meaningful Use program. HL7 continues to forge interoperability standards with the "Fast Healthcare Interoperability Resources (FHIR) standard" which holds great promise for accelerating the sharing of clinical data for specific uses.[105]

DATA TYPE	CODING SYSTEM	DESCRIPTION
diagnoses, signs, symptoms	CD-9, ICD-10-CM	International Classification of Disease – Clinical Modification
procedures	CD-10-PCS	International Classification of Disease – Procedure Coding System (U.S. specific)
laboratory results, assessment risk category	LOINC	Logical Observation Identifiers Names and Codes
medications	RxNORM	Normalized names for clinical drugs
procedures, devices, attributes (e.g. risk level), treatment and Discharge location, Route of administration (e.g. medication)	SNOMEDCT	Systematized Nomenclature of Medicine -- Clinical Terms
individual characteristics, attributes (race, ethnicity, etc.)	CCD	Continuity of Care Document

Table 7.4: Example HL7 Clinical Data Standards for Meaningful Use Program[106]

In October 2015, the American healthcare system caught up with much of the rest of the world with transition from ICD-9 to ICD-10 for diagnosis and procedure codes. The monumental change was actually delayed on several occasions due to the complexity of the task and due to the timing of other major changes in electronic systems required by the Meaningful Use program. CMS required the change for all those providers billing for the Medicare and Medicaid programs. The code set expanded dramatically from the 16,000 individual ICD-9 codes to the 60,000+ ICD-10CM codes, enabling a considerably more granular description of diagnoses and procedures. A major feature was the addition of more specific descriptions, such as sidedness (right or left) and specificity (relative location). For example, there are now two ICD-10 codes for "right humeral head fracture" and "left humeral head fracture" where previously there was just one ICD-9 code for "humerus fracture."

Even while employing new standards of data codification, physicians and researchers know that a tremendous amount of detail remains "hidden" in the text of operative notes, medical progress notes, radiology reports, pathology reports, etc. and never gets assigned a code. Important concepts such as the severity of wound infection or bleeding, extent of a rash or frequency of pain are often found in a descriptive format and not discrete data elements. These and other "hidden in plain sight" artifacts are very important for differentiating the quality of care and patient outcomes. Data scientists and computer specialists are actively working on tools, such as natural language processing, to help transform this text into discrete data which could be used for performance and outcome measurement.

7.6.1 Medical Data Quality

Going forward, medical data is expected to perform double duty, to include applications beyond those that the clinical system originally envisioned. Traditionally, medical care was delivered and reimbursed one patient at a time. Accordingly, clinical and financial data systems were designed to manage one patient at a time, with little attention given to the outcomes of aggregate populations. Now, there is tremendous interest in secondary use of data such as clinical pathway performance reporting, comparative effectiveness research, post-marketing drug safety research, population management and the development of predictive models.

With the looming prospects of multi-purpose data, quality of data must be reexamined for all categories of use. The quality of clinical systems is inherently a work in progress, where the definition of quality is highly dependent on use. Researchers from the Department of Bioinformatics at Columbia University completed a review of methods of data quality assessment in the context of EHR data reuse for research. In 2013, they described five dimensions of data quality including completeness, correctness, concordance, plausibility, and currency, and seven broad categories of data quality assessment methods: comparison with gold standards, data element agreement, data source agreement, distribution comparison, validity checks, log review, and element presence. When comparing their quality and assessment measurements, with available

Pathways

data sets from medical institutions, they concluded that, *"There is currently little consistency or potential generalizability in the methods used to assess EHR data quality. If the reuse of EHR data for clinical research is to become accepted, researchers should adopt validated, systematic methods of EHR data quality assessment."*[107] Since that time there has been continued work on this important area.

CMS Meaningful Use program and subsequent MACRA and MIPS programs have been instrumental in driving the adoption of data standards, primarily those envisioned by HL7. However, it still is relatively early in the evolution of our healthcare data systems. We are now witnessing rapid development of hospital and provider delivery systems, innovations in telemedicine, contracting and insurance design and consolidation of EHR companies. These forces pose additional impact on data quality. See Table 7.5 for a partial listing of the many factors effecting healthcare data quality.

EHR DATA TYPE	DESCRIPTION	IMPROVEMENTS	CHALLENGES
EHR problem list	List of ICD 10 or SNOMED codes; SNOMED codes are allowed by HL7 but uncommonly used.	Transition from ICD9 to ICD10 (Oct. 2015) has added granularity and specificity.	Dates of onset usually auto-set to the date problem recorded, not necessarily the date of diagnosis, which may affect treatment or payment; often the result of EHRs auto-populating; often not purged from inactive problems or refined to more specific diagnosis.
EHR Medication list	List of drug names and complete "sig" information regarding doses, refills, etc.	Improving standardization of sig details in recent years.	Mix of RxNorm and NDC codes in use; "discontinue" dates often unspecified.
EHR demographics	Birthdate, medical Record number(MRN), gender, location data.	Most health systems now have master patient indexes (MPI) to integrate access to data for patients with multiple MRNs.	Race, ethnicity data often incomplete.
EHR Social history	Tobacco, alcohol use.		Often not updated; lack of rigor in use of standard codes for smoking and alcohol use.
EHR Allergies and adverse reactions	List of drugs or drug components causing adverse reactions.		Lack of standards describing specific adverse reactions and severity.
EHR Operative Notes	Text document describing procedures done, some coding attached.		Description of complications or adverse events captured in text but not converted to discrete codes.
Claims – office visits	ICD diagnosis and CPT procedure codes for office visits.		Variable training and use patterns for codes across medical groups can make comparisons challenging.
Claims – hospital episodes	ICD, DRG and CPT procedure codes, often multiple for each hospitalization.	Professional coders in most hospitals with relatively good consistent use of explicit rules from payers.	Discharge diagnosis reported; usually no information on initial complaint for hospitalization.
Claims – pharmacy benefit management (PBM)	Listing of medications dispensed and processed / paid by insurance carrier.	Includes pharmacy claims across providers who may not be on same EHR.	Often lacks explicit information on discontinuation; lose trail of information when patient switches insurers or PBMs.

Table 7.5: Data Sources and Factors Affecting EHR and Claims Data Quality and Completeness

7.7 Using Machine Learning in the Clinical Discovery Process

One primary method to discover positive or adverse trends and correlations within complex, multi-dimensional data is Machine Learning. Machine Learning methods allow for unsupervised learning where the researcher doesn't pose a hypothesis to be proven or disproven. The data is allowed to speak for itself, where Machine Learning reveals the truths that lie within.

The researcher is presented with a wealth of statistically measured insight which is then subject to their interpretation. The researcher must decide what is relevant and actionable within the scope of their inquiry and workflow. In the setting of hospital care, Machine Learning can help reveal correlations between certain medications and outcomes. Examples such as length of stay, use of specific surgical instrumentation or devices, incidence of adverse events, cost of certain imaging strategies and outcomes of care.

Machine Learning has been particularly useful in the generation and optimization of hospital care pathways. As we discussed above, clinical leaders in a large health system create and deploy common care pathways across multiple related hospitals to be reduce unnecessary variation and improve quality. Machine Learning can help identify those specific drugs, devices, nursing protocols, consultations, and patient characteristics which correlate with favorable patient outcomes such as lower lengths of stay, lower cost and avoidance of readmission.

Figure 7.2 illustrates the following outline of a Machine Intelligence workflow analyzing inpatient surgical admission. The example workflow demonstrates how an analyst and clinician might work together to complete a CP; the analyst's expert familiarity with the Machine Learning software platform and the clinician with expert working knowledge of the clinical domain can complete a data analysis session within a few hours.[8]

1. A logical approach is to first explore the general characteristics of the population of patients, understanding the number of cases, number of surgeons, distribution across hospitals, length of stay (LOS) and cost characteristics. A large number of cases (100+) is always better for Machine Intelligence analysis. Typical cohorts will include thousands of patients undergoing a given surgical procedure, over multiple hospitals across a common time frame.

---

[8] More detail about findings is discussed in the case studies on colon surgery and cholecystectomy.

2. In the second stage of inquiry, we seek to identify a cluster of cases representing the best outcomes. In this analysis, the users sought to find cases which were in the lower 50th percentile for length of hospital stay, lowest 50th percentile for cost of care and patients who had no readmission within 30days of hospital discharge. Spending time reviewing the hospital event of these multiple small groups of patients (approximately 30 – 100 patients each) gives reviewers an excellent understanding of the workflow of these patients, resources used and timing of every type of service. Based on this knowledge, comparing these subgroups, we can start to confirm known characteristics of "best" patients and also find new correlations which might turn out to be new "best practices" in the hospital system.

3. Create a draft 'best practice pathway" by selecting auto-generated pathway of the subgroup representing the lowest LOS and lowest cost. Edit the draft pathway by adding and deleting specific event types based on identified best practices.

4. Fine tune the pathway by comparing known subgroups against it – perhaps groups with low and high LOS as well as extremes of cost performance. Compare the impact of specific event types such as use of specific medications or surgical supplies, pre-operative testing, etc. Make final selections of all events to be included in the care.

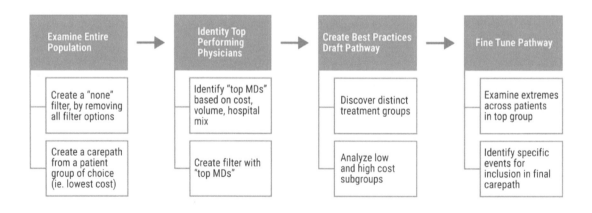

Figure 7.2: Example Sequence of Data Analysis for Inpatient Surgery
(Courtesy of Mercy Health).

Figure 7.3: Example Detail of Clinical Care Pathway for Inpatient Surgery Laparoscopic Cholecystectomy

7.7.1 Machine Learning in Physician Adherence Monitoring and Reporting

Successful implementation of a clinical pathways program includes feedback to physicians, nurses, pharmacists and other providers on real world experience of their patients. Machine Learning is an excellent method for measuring and reporting the "adherence" to a multi-dimensional care pathway. Information is usually displayed as comparisons at the hospital level or the provider level. A typical care pathway usually can be very detailed, with dozens of specific events. The calculation of "adherence" to the overall pathway includes analysis of all of these events. Figure 7.4 compares the performance of a single inpatient surgery over 11 different hospitals. Figure 7.5 shows the distribution of care for a specific surgical case for one surgeon. Figure 7.6 shows an example report calculating the potential financial impact of converting from usual care to "best care" among the top 3 physicians.

As physicians and patients alike continue to demand more detail about the quality and outcomes of medical care, expect health systems and insurers to provide Machine Learning and other sophisticated methods of data analysis and reporting. The vast data stores now available provide opportunity for the routine analysis and discovery of best care methods. Expanded use of clinical pathways and adherence monitoring made possible by advanced analytics have now become the foundational elements needed to eliminate unnecessary clinical variation and promote the best possible clinical outcomes for patients.

Operational Dashboard — facility

facility	num	adh	stay	cost
Medical Center ABCD	126	31.7%	5.41 2 - 53	$7,445.20 $2,861.75 - $70,128.81
Medical Center EFGH	86	30.7%	6.38 2 - 22	$7,696.17 $3,151.14 - $28,064.79
Medical Center IJKL	77	36.6%	4.71 1 - 17	$7,275.12 $1,693.41 - $39,083.94
Medical Center MNO	74	29.3%	6.54 2 - 17	$10,053.10 $5,337.52 - $24,282.71
Medical Center PQRS	71	29.5%	4.42 2 - 14	$6,407.14 $3,664.02 - $17,278.78
Medical Center TUV	23	26.2%	4.65 2 - 20	$7,497.32 $4,198.88 - $20,694.56
Medical Center WXYZ	19	30.4%	5.68 2 - 16	$6,903.58 $3,329.35 - $16,613.33
Medical Center 123	16	28.2%	4.06 2 - 8	$6,414.09 $4,101.25 - $9,764.75
Medical Center 421	14	31.3%	5.79 3 - 13	$6,470.76 $3,685.54 - $15,350.02
Medical Center 897	8	28.0%	6.75 4 - 10	$9,874.32 $5,309.28 - $13,230.10
Medical Center 350	5	35.2%	3.60	$6,695.42

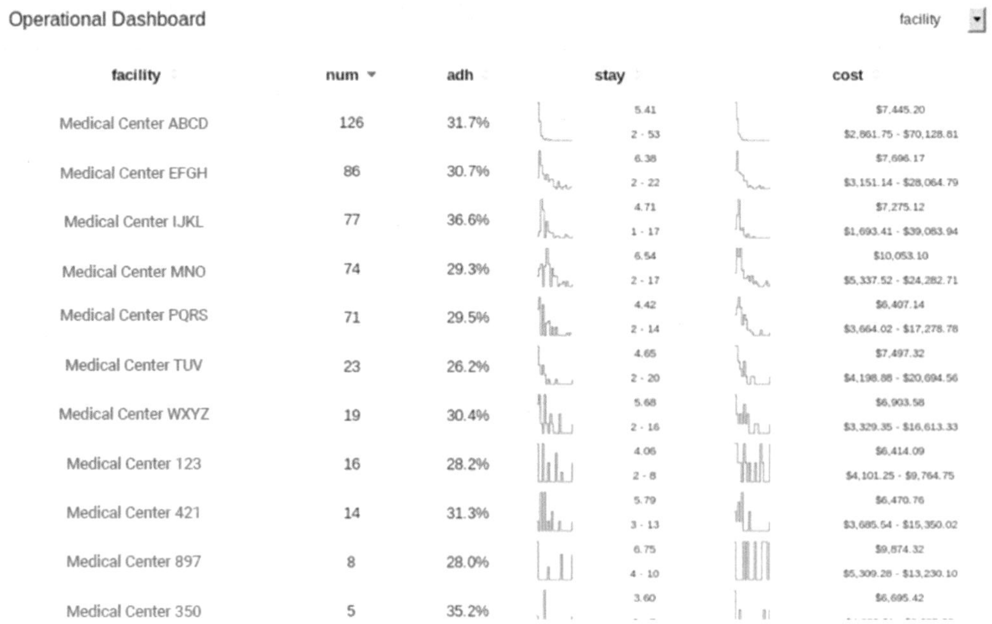

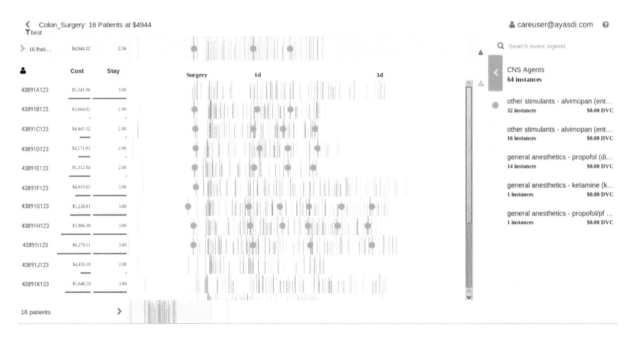

Figure 7.4: Operational Dashboard of a Surgical Procedures at Eleven Hospitals

Figure 7.5: Detail of 16 Patients Cared for at One Hospital (Colon Surgery)

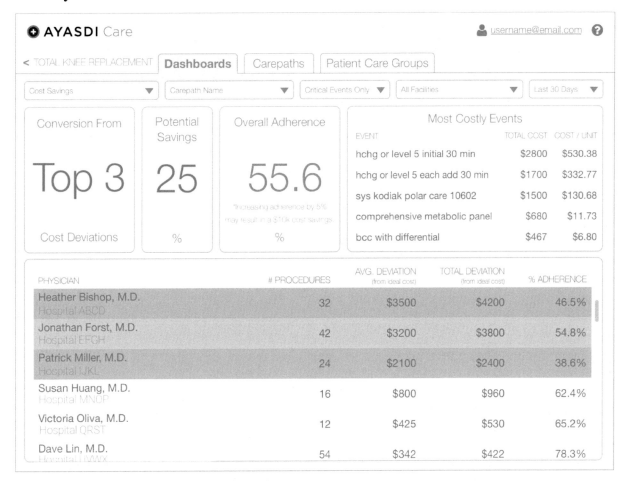

Figure 7.6: Cost Savings and Estimated Impact of Converting Care to the Pathway

Chapter 7

7.8 Case Study 12: Total Knee Replacement

Title: Total Knee Replacement – Variation Analysis

7.8.1 Contributors:

Mercy Health System, St. Louis, MO

7.8.2 Case Study Highlights

- Physician and nursing leaders analyzed 1,314 total knee replacement surgeries over 10 hospitals to identify efficiencies and best practices to significantly update their care pathway.
- Use of pregabalin dosed two hours pre-operatively correlated with significantly lower length of stay.
- Surgical supplies, particularly selection of joint prosthesis was a major cost driver and varied significantly across surgeons.
- Timing of compression devices to prevent deep vein thrombosis varied, leading to action plan to promote standardization.
- The health system updated its clinical pathway in record time with inclusion of best practices from several hospitals.

Mercy Health is a 33 hospital system distributed over four states, based in St. Louis, MO. Health system leaders are dedicated to improving care across all hospitals through the sharing of best practices and creation of care pathways for many surgeries and medical diagnoses requiring hospital care. Total knee replacement (TKR) is a high volume surgery performed in many of their hospitals and was known to have variable cost and length of stay within individual hospitals and across the health system. Orthopedic surgeons across the country have continued to innovate with new pre-operative preparation, surgical techniques, and pain management regimens. Device makers have continued to modify and diversify joint implant hardware. Mercy's orthopedic service line team determined it was a good time to update their current pathway for total knee replacement, particularly in light of CMS bundle payment program which began in 2016 for selected hospitals.

A Machine Intelligence (MI) platform was used to analyze performance across ten Mercy hospitals. These included larger urban teaching hospitals, suburban community hospitals and rural facilities. Mercy Health System maintains a large centralized data warehouse and data lake with a host of analytic tools. Data from each hospitals' EHR flows into the central data lake on a regular basis. Database managers performed their routine data quality and completeness review before uploading the data to the Machine Intelligence platform.

The goal of the MI analysis is to identify the TKR cases which met "best care" criteria. Best care being defined as cases which:

- Fell within the lowest 50th percentile for length of stay (LOS).
- Represented the lowest 50th percentile for cost.
- Patients were not readmitted within 30 days of discharge after surgery.

Among the best care subset of TKR cases, the MI platform performed similarity mapping to generate 6 specific groups of patients. Each of these groups had similarity among them. Table CS12.1 shows the characteristics of each group.

GROUP	#PATIENTS	DIR.VAR.COST	LOS	DIABETES	HYPERTENSION
1	67	$7,595	2.42	3.0%	25.4%
2	65	$6,852	2.29	1.5%	58.5%
3	47	$6,907	2.45	4.3%	53.2%
4	40	$6,190	2.50	2.5%	17.5%
5	33	$5,798	2.70	0.0%	12.1%
6	31	$7,634	2.06	12.9%	61.3%

Table CS12.1: Total Knee Replacement "Best Care" Groups

7.8.3 Results

The clinical evaluation group became interested to understand the details of group #6 which had the lowest length of stay. The MI platform automatically derived comparisons on multiple parameters for Group 6 compared to all other cases of TKR. In analyzing what parameters differentiated the group the most, it was quickly discovered that Group 6 patients had a significantly higher use rate of "CNS drugs" (central nervous system). In particular, 30 of the 31 (96.8%) patients in Group 6 had received pregabalin (trade name Lyrica, Pfizer, Inc.) whereas only 16.3% of all other patients had received the drug during their hospital stay. This was clearly statistically significant with p-value= 1.73e-21 (see Figure CS12.1).

Specifically, the software created a display of the timing of the use of pregabalin for all 31 patients in Group 6. Figure CS12.2 shows that these patients received a 75mg dose of pregabalin two hours before surgery. This use of pregabalin was ordered primarily at one community hospital. These orthopedic surgeons had adopted this best practice for pain control after learning about it at a surgical conference led by national experts a few months earlier. The surgeons found that patients receiving the pregabalin had improved pain control, enabling earlier post operative ambulation and hospital discharge.

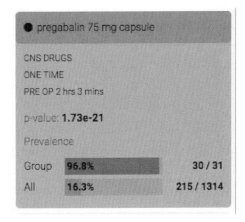

Figure CS12.1: Auto-calculation of Pregabalin Medication Use in Group 6 Patients

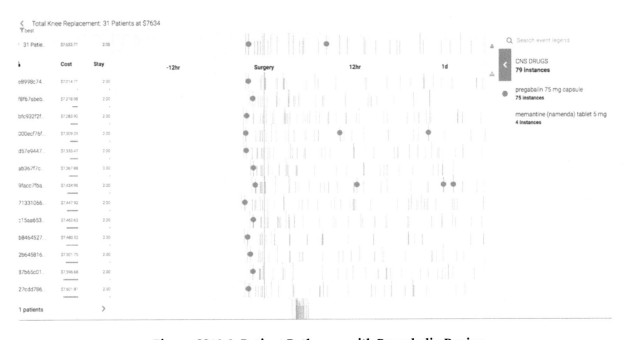

Figure CS12.2: Patient Pathways with Pregabalin Dosing

Over a period of two hours the TKR pathway team analyzed the data to investigate other differentiating features within and among the best care groups compared to the entire cohort of 1,314 patients.

The next most pressing issue is understanding the significant difference in cost between patients in Group 6, with the lowest LOS, but highest cost and Group 5, which had the highest LOS, but the lowest cost. It became immediately apparent that the selection and cost of the knee prosthesis itself was significantly different in the two groups. In Group 6, a high cost ($2,991.59 total direct cost) prosthesis was used in the majority of patients, whereas in Group 5, a lower cost, ($1997.31 total direct cost) prosthesis was used in the majority of cases. (see Figure CS12.3).

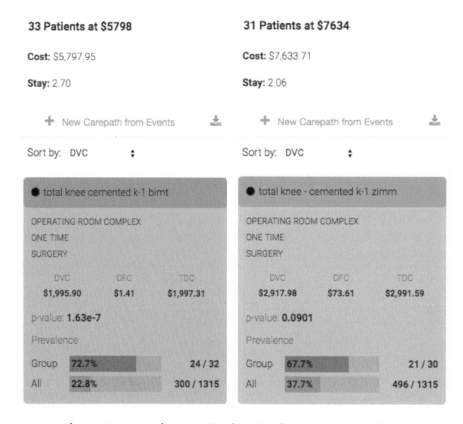

Figure CS12.3: Joint Prosthesis Selection Cost Comparison

The orthopedic clinical pathway team was able to further analyze trends in other aspects of care including use of compression devices for prevention of deep vein thrombosis (blood clot complications), use of anti-nausea medications and narcotics for pain control, as well as timing of removal of urinary catheters, patient ambulation and physical therapy. The MI platform automatically created a "consensus pathway" which

Pathways

they edited to include the specific features they wished to highlight. Figure CS12.4 shows the pathway with specific events recommended to achieve best care outcomes. Using automated reporting, the team analyzed the "adherence" to the consensus pathway to evaluate current practice at the level of individual surgeons and rolled up to the level of individual hospitals. The adherence pathway quickly identified those hospitals and surgeons which varied the greatest (see Figure CS12.5). Each surgeon received a Individual Physician Adherence Report detailing their cases relative to the consensus pathway (Figure CS12.6).

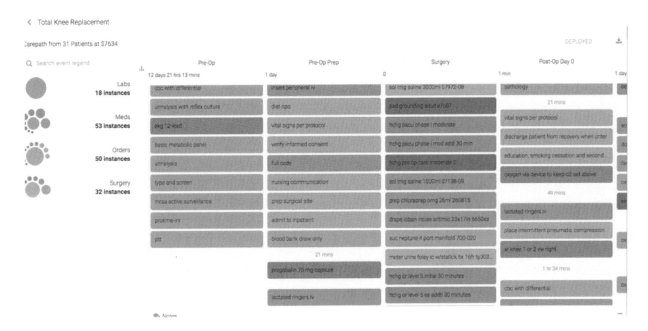

Figure CS12.4: Consensus Pathway for Total Knee Replacement

< Total Knee Replacement

Dashboard Carepaths Patient Groups

Operational Dashboard
physician ⇕ summary for: Carepath from 31 Patients at $7634 ⇕

primary physician	num	adh	stay	radm	cost	htn	dia
Physician 91.	10	44.5%	days 3 days · 4 days	20.0%	$11,962.44 $4,926.43 · $20,657.55	40.0%	30.0%
Physician 178.	31	69.5%	days 2 days · 7 days	3.2%	$8,700.51 $7,424.96 · $13,511.96	71.0%	32.3%
Physician 94.	30	65.8%	days 2 days · 5 days	3.3%	$8,304.38 $7,333.47 · $10,627.65	63.3%	6.7%
Physician 8.	33	64.7%	days 2 days · 4 days	3.0%	$8,323.04 $7,314.71 · $11,674.71	69.7%	33.3%
Physician 161.	15	55.6%	days 2 days · 5 days	0.0%	$9,727.80 $8,711.01 · $13,861.69	46.7%	20.0%
Physician 191.	47	54.2%	days 2 days · 6 days	4.3%	$9,638.33 $8,732.90 · $15,913.87	61.7%	14.9%
Physician 26.	12	53.9%	days 3 days · 5 days	0.0%	$9,192.56 $4,446.80 · $10,656.13	58.3%	25.0%
Physician 45.	6	53.6%	days 1 day · 2 days	0.0%	$8,033.76 $7,297.70 · $8,619.75	83.3%	16.7%
Physician 248.	15	53.2%	n/a 3 days 3 days · 3 days	6.7%	$10,467.36 $5,481.98 · $14,127.34	20.0%	13.3%
Physician 152.	3	52.5%	3 days 2 days · 4 days	0.0%	$6,296.71 $5,862.69 · $7,106.43	66.7%	33.3%
Physician 85.	47	52.2%	days 2 days · 14 days	0.0%	$7,359.78 $5,422.96 · $12,479.09	23.4%	4.3%
Physician 68.	5	51.0%	n/a 3 days 3 days · 3 days	20.0%	$11,174.42 $8,106.30 · $22,123.36	40.0%	20.0%
Physician 114.	1	49.7%	n/a 3 days 3 days · 3 days	0.0%	n/a $8,784.74 $8,784.74 · $8,784.74	100.0%	0.0%

Figure CS 12.5: Physician-level Adherence Reporting

Physician detail for Physician 69.
Carepath from 65 Patients at $8019_04/13/2016 ⇕

45.2 % adherence	67 encounters	4.48 % readmission	5.97 % diabetic	56.7 % hypertensive

cost distribution   length of stay distribution

event	category	sub category	time	adherence ▾
TOTAL KNEE - CEMENTED K-1 ZIMM	Surgery	OPERATING ROOM COMPLEX	SURGERY	74.6%
BASIC METABOLIC PANEL	Labs	LAB	POST OP 3 hrs 16 mins	74.6%
IP CONSULT TO HOSPITALIST	Orders	CON	POST OP 3 hrs 16 mins	73.1%
oxyCODONE CR (OXYCONTIN) tablet ...	Meds	ANALGESICS	POST OP 1 day 17 hrs 49 mins	71.6%
CEFAZOLIN 2000 MG INFUSION SO	Meds	ANTIBIOTICS	POST OP 14 hrs 53 mins	71.6%
BASIC METABOLIC PANEL	Labs	LAB	PRE OP 13 days 21 hrs	71.6%

Figure CS12.6: Individual Physician Adherence Report

Pathways

Using MI software, the orthopedic pathway team analyzed their pathway performance in greater detail than ever before. They discovered best practices from among their own hospitals which they did not know existed. Being able to use the MI platform's ability to automatically cluster similar patients into groups for analysis and systematically analyze the entire group for differences, improved efficiency greatly. The pathway team brought a list of best practices and insight back to the health system clinical excellence committee with specific recommendations for updates to the pathway. This included addition of pregabalin 75mg preoperatively and an enhanced decision algorithm for selection of knee joint prostheses. The surgeons were grateful to have clinical performance and cost data integrated and presented in an actionable manner.

Chapter 7

7.9 Case Study 13: Colectomy Surgery

Title: Colon Surgery – Variation Analysis

7.9.1 Contributors

Intermountain Healthcare, Salt Lake, City, UT

7.9.2 Case Study Highlights

- Use of Alvimopan dosed one hour pre-operatively correlated with significantly lower length of stay. This appears to be shortening post-operative ileus, enabling earlier return to oral nutrition and bowel function.
- Early use of ketorolac for pain control was associated with lower length of stay.
- Frequent post-op ambulation, early removal of foley catheter and early intake of oral fluids was associated with shorter length of stay.
- The health system used the Ayasdi Machine Intelligence software for confirmation of new pathway changes and identification of best practices.

7.9.3 Introduction

Intermountain Healthcare is a twenty-two-hospital system, based in Salt Lake City, Utah, spanning urban, suburban and rural communities. The health system is well known for its innovations related to patient safety and standardization of care. They have incorporated electronic clinical decision support, physician order sets, nursing care plans, patient education and other tools into "care process models" for high volume and high complexity medical diagnoses and surgical procedures. The system now prides itself on the systematic use of dozens of inpatient pathways which are shared across the system.

In the field of colon surgery, Intermountain has developed a recognized center of excellence with clinical leaders participating in national guideline initiatives. Their multidisciplinary surgical services quality team has worked to improve small intestine and large intestine surgery for over 8 years. They were an early adopter of the national movement calling for Enhanced Recovery after Intestinal Surgery (ERAS), a set of key interventions to improve surgical outcomes and patient experience. ERAS focuses on patient education, shared decision making, optimized anesthesia, multimodal non-narcotic analgesia, early mobilization and early return to oral feeding after intestinal surgery. In 2014, after years of analysis of these many aspects of care, using traditional spreadsheets, the surgical services quality team published an update of their clinical pathway for intestinal surgery to include many of the tenets of ERAS.[108]

Intermountain Healthcare evaluated a Machine Intelligence platform, to see if it could replicate the findings of their evidence based care process model for colon surgery.

7.9.4 Results

After a short period of data loading, the analysis of over 4,500 colon surgeries spanning 2010–2015 was completed in approximately two days. Table CS13.1 and CS13.2 summarize key findings. The team found some evidence of many of the optimal care interventions in the 2010-2014 surgeries and evidence that key interventions were being put into practice more consistently in their hospitals since the 2014 publication of the updated care process for intestinal surgery. The Machine Intelligence platform was used to identify groups of patients with similar care across multiple hospitals. One method of analysis defined a "best care" filter to find practice patterns achieving the lowest length of stay and lowest cost cases while still avoiding 30-day re-admissions after hospital discharge. The non-opioid pain medication, ketorolac, was found in some groups pre-2015 and now was commonly used in 2015. Similarly they found early ambulation, early foley catheter removal (<24 hours post-op) and early oral intake of fluids post-op also correlated with the most favorable outcomes.

Most gratifying was identification of the recent adoption of the drug alvimopan, which was for the first time included in the 2014 pathway update. Alvimopan is a mu-opioid receptor antagonist which blocks the effect of narcotic medications in the wall of the intestines. This helps overcome a major complication of opioid use, the development of ileus (slow intestinal motility) with constipation. In colon surgery patients, a post-operative ileus is expected from the surgery alone and is often made worse by the use of narcotics administered for pain control. Some surgeons became early-adopters of the use of alvimopan for their patients undergoing colon surgery for colon cancer, inflammatory bowel disease and other bowel disorders after leading a research study on use of alvimopan a few years earlier. The analysis quantified the beneficial impact of this best practice. The number of patients receiving alvimopan rose dramatically in 2015 and was correlated with lower length of stay and lower cost. See Figure CS13.1 which demonstrates the findings. Patients typically received a dose of alvimopan approximately one hour prior to surgery and again shortly after surgery began.

COLON SURGERIES	ALVIMOPAN	KETOROLAC	AMBULATION	FOLEY CATHETER	ORAL FLUIDS WELL TOLERATED
2010-2014 n=3,700	rare use	low use	less frequent	low documentation rate	low documentation rate
2015 "Best Care" lower cost, lower LOS n=536	common use	higher use	more frequent	removed earlier	earlier use of oral fluids

Table CS13.1: Colon Surgery Key Aspects of Care

	PRE-OP LABS	MIDAZOLAM	ODANSETRON	SURGICAL SUPPLY GROUNDING PAD
$4738 cost/case 2.47 days LOS 47 patients	lower frequency	lower use rate	more commonly "PRN" dosing	higher cost item
$4571 cost/case 2.07 days LOS "Best Care" n=14 patients	higher frequency	higher use rate	more commonly scheduled dosing	lower cost item

Table CS13.2: Subgroup Analysis of Laparoscopic Sigmoidectomy in 2015

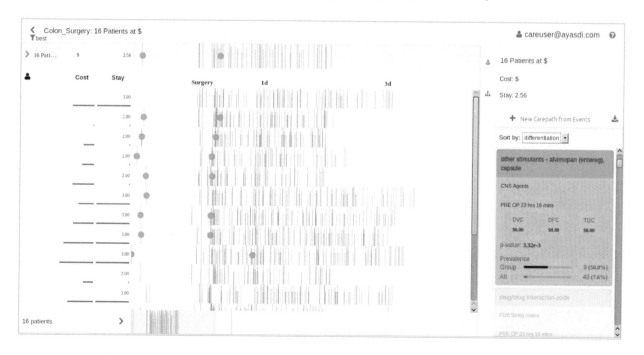

Figure CS13.1: Alvimopan Use Pre- and Post-op Associated with Low LOS

Findings from the analysis confirmed that many of these ERAS best practices were associated with lower LOS and lower cost colon surgeries. For example, the ERAS initiative encourages early oral nutrition after surgery with clear liquids on the day of surgery and solid foods on postoperative day 2. In addition, the team performed subgroup analysis to explore other trends surfaced by the Machine Intelligence software. The MI software also identified some practice patterns of interest related to the use of anti-anxiety and anti-nausea medications, which may warrant further analysis to determine their impact on clinical outcomes. This is illustrated in Table CS13.2 in subgroups of patients undergoing laparoscopic sigmoidectomy. Use of the intravenous drug, midazolam and the anti-nausea drug ondansetron were consistently used in patients with lower length of stay and lower cost. The visualization of clinical events using Ayasdi Care showed that patients receiving regular dosing of ondansetron correlated with lower length of stay.

In aggregate, the analysis does show that the surgical teams at Intermountain did maintain pro-active focus on pain management, postoperative oral nutrition and other clinical practices as envisioned in the ERAS guidelines. This does appear to facilitate earlier discharge of patients. Other events such as pre-operative testing of blood chemistries and the intraoperative use of specific surgical supplies (e.g. grounding pad) were also correlated with lower cost cases.

This analysis of colon surgery data using Machine Intelligence software helped confirm and measure the impact of specific care activities and helped identify new opportunities for clinical standardization. Intermountain Healthcare will continue to systematically update their large number of active care process models. They expect to enable their talented group of analysts to become even more productive while expanding the scope and volume of analysis with the use of advanced analytics.

Chapter 8: Population Health Management

"One touch of nature makes the whole world kin."
-William Shakespeare

8.1 Chapter Preview

- Discussed population management and its relationship to Machine Learning.
- Federal government mandates under ACA and HITECH as motivators for various aspects of population management.
- Risk assessment, clinical registries and quality measures are explored with examples provided.
- Examined are data sources and EHR methods for clinical registries.
- Case Studies
    - Case Study 14: Syria Polio Vaccination Campaign
    - Case Study 15: Smartphone Gait Data Elucidates Parkinsonism Progression
    - Case Study 16: Population Management Transformation

8.2 Introduction

In 2008, Don Berwick, MD and colleagues made their famous call for healthcare reform to pursue the "triple aim". They stated,

"Improving the U.S. healthcare system requires simultaneous pursuit of three aims: improving the experience of care, improving the health of populations, and reducing per capita costs of healthcare. Preconditions for this include the enrollment of an identified population, a commitment to universality for its members, and the existence of an organization (an "integrator") that accepts responsibility for all three aims for that population. The integrator's role includes at least five components: partnership with individuals and families, redesign of primary care, population health management, financial management, and macro system integration."[109]

Many of these concepts are now the guideposts of redesign for the healthcare systems in the U.S. and abroad. The notion of "population" emphasizes some commonality of a group that need not be restricted by geography, such as a group of diabetic patients, or enrollment in a specific health insurance plan. For our purposes the definition of population health is "the health outcomes of a group of individuals, including the distribution of such outcomes within the group".[110] The purpose of population health management (PHM) then is to optimize the health of a defined group within a pool of healthcare and social resources.

8.3 Population Health Management

Population management is an important factor in improving healthcare outcomes. Considering that "approximately half (117 million) of US adults have at least one of 10 common chronic conditions (i.e. hypertension, coronary heart disease, stroke, diabetes, cancer, arthritis, hepatitis, weak or failing kidneys, asthma, or chronic obstructive pulmonary disease [COPD])"[111], the benefits in the ability to identify, track and treat specific populations are obvious.

Given that, 5% of the population accounts for 49% of healthcare costs, identifying those population clusters which have the greatest impact on change in healthcare outcomes becomes imperative.[112] As discussed previously, the motivation for the move away from fee-per-service based medicine to value based medicine (VBM) "are improving quality of healthcare and using healthcare resources efficiently."[113] Population health management (PHM) is one tool enabling the VBM goal.

A population is generally defined by two parameters:

1. The subject of study
2. The boundary condition(s)

For example, a medical population might have as a subject of study, "diabetic patient outcomes using clinical pathway X", and a boundary condition, "those men and women insured through a commercial insurance pool and receiving primary care from a specific medical group". Without clear specification of both parameters, coming to meaningful conclusion in a population management program is problematic.

The types of data needed generally fall into three classes:

1. Population member outcomes data.
2. Social and medical conditions surrounding the population member that may be uniquely variable per member.
3. Costs per member of population related to the population subject of study or boundary, or both.

In most cases, the job of PHM starts with the aggregation of patient data from multiple health information technology sources. Once aggregated, the PHM should ideally analyze the data and provide actionable patient reporting in a consolidated user interface for front line healthcare staff. This activity provides evidence based solutions to care providers which can improve both clinical and financial outcomes. The success goal is seeking out and monitoring individual patients within the group and applying knowledge learned to improve health outcomes to the whole group.[114]

"An effective PHM toolset must be able to perform a number of key tasks, including[115]:

- *Aggregating data across the continuum of care. This includes clinical applications, claims systems, administrative systems, health information exchange, remote monitoring devices, consumer mobile applications, patient reported surveys, biometric sensors, etc.*
- *Tracking, aggregating and analyzing a vast spectrum of clinical and financial data, following a patient's journey from prognosis, prevention and treatment to maintenance and wellness management.*
- *Measuring performance scores and analyzing clinical outcomes to help enhance quality, cost and efficiency of care delivered at both an individual and population level.*
- *Applying risk stratification algorithms to patients in a given population to derive better and more targeted health management programs.*
- *Delivering information to care team members and decision makers when and where they need it.*
- *Assessing cost and quality metrics of population health programs to deliver return on investment projections and scores."*

8.3.1 Machine Learning in Defining Populations

Machine Learning techniques can be used to determine in real-time, whether a patient is, or isn't a member of a population. ML techniques are capable of providing in real-time a clinical response which enables better patient population risk assessment, care gaps identification, and patient intervention models.

Consider a hypothetical situation regarding prescription opiates and fear of addiction and a care system augmented with Machine Learning. The identified population might be patients where potential for opiate addiction is likely for a particular type of prescribed drug. The boundary condition, for example, is patients taking the drug longer than 2 weeks. ML is used to both predict which patients are at greatest risk of addiction and is used for ongoing, real time monitoring.

Using a clinical registry, a training data set is created across all opiate users of a particular type of prescription drug; including not only clinical data, but social interaction data, genetic and family history, and other behavioral data about patients and outcomes. Co-pays to multiple doctors and attempts at getting multiple prescriptions from the patients' insurance is also fed into the ML prediction data set. Machine Learning and topological data analysis (TDA) is performed to identify vectors most indicative of addiction over specific timeframes.

Data is captured in real time and analyzed by cloud-based ML predictive models that can evaluate the individual patient's likelihood of addiction by evaluating in real time risk factors and conditions, sending warnings if necessary to the patient and doctor. As a stipulation of obtaining the drug, and with patient agreement and cooperation, an opioid prescription for a patient at high risk of addiction includes a requirement that the vectors most indicative of addiction are monitored by smartphone app. Prescription refill data is merged with physiological characteristics, such as sleep disruption, breathing, light sensitivity and alertness which are tracked with sensor technologies and wireless communications. Additionally, location tracking may be employed attempting to indicate social withdrawal or distinct changes in routine. Real time monitoring and ML calculations then provide feedback to population management staff who can intervene with any patient exhibiting addiction behaviors. In this manner, the medical group can tailor pain management care to patients and limit the risk of addiction and patient harm.

8.4 Clinical Registries and Quality Measures: Creating a Value Based Medical System

The HITECH Act and the ACA after it helped formalize and operationalize all of the tenets of the "triple aim." Population health management supported by EHRs, registries and quality measures is now a major initiative in virtually every healthcare system in the United States.

Under HITECH, "meaningful use" of health information technology is defined by five health outcomes policy priorities including a specific call for improving population health:[116]

1. *Improving quality, safety, efficiency, and reducing health disparities*
2. *Engage patients and families in their health*
3. *Improve care coordination*
4. *Improve population and public health*
5. *Ensure adequate privacy and security protection for personal health information*

The use of clinical registries enables much of this work. "A clinical data registry records information about the health status of patients and the healthcare they receive over varying periods of time. Clinical data registries typically focus on patients who share a common reason for needing healthcare."[117] Registry can refer to both programs that collect and store data and the records that are created. It's clear that the creation of data registries is advancing, and with them the availability of quality data for improving the care of individual patients as well as providing insight into medical efficacy at the aggregate level. This is consistent with the related goals of clinical effectiveness research (see Chapter 6).

Medical registries can serve many different purposes. Listed below are a number of examples:[118]

1. For a clinician, registries can collect data about disease presentation and outcomes on large numbers of patients rapidly, thereby producing a real-world picture of disease, current treatment practices, and outcomes.
2. For a physician organization, a registry might provide data that can be used to assess the degree to which clinicians are managing a disease in accordance with evidence-based guidelines, to focus attention on specific aspects of a particular disease that might otherwise be overlooked, or to provide data for clinicians to compare themselves with their peers.
3. For patients and patient advocacy organizations, a registry may increase understanding of the natural history of a disease, contribute to the development of treatment guidelines, or facilitate research on treatment.
4. From a payer's perspective, registries can provide detailed information from large numbers of patients on how procedures, devices, or pharmaceuticals are actually used and on their effectiveness in different populations. This information may be useful for determining coverage policies.
5. For a drug or device manufacturer, a registry-based study might demonstrate the performance of a product in the real world, meet a postmarketing commitment or requirement, develop hypotheses, or identify patient populations that will be useful for product development, clinical trials design, and patient recruitment.

Given that patients receive care from different medical providers over time, it's important the clinician has global access to the registry. In general the input and output of a patient's data to and from a registry (with widely varying degrees of automation) is as follows[119]

1. Each time a patient participating in a registry sees their clinician or is admitted to a hospital, specific data about their health status and the care received is recorded.

2. The clinician, through an EHR device sends encrypted data about the patients to the clinical data registry over a highly secure web portal.

3. As data is entered, the clinical registry performs a number of quality checks before the data becomes part of the data set, such as correctness and completeness of the data. If something is missing or outside of the expected range, either registry staff or electronic feedback is sent to the clinician requesting them to review and verify the data.

4. Providers from multiple specialties or services will typically contribute to and receive information from the registry. But more important is retrieving the analytic interpretations of the population data and the potential conclusions that can be drawn from aggregate comparisons.

8.4.1 Registries Used to Capture Measures of Quality

As discussed in Chapter 7, paper medical records and early EHRs were designed to care for one patient at a time, where little thought was put into aggregate analysis; there was little or no functionality provided for population management. Before broad adoption of EHRs in 2011, even simple lists of all of the diabetic or heart failure patients in a medical practice were hard to come by. Prior to that, some practices did receive lists of their chronic disease patients from one or more individual insurance companies if they participated in managed care programs such as Health Maintenance Organizations. Rarely available were lists of patients with common diagnoses across their entire medical practice since most practices interface with many different insurance companies and they depended on the insurance companies for the lists.

As discussed above, medical practices have business and legal requirements to meet quality performance goals for diabetic, hypertensive and other patient populations. Increasingly, insurance programs provide incentives and penalties to providers based on measures of quality using the HEDIS (Health Employer Quality Data Information Set), the National Quality Forum (NQF) and CMS Quality Measures or its predecessor, the

CMS Physician Quality Reporting System (PQRS).[120] Now, physicians use standard tools in their EHRs to generate a list of chronic disease or other cohorts of patients in their care. In fact, generating a patient list is one of the features which EHRs must provide to meet the EHR certification standards for CMS incentive programs. Usually these patients' lists or simple registries contain dozens or even hundreds of patients from a physician's practice. The number of data elements is generally small, 10 – 50 data elements per patient. See Figure 8.1, the High Risk Heart Failure Registry tool available within the Epic EMR. These registries are typically designed to serve the needs of quality reporting programs and usually focused on process measures. The Epic EMR registry does include an advanced analytic feature – inclusion of a "general risk" score and is color coded, indicating high risk in red. This risk score is pre-calculated using additional data and then merged with the other registry information to help clinicians select patients for individualized attention.

8.4.2 Examples of Clinical Registries, Data Types and Quality Measures

For example, a diabetic measure may include glycemic control (HBA1C < 7.0), blood pressure control (<140 /90), annual retinal eye examination (performed or not performed). See Figure 8.2 for a list of common quality measures in cardiology. Most quality measures do not vary based on severity of disease and focus on relatively short timeframes (occurrence of care activities within one calendar year). For these reasons, commonly used disease registries are simple, with relatively small data size per patient. This is in great contrast to the data sets used in Machine Learning analysis, which typically have thousands of patients in rows and hundreds or thousands of individual data columns per patient.

Figure 8.1: Disease Registry: High Risk Heart Failure Patients Report from Epic EMR

PQRS MEASURE NUMBER	NQF MEASURE NUMBER	TITLE	DEFINITION
5	0081	**Heart Failure Angiotensin** Converting Enzyme (ACE) Inhibitor or Angiotensin Receptor Blocker (ARB) Therapy for Left Ventricular Systolic Dysfunction (LVSD)	Percentage of patients aged 18 years and older with a diagnosis of heart failure (HF) with a current or prior left ventricular ejection fraction (LVEF) < 40% who were prescribed ACE inhibitor or ARB therapy either within a 12 month period when seen in the outpatient setting or at each hospital discharge
6	0067	**Coronary Artery Disease (CAD) Antiplatelet Therapy**	Percentage of patients aged 18 years and older with a diagnosis of coronary artery disease (CAD) seen within a 12 month period who were prescribed aspirin or clopidogrel
7	0070	**Coronary Artery Disease (CAD)** Beta-Blocker Therapy Prior Myocardial Infarction (MI) or Left Ventricular Systolic Dysfunction (LVEF < 40%)	Percentage of patients aged 18 years and older with a diagnosis of coronary artery disease seen within a 12 month period who also have prior MI OR a current or prior LVEF < 40% who were prescribed beta-blocker therapy
226	0068	**Ischemic Vascular Disease (IVD)** Use of Aspirin or Another Antithrombotic	Percentage of patients 18 years of age and older who were discharged alive for acute myocardial infarction (AMI), coronary artery bypass graft (CABG) or percutaneous coronary interventions (PCI) in the 12 months prior to the measurement period, or who had an active diagnosis of ischemic vascular disease (IVD) during the measurement period and who had documentation of use of aspirin or another antithrombotic during the measurement period
236	0018	**Controlling High Blood Pressure**	Percentage of patients 18-85 years of age who had a diagnosis of hypertension and whose blood pressure was adequately controlled (<140/90 mmHg) during the measurement period
392	2474	**Cardiac Tamponade and/or Pericardiocentesis Following Atrial Fibrillation Ablation**	Rate of cardiac tamponade and/or pericardiocentesis following atrial fibrillation ablation. (This measure is reported as four rates stratified by age and gender.)

Table 8.1: Medicare Quality Measures[121]

8.5 Data sources – EHR, Insurance Claims, PROs and Limitations

Population management requires relevant and timely data for a group of patients which can be reliably updated over time. Depending on practice size and sophistication, physicians, pharmacists and case managers have widely varying access to good information. Some issues such as diabetic glycemic control, measured by HBA1C blood test or blood pressure control will require data from the EHR. These details, lab values and blood pressure values will not be available through insurance claims data alone. If a physician is part of a large EHR installation with cardiologists, endocrinologists and other specialists contributing to the care of the same patients, then they will have access to lab and blood pressure values ordered or measured by all of the physicians in the group. However, if the physician is a solo practitioner or is in a single specialty group without EHR connectivity to other specialists, then their access to these data will likely be limited to only the values acquired through their own office visits. Partly for these reasons significant consolidation in medical practices and growth of physician networks with large data warehouses to improve quality of care is occurring.

Even with large EHR data sharing arrangements, there continue to be important uses of insurance claims data for population management. Certain aspects of primary care and chronic disease quality measures rely on knowledge gained through claims. One example is the performance of diabetic retinal eye examinations – usually performed by optometrists and ophthalmologists, often not in the same group or EHR instance as primary care physicians. Similarly, colonoscopies for colon cancer prevention are usually performed by gastroenterologists at outpatient surgical centers or hospitals which are not part of the primary care EHR environment. Patients with emergency care or hospitalizations outside the providers' network, such as a heart attack or heart failure admission out of state, are important events which usually fall outside the EHR instance of the primary care provider. Regular updates of insurance claims data now are commonly integrated into the providers' data warehouse and information used for population management. In just a few years is has become common for medical groups with Medicare Shared Savings contracts to receive CMS monthly claims data feeds to the ACO provider organization.

There is good recognition that optimal chronic disease management requires actively engaged patients and families to ensure compliance with medications, diet and exercise prescribed by providers. New information streams of patient reported outcomes (PROs) are growing quickly. Treatment of diabetes, coronary artery disease, heart failure, hypertension, asthma, COPD, rheumatoid arthritis and other conditions have greatest success when patients actively monitor glucose values, blood pressure, weight, peak flow meters, medication dosing and physical activity on a daily basis. Increasingly, patients are logging these PROs with home based monitoring using web-based tools such as smart phones and blue-tooth enabled glucose meters, scales and other devices. Some health systems are expanding their data systems for population management by integrating EHR, claims and PROs and actively tracking patient compliance. Increasing complexity of data is an opportunity to gain insight into what works for certain conditions and subpopulations of patients. Machine Learning can be used to efficiently translate these growing data sets into actionable outreach by providers and feedback to patients.

8.5.1 Improving Data Quality: Examples of Risk Adjustment Tools

Prior to the ACA, insurers would reject patients who they considered "too risky". Currently, the ACA prohibits risk selection by insurers, and addresses risk variation among patients through Risk Adjusted financing. For example, CMS uses risk adjustment to calculate patient and group level budgets and then transfers funds from ACOs with lower-risk enrollees to ACOs with higher-risk enrollees. Excerpted below are a few items that discuss the goals and methods of risk adjustment. The interested reader is encouraged to refer to the original paper from the Henry J. Kaiser Family Foundation for a more complete and thorough discussion on risk adjustment.[122]

- *"The goal of the risk adjustment program is to encourage insurers and providers to compete based on the value and efficiency of their programs rather than by attracting healthier enrollees."*
- *"To the extent that risk selecting behavior by insurers – or decisions made by enrollees – drive up costs in the health insurance marketplaces (for example, if insurers selling outside the Exchange try to keep premiums low by steering sick applicants to Exchange coverage), risk adjustment also works to stabilize premiums and the cost of tax credit subsidies to the federal government."*
- *"Under risk adjustment, eligible insurers are compared based on the average financial risk of their enrollees. The HHS methodology estimates financial risk using enrollee demographics and claims for specified medical diagnoses. It then compares plans in each geographic area and market segment based on the average risk of their enrollees, in order to assess which plans will be charged and which will be issued payments."*

Clinicians and administrators have great interest in risk adjustment of their patient populations. It is not unusual for a physician to argue that their "patients are sicker" than those cared for by another physician. Academic medical centers typically demand higher payments from insurers based on this reasoning. Disease severity adjustment is a form of "risk adjustment," the tools of which must be carefully constructed to meet the needs of the intended use. Tools for physiologic severity of illness may be quite different from tools designed to express relative "severity" of cost burden of health conditions.

The Diabetes Complications Severity Index (DCSI) was developed from a large primary care registry of ambulatory diabetic patients in Washington State. It uses a weighted scale (0-2) to score presence or absence of specific cardiovascular, neurologic, renal and other conditions based on over 60 ICD-9 codes.[123] It was shown to be helpful in predicting both hospitalization and death. The DCSI has acknowledged limitations of generalizability since it was developed in a single health system and the ICD-9 codes it uses have now been superseded by ICD-10. As a predictive tool, it performed only slightly better than a simple count of complications. It is now common practice to use simple counts, lab values and physiologic values (blood pressure and BMI) to organize diabetes disease management activities in many physician offices. Case managers use these tools to reach out to diabetic patients in greatest need for additional care.

For hospitalized patients admitted to the intensive care unit, the APACHE II score has become a widely used metric of illness severity.[124] The "Acute Physiology and Chronic Health Evaluation II" is measured upon each admission or readmission to the ICU but is not intended for re-calculation during the ICU stay. It was first developed in 1981 and has undergone subsequent revisions. Using twelve common measurements, APACHE II provides a score from 0 to 71. Patients with higher scores have more severe disease and a higher risk of death. APACHE III was published in 1991 including additional variables such as ICU admission diagnosis and patient location prior to admission. It provides a more granular score (0-299) and has refined predictive uses. APACHE III was validated through patient cohorts in forty hospitals in the U.S.[125]

	PHYSIOLOGICAL MEASUREMENTS OF APACHE II SCORE
1.	AaDO2 or PaO2 (depending on FiO2)
2.	Temperature (rectal)
3.	Mean arterial pressure
4.	pH arterial
5.	Heart rate
6.	Respiratory rate
7.	Sodium (serum)
8.	Potassium (serum)
9.	Creatinine
10.	Hematocrit
11.	White blood cell count
12.	Glasgow Coma Scale

Table 8.2: Apache II Score

As mentioned above, CMS and other large payers use risk adjustment in determining payments to providers. One of the most commonly used risk adjustment tools in the U.S., in recent years, is the "Hierarchical Condition Category" or MC-CMS-HCC model. CMS explains that "Risk adjustment is a method of adjusting capitation payments to health plans, either higher or lower, to account for the differences in expected health costs of individuals."[126] The CMS-HCC model has been used since 2004 in the Medicare Advantage program to set each Medicare enrollee's monthly capitation rate. Approximately 25% of all Medicare patients are enrolled in Medicare Advantage plans in which CMS pays private insurance companies to manage the care of enrollees. Although Medicare cautions users that the HCC model is built to enable fair payments at the aggregated group level, many providers also have adopted HCC to rate individual patients and prioritize care and outreach.

The CMS-HCC risk adjustment model uses demographic information (age, sex, Medicaid dual eligibility, disability status) and a profile of major medical conditions in the base year to predict Medicare expenditures and set payment rates in the next year. CMS calculates a Risk Adjustment Factor or RAF score for each enrollee each year. The diagnoses used for a given patient come from the claims from face to face encounters with qualified practitioners during the prior calendar year. Correct and completed coding for chronic conditions such as emphysema, heart failure, atrial fibrillation, multiple sclerosis, Parkinson's disease and chronic hepatitis have major impact on RAF scores for patients so many medical groups have expanded their provider education on proper coding. CMS-HCC is updated routinely to stay relevant and as accurate as possible in its attempt to reasonably predict insurance risk for the Medicare Advantage contracting plans. It is periodically re-calibrated using the fee for service (FFS) Medicare population. FFS experience is used since this population, unlike the Medicare Advantage population, submits the most complete Medicare claims data, including both diagnoses and expenditures.

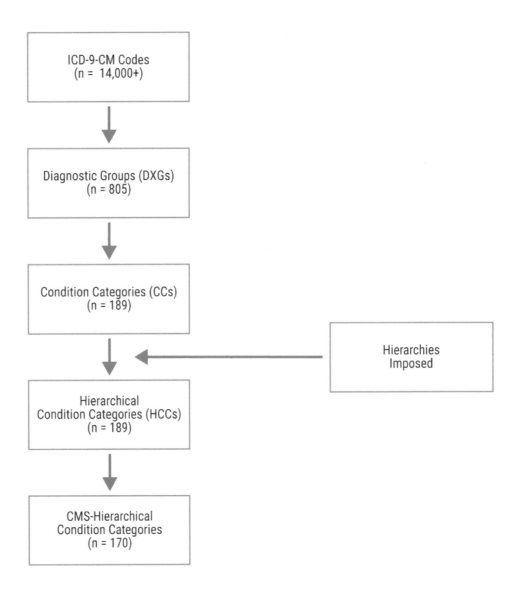

Figure 8.2: CMS HCC Model- Aggregation of Diagnosis Codes

Related condition categories (CCs) are arranged hierarchically, such that a patient's code reflects only the most severe expression of similar diseases. For example (Figure 8.3), ICD-9-CM Ischemic Heart Disease codes are organized in the Coronary Artery Disease hierarchy, consisting of four CCs arranged in descending order of clinical severity and cost, from CC 81 Acute Myocardial Infarction to CC 84 Coronary Atherosclerosis/Other Chronic Ischemic Heart Disease. If a patient's physicians have used more than one of these diagnosis codes during the past year, only the most severe is used to calculate that patient's HCC score.[127]

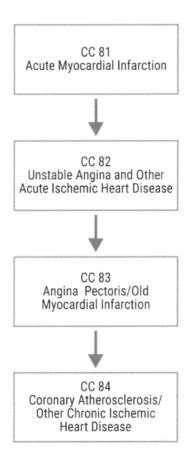

Figure 8.3: Hierarchical Condition Categories for Coronary Artery Disease[9]

---

[9] Created from ICD-9-CM ischemic heart diseases codes, version 12 CMS-HCC model

8.5.2 Prediction Methods: Current Applications

To a great extent, provider organizations have been successful in the early years of the Medicare Shared Savings contracts and other commercial capitation arrangements by "harvesting low hanging fruit". They have done this by tightening up existing work flows, limiting hospital readmissions by arranging common sense follow up care and completing basic preventive care such as cancer screening and immunizations. But health systems are under continued pressure to ratchet down costs and further improve quality, to deliver higher "value" care. In order to accomplish this challenge, providers are hoping to be able to predict which patients will become sicker and which are most likely to consume more care in the next 6 to 12 months. Ideally, prediction software should answer the following questions:

- Which patients will have progression of their chronic condition(s)?
- Which patients are most likely to be admitted to the hospital?
- Which patients are most likely to respond to treatment?
- Which patients are prone to have injury or complications from treatment?
- Which patients are prone to poor medication or treatment adherence?
- Which patients are likely to respond to first line treatments and which should go directly to second order therapies or receive advanced treatments sooner?
- Which hospitalized patients are most likely to experience a wound infection or suffer from sepsis?
- Which ambulatory patients are likely to seek emergency room care?

Answers to these questions can enable providers to create personalized treatment plans and tailor care management. Access to data and routine application of algorithms in a real-time environment are key to creating actionable prediction tools. The most effective strategies will integrate this information directly into clinical registries used by case managers and EHR clinical decision support tools used by physicians. This can enable timely outreach to patients at risk and enable physicians to order treatments most likely to help the patients.

Commercially available tools for predictions of healthcare consumption are now available. In England, the Health Numerics-RISC® service from Optum Health predicts the risk of patients having unplanned hospital admissions for chronic illness in a 12 month period.[128] The models used in this product were developed using logistic regression to identify independent variables impacting likelihood of hospital admission in the National Health Service. The models were built using multiple data sources from more than 70 million records from urban and rural populations in five Primary Care Trusts (PCTS).

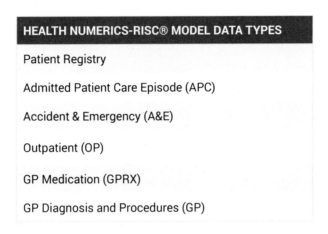

HEALTH NUMERICS-RISC® MODEL DATA TYPES

Patient Registry

Admitted Patient Care Episode (APC)

Accident & Emergency (A&E)

Outpatient (OP)

GP Medication (GPRX)

GP Diagnosis and Procedures (GP)

Table 8.3: Health Numerics-RISC® Model Data Types

Large health insurers in the United States, similarly, are seeking to better characterize their populations. See the case study below on Machine Intelligence for examining the populations of patients to best understand how insurance plan design can affect health seeking behaviors. Machine Learning approaches can encompass many more factors including clinical, demographic, social and other characteristics for more precise population segmentation.

Predicting the progression of illness or complications in real time, within an individual's hospitalization, can be very challenging. Complications like wound infections, ventilator-associated pneumonia; falling and sepsis require advanced analytics. Some relatively simple prediction tools have been in use for years. One risk-stratification tool is the Anesthesia Society of American Classification system for pre-operative planning.[129] It helps physicians select the level of care and setting (outpatient surgical center or inpatient operating room) needed to handle potential complications and intensity of care appropriate for each patient. Many hospitals are focused on predicting which patients are likely to be re-admitted after hospital discharge. This is partly due to penalties from CMS under which hospitals may not receive reimbursement for readmission for specific diagnoses such as heart failure, acute myocardial infarction and pneumonia. One example is an algorithm using the Charlson Score of illness burden along with the complexity of medication regimen (e.g. fewer or greater than 6 medications at time of initial admission).[130] In this study by Logue and colleagues at a community hospital, patients with high Charlson scores and more than six medications had a 19% likelihood of readmission within 30 days whereas those with low Charlson scores and fewer than six medications had only a 9% rate of readmission.

ASA PHYSICAL STATUS CLASSIFICATION SYSTEM Last approved by the ASA House of Delegates on October 15, 2014		
YEAR	NAME	WORK
ASA I	A normal healthy patient	Healthy, non-smoking, no or minimal alcohol use
ASA II	A patient with mild systemic disease	Mild diseases only without substantive functional limitations. Examples include (but not limited to): current smoker, social alcohol drinker, pregnancy, obesity (30 < BMI < 40), well-controlled DM/HTN, mild lung disease
ASA III	A patient with severe systemic disease	Substantive functional limitations; One or more moderate to severe diseases. Examples include (but not limited to): poorly controlled DM or HTN, COPD, morbid obesity (BMI ≥40), active hepatitis, alcohol dependence or abuse, implanted pacemaker, moderate reduction of ejection fraction, ESRD undergoing regularly scheduled dialysis, premature infant PCA < 60 weeks, history (>3 months) of MI, CVA, TIA, or CAD/stents.
ASA IV	A patient with severe systemic disease that is a constant threat to life	Examples include (but not limited to): recent (< 3 months) MI, CVA, TIA, or CAD/stents, ongoing cardiac ischemia or severe valve dysfunction, severe reduction of ejection fraction, sepsis, DIC, ARD or ESRD not undergoing regularly scheduled dialysis
ASA V	A moribund patient who is not expected to survive without the operation	Examples include (but not limited to): ruptured abdominal/thoracic aneurysm, massive trauma, intracranial bleed with mass effect, ischemic bowel in the face of significant cardiac pathology or multiple organ/system dysfunction
ASA VI	A declared brain-dead patient whose organs are being removed for donor purposes	

*The addition of "E" denotes Emergency surgery: (An emergency is defined as existing when delay in treatment of the patient would lead to a significant increase in the threat to life or body part)

Table 8.4: American Society of Anesthesiology Physical Status Classification System[10]

[10] These definitions appear in each annual edition of the ASA Relative Value Guide®. There is no additional information that will help you further define these categories.

8.5.3 Opportunities for Machine Learning

Better population segmentation and disease prediction tools are sorely needed across the health delivery system. By their very nature traditional severity adjustment and risk prediction tools have limitations. Now that very large claims and clinical datasets are becoming readily available, insurers and health systems have the opportunity to improve upon existing tools and move these measurements closer to real time using Machine Learning. With the addition of novel data sources such as remote patient monitoring and social behavioral metrics, the potential for new prediction tools is very promising.

DISEASE SEVERITY AND RISK PREDICTION TOOLS	SETTING	STRENGTHS	LIMITATIONS
Diabetes Complication Severity Index	Primary care	Single disease	Built on diagnosis code data from a single state, quickly outdated
Acute Physiology and Chronic Health Evaluation (APACHE)	Intensive care unit admission	Includes 12 physiologic parameters	Not intended for re-calculation
Hierarchical Condition Category (HCC)	Capitation payment calculation, population level	Use of large, standardized claims data set	Based on diagnosis codes only; always at least one year retrospective
Health Numerics-RISC®	Hospitalization prediction	Focus on patients with chronic illness	Based on care in England
American Society of Anesthesiology Physical Status Classification System (ASA score)	Peri-operative risk	Simplicity; semi-structured	Subjective assessment made by individual clinician at one point in time
Machine Intelligence	Potentially applied across many settings	Continuous re-calculation and refinement on hundreds or thousands of parameters for each population of interest	Not yet widely integrated into data stream and workflow

Table 8.5: Disease Severity and Risk Prediction Tools

The prediction of impending sepsis is a complex problem facing some 230,000 patients in the U.S. each year.[131] Septic shock causes some 40,000 deaths each year. It is an area of intense research. Researchers and data scientists at Johns Hopkins University published a prediction tool, the TREW Score based on 23 clinical data elements which outperformed standard algorithms.[132] This algorithm outperformed older methods but still achieved only a 0.67 specificity. Timely care of sepsis, in particular, achieving the first 3-hour "bundle" and 6-hour bundle of care can save lives and improve patient outcomes. Future directions include more precise prediction based on larger data sets including genetic markers, molecular diagnostics and detailed physiological measurements (e.g. arterial pulse contour analysis). Major collaborations are underway to establish a learning healthcare system organization including a project team sponsored by the High Value Healthcare Collaborative.[133] Machine Learning may become a key tool in moving the field forward.

Predicting onset as well as progression of chronic diseases is considered the Holy Grail for many working in the population health management community. New data sources are now becoming available for analysis. For example, the Michael J. Fox Foundation is pioneering the use of data from smart phones and other devices to better understand the deterioration of gait of patients with early Parkinson's disease.[134] Early detection could enable family and physicians to craft fall prevention and treatment strategies tailored to keep patients safe, in their home environments for as long as possible. Identifying cohorts early in the disease is expected to open new opportunities for drug treatments, surgery and preventive strategies to slow progression and potentially cure this disease. See the case study below for this example of analysis on large, patient-generated datasets. There is tremendous interest in the use of genetic markers to predict risk of onset and progression of chronic diseases. See Chapter 6, on Machine Intelligence for precision medicine to learn about research at the Mount Sinai Medical Center in New York City which identified three genetic subtypes of Type II diabetes and the European academic-industry collaboration centered at the University of Southhampton in England which has used Machine Learning to uncover 5 subtypes of severe asthma.

There is an enormous appetite for better predictive models in healthcare. Application of the first generation of risk stratification tools to assist physicians in clinical decision making and planners for creating health insurance programs and care delivery systems to meet the needs of populations are increasingly available. It is the tailoring of prediction models to specific populations where the next phase of development lies. The opportunity to apply Machine Intelligence and other methods of analysis to very large and complex healthcare data sets will become the norm for the creation and routine updating of population management tools over the next decade.

8.6 Case Study 14: Syria Polio Vaccination Campaign

8.6.1 Contributor:

Stefan Heeke, Executive Director, SumAll Foundation

8.6.2 Case Study Highlights:

- The goal of the study is to identify risk factors associated with missing the second dose of polio vaccination for children in war torn Syria.
- Using Machine Intelligence and a multiple factor database, a systematic cluster analysis of polio vaccinations for Syria's children is performed.

8.6.3 Introduction

Using the most advanced analytical tools available is a necessity for any organization, and SumAll.org has employed powerful topological data analytics software that delivers both visual and statistical analytics. By using this software, SumAll.org is able to quickly identify and explore relationships that, without the software, would take significant resources to complete. This provides an opportunity to more quickly develop and implement life saving interventions, creating real world impact on today's toughest problems.[135]

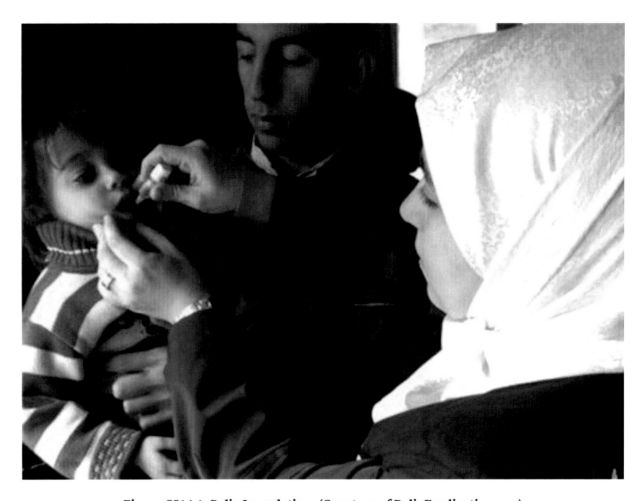

Figure CS14.1: Polio Inoculation. (Courtesy of PolioEradication.org)

8.6.4 The Analysis

SumAll.org used Machine Intelligence software to perform a quick systematic cluster analysis of a Polio vaccination campaign in Syria for children, with data provided by HumanitarianTracker.org. This humanitarian effort in a conflict zone reaches millions of people per campaign, however there is a need to quickly and easily understand which locations are most impacted from the constantly fluctuating refugee population. This is especially important as follow-up doses are necessary for the Polio vaccine to be effective in protecting the population. Analysis with visual based TDA software differs from simply counting the number of doses by region as the software is taking into account all available features in the data set, not just ranking doses. In a traditional analysis of this data one would first need to examine each district and try to locate outliers in terms of each feature class. After that, one or several hypotheses would need to be formed and tested, which in this case would involve testing and validation between over 100 districts.

The Machine Intelligence software is capable of interacting with all of the available feature classes at once and the results are then visualized in such a way that any interesting behavior in the data can be quickly identified. This means that there is no need to have a formulated hypothesis to find important and significant information in your data set. Moreover, once the interesting data is identified, Topological Data Analysis supplies all the necessary statistical results to validate significance. The systematic cluster analysis first creates nodes that contain statistically similar rows from a given dataset. Statistically similar nodes are then connected by "edges", resulting in a structured architecture that can be used to identify interesting relationships. These relationships can then be further explored both visually and with high-level statistical comparisons. For example, when node clusters exhibit a behavior that is not similar with the majority of the population, they show up as "flares" or protrusions in the node network. These are visually apparent, and once identified the flares can be selected for statistical analysis.

8.6.5 The Results

SumAll.org identified two statistically distinct groups where "Not Reached Doses" were the largest defining factor, with statistically significant districts within each group. There were no significant differences for those receiving their first dose. Based on insight from the vaccination team, it is likely the reason why children are not reached for follow-up doses is because of the high fluidity of refugee populations at vaccination sites.

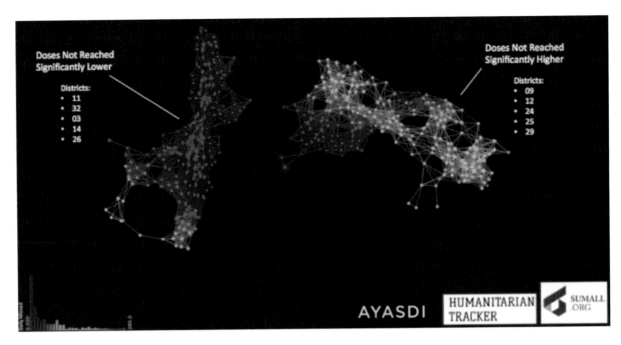

Figure CS14.2: Polio Vaccination Campaign in Syria– Follow Up Doses Not Reached

8.6.6 The Impact

By understanding where children are most likely not reachable for follow up doses, SumAll.org is able to work with Humanitarian Tracker and help examine strategy to ensure that all individuals are receiving their doses. "Children in Syria have a right to be vaccinated, and it's even more critical because Polio is a preventable disease." Taha Kass-Hout, Humanitarian Tracker Founder and CEO.

For humanitarian aid organizations strapped for time and resources, the ease and efficiency of reliable statistics and reporting can become crucial, and in cases such as this, Machine Intelligence software can significantly cut down on the investment needed for analysis. Moving beyond a tabular report, TDA provides a statistical and visual aid that, with other techniques would take a significant amount of time and resources. By saving this time, organizations can keep their focus on providing the aid and saving lives.

8.7 Case Study 15: Smartphone Gait Data Elucidates Parkinsonism

8.7.1 Contributors:

Dr. Christian Bracher, Research Fellow, Bayes Impact

Ken Kubota, Director of Data Science at The Michael J. Fox Foundation

8.7.2 Case Study Highlights:

- Data collected from smartphones was pooled for groups of patients with Parkinson's Disease and for a group of healthy volunteers
- TDA analysis showed distinct differences in patterns of ambulation between patients with Parkinson's disease and normal patients
- Among Parkinson's patients, at least two subgroups were identified which could help predictive tools to facilitate early diagnosis and improved treatment.

8.7.3 Introduction

The Michael J Fox Foundation has made available accelerometer and gyroscopic data collected from smart phones used by subjects with Parkinson's disease (PD) and by healthy controls that took part in the study. By applying Machine Intelligence software to the data set it shows that data collected from smart phones can differentiate between subjects with Parkinson's disease and healthy controls. In addition, we also showed that there may be two patient sub-groups of Parkinson's patients as defined by the data collected from the smart phones.

Smart phones are increasingly being used to track many aspects of our lives. They are used to track our geo-locations, our buying habits, websites we frequent and even the games we play. The healthcare sector has been very active in using wearable devices as a way to track personal activity. Recently, there are efforts to use more of these types of mobile devices to track health of patients. Parkinson's affects over 60,000 Americans each year (not counting the many who go undetected) and 7-10 million worldwide; with medication costs averaging $2,500 a year per person, and surgery costs up to $100,000 dollars per patient, this is an important disease for early diagnosis and proactive monitoring.

Two-thirds of U.S. consumers carried smartphones and healthcare organizations are beginning to use smartphones as a way to track patient health. Seeing trends in smartphones and healthcare converging, the Michael J. Fox Foundation (MJFF) launched a Parkinson's Data Challenge in early 2013. The initiative made available accelerometer and gyroscope data from smartphones carried by both Parkinson's patients and healthy control volunteers. Data was collected from 9 participants with Parkinson's disease and 7 age and gender matched healthy controls. Participants carried Android smartphones that ran an app that collected information from the sensors and microphone for 4-6 hours per day. The data collected included audio, accelerometry of 3 axes, compass data in 3 axes, ambient light. An application running on the smartphones captured data from the phone's accelerometers, microphone, battery, compass, GPS, light sensor and proximity sensor. A total of over 6,000 hours of data were collected.

8.7.4 Results

Analysis using Machine Intelligence software with topological data analysis (TDA) took just a few hours to complete. The resulting data network revealed two subpopulations of Parkinson's patients within the smartphone data (Figure CS15.1). The software incorporates algorithms to measure similarity across the research subjects. The data set included hundreds of data elements per individual. Each data entry is associated with a time stamp or other distance parameter. Researchers are now interested in combining these data with other clinical parameters of disease duration, difficulty with activities of daily living, medication dosing and adverse event information such as history of falling, dropping items, etc.

Years from now, we could expect that smartphone data from Parkinson's patients would stream directly to an automated data analysis center using Machine Learning software. Real time data processing could provide patients and physicians with trended information about each patient relative to a large number of other patients with and without Parkinson's disease. The system could continuously learn and refine its predictive capabilities. These systems will enable more accurate dosing of medications based on timely information collected passively from smartphones. Physicians will quickly learn which medications are helping and which are not helping patients with specific types or patterns of Parkinsonism. Dose adjustments could be made more accurately and improve patient safety by avoiding adverse drug reactions altogether. Non-medication strategies such as strength and balance training techniques could be refined with this method. Based on individual characteristics, physicians will be better equipped to help families predict what the trajectory of functional decline lies ahead. This will empower patients and families to choose treatments and adapt living arrangements to maximize health and wellness in the face of a progressive neurologic disease.

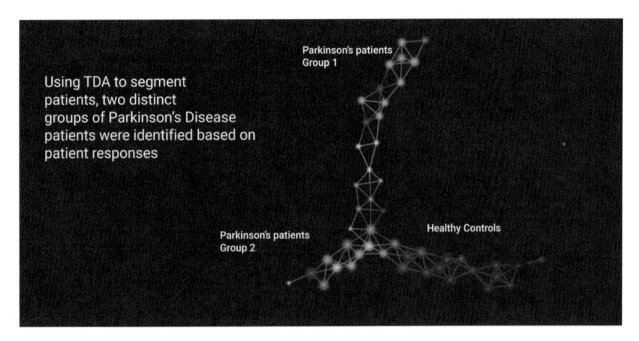

Figure CS15.1: MJFF Patient Stratification–
TDA Analysis of Smartphone-Acquired Data Shows Two Possible Subtypes of PD.

8.8 Case Study 16: Population Health Transformation

8.8.1 Case Study Highlights

- Using Machine Intelligence tools, clinical leaders in Accountable Care Organizations are organizing care for population health management by routinely identifying patients at greatest risk of declining health and incurring high costs.
- Automating patient enrollment into enhanced care programs based on calculated criteria can insure timely patient interventions focused on prevention.
- A "center of excellence for analytics" including Machine Learning software can accelerate standardization of population health services.

8.8.2 Introduction

Providers and payers caring for Medicare patients are seeking better methods for identifying patients at greatest risk for developing poor health outcomes and high cost care. One large health system had grown by acquisition of medical groups and hospitals. It manages a number of risk contracts with CMS which now are focused on total population costs. Altogether, they have just over 115,000 patients under risk contracts. The Accountable Care Organization (ACO) provider groups are seeking to both deliver needed care more efficiently and predict and intercede on preventable health decline and complications. They need new tools for better characterizing their defined patient group and anticipating which patients will benefit from treatment adjustments, fall risk prevention, cancer screening, mental health counseling, in-home monitoring, medication adherence coaching, appointment reminders and end-of-life planning. Through better preventive care, they hope to find cancers at a curable stage, avoid injuries, achieve better pain control, limit progression of organ failure and enhance quality of life.

They knew that change was needed in their organization despite early successes in the Medicare Shared Savings programs by several of their ACO groups. They realized that across all of their groups they had many best practices and were now willing to share and consolidate services wherever needed. A major area of weakness was in their capacity to stratify their population in a consistent and standard manner. They relied on physician referrals to their patchwork of many case management and disease management programs which they felt were underutilized. Table CS16.1 summarizes some key aspects of their current case management programs with their goals for transforming their organization to one focused on population health.

CURRENT CASE MANAGEMENT PROGRAM	POPULATION HEALTH TRANSFORMATION
Physician referrals required for entry into programs	Continuous multi-factor risk profiling of 100% of population with automatic enrollment
PCP directed, reactive, episodic	Team Based, patient activated, anticipating needs
National Evidence Based Guidelines	Patient centric goals of care, continuous data-driven care paths to best utilize in-network resources
Focus on high risk group for cost savings	Savings by managing predicted risk transitions at all levels
Prior cost based financial risk prediction	Predictive clinical and financial risk modeling
12 month risk planning	3-5 year risk trajectory modeling and planning

Table CS16.1: Goals for Population Health Transformation

8.8.3 New Methods for Population Analysis

The smaller ACOs found that their relatively small number of Medicare lives under management made use of statistical analysis very imprecise. They chose to evaluate new methods for population analysis with focus on cost of care. Using Machine Learning software they analyzed the entire population of Medicare risk patients across the health system. Figure CS16.1 and Figure CS16.2, show their first findings from the network level assessment. Their first step was to assign a simple "co-morbidities" score for each patient. The comorbidity score simply added up the number of co-morbidities for each patient. They chose to use the Medicare claims extract alone since it was common across all patient groups.

In Figure CS16.1 we see the graphical network generated using similarity analysis and colored by the co-morbidity score. The software automatically segmented the patients into clusters of patients with similar attributes, in this case disease conditions. This is an unbiased segmentation where there have been no constraints or guidance on the taxonomy for segmenting the population. We can see that there are four naturally occurring segments. The software allows interrogation of the groups using color. In Figure CS16.1, red indicates a higher number of co-morbidities compared to blue with lower co-morbidities. There appears to be a small concentration of high comorbid patients in the top right hand segment but otherwise quite heterogeneous across the board in the mid-range of number of comorbidities. The highest was 10 co-morbidities and the average for the entire population was 5.10.

In Figure CS16.2, they changed the color scale to represent costs based on actual Medicare payments. The groupings light up with well demarcated groups of red and blue. The highest cost groups are shown with labels. The largest grouping of high cost patients was characterized by a combination of diabetes and ischemic complications (e.g. heart attack, peripheral arterial disease). They identified a mid-sized group of diabetics with osteoporosis and a group of cancer patients also in the high cost range. A smaller cluster of high cost depressed patients formed a distinct grouping. Based on these data, the population health team began review of their current disease management and outreach programs.

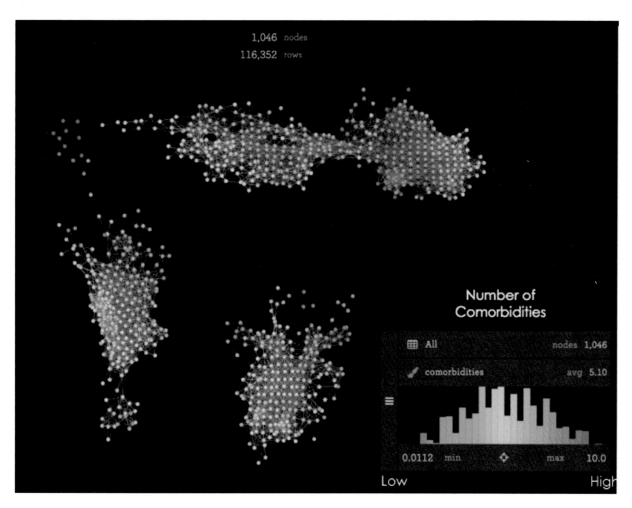

Figure CS16.1: Comorbidity Analysis of 116,352 Medicare Patients

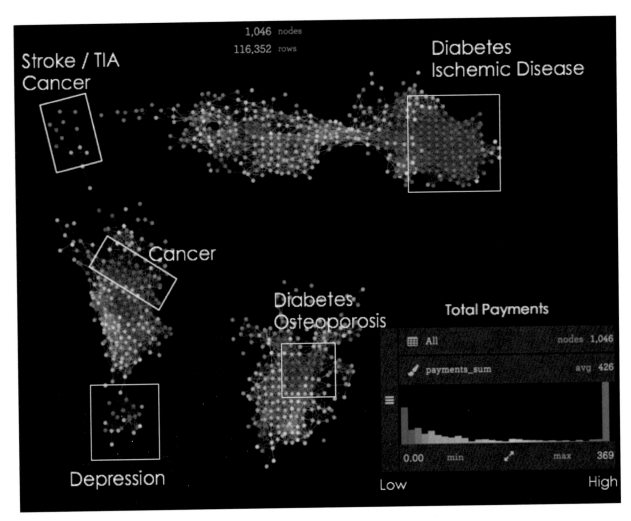

Figure CS16.2: Cost Analysis Base on Medicare Expenditures

8.8.4 Action Steps

Using the software to explore the data display networks further, the team discovered that the group of diabetic patients had a high rate of falls resulting in trauma. These patients underwent emergency room care and hospitalizations for fracture, some requiring hip replacement and extended rehabilitation stays. It appeared these patients had a high rate of diabetic neuropathy and resulting numbness in their feet, which made falls more likely. They modified their selection for intensive diabetes outreach to focus on patients with these attributes with hope of preventing these injuries and expenses.

The health system had previously instituted an expedited stroke care program in their main group of community hospitals. The data analysis helped prove the tremendous value of this initiative. Based on the relatively low cost of stroke expenditures they decided to move the stroke programs from "pilot status" to a fulltime operational initiative by expanding the program to all of their hospitals. Health system leaders have promoted their stroke care program as a demonstration of "value-based care" enabling better recruitment of neurologists to the health system and enhanced contracts with commercial insurers.

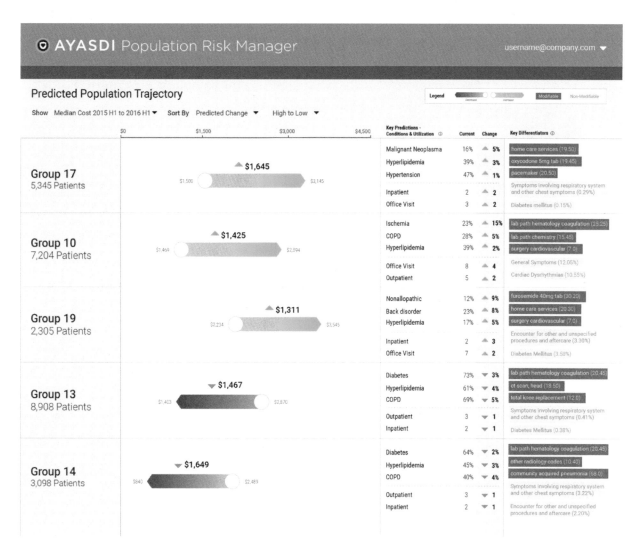

Figure CS16.3: New Population Risk Applications

8.8.5 Machine Learning Becoming Mainstream

The health system is proceeding with the next phase of its population health strategy, enabling them with the ability to better predict which patients will benefit the most from enhanced care strategies. Figure CS16.3 shows a small portion of their newly designed dashboard for predictive analysis. Using Machine Learning applied to claims data, they can now routinely update their patient risk profiles, identifying patients most likely to be readmitted to the hospital within the next 6 months or most likely to become expensive utilizers of care in the next year. Current plans are to add electronic medical record data to begin predictions of those patients likely to progress in disease severity such as chronic kidney disease. They are examining models to identify patients at risk for healthcare associated complications such as Clostridium Difficile (C. Diff.) colitis. The health system is restructuring their support systems for the physician groups and hospitals including a center of excellence for analytics. They have found efficiencies in standardizing their data warehouse and analytics personnel who are now equipped with state-of-the art software including Machine Intelligence.

Chapter 9: Machine Intelligence for Precision Medicine

"How many things are there which I do not want"
-Socrates

9.1 Chapter Preview

- The relationship between precision medicine, genetics and Machine Learning are discussed
- Introduced is a short primer on human genetics and how Machine Learning is the obvious assistant to a geneticist.
- Complications of the genome and its use as a diagnostic tool
- Examples of the influence genetic research is having treatment pathways and models of care
- Case Studies
  - Case Study 17 – Genetic Subtyping of Type 2 Diabetes
  - Case Study 18 – Patient Stratification for Precision Medicine

9.2 Introduction

It truly is the dawn of the era of precision medicine. For purposes of this discussion we will use the terms "precision medicine" and "personalized medicine" interchangeably. Large data sets of clinical and research information can be interpreted with advanced, unsupervised analytic methods, such as Machine Learning, to "enable the data to speak". Gone are the days of sole reliance on the slow and uneven pace of hypothesis-driven inquiry and long cycle time for analysis and publication. Knowledge networks will be the underpinning of the learning health system enabling patients and physicians to treat current illness and prevent disease progression, malignancy and organ failure. The promises of personalized medicine are awe inspiring; the challenges are formidable, but manageable.

Since the ambitious first mapping of the human genome was completed in 2003, progress on truly understanding the blueprint of our make-up is expanding rapidly. In 2008, the President's Council on Advisors on Science and Technology (PCAST) defined "personalized medicine" as "the tailoring of medical treatment to the individual characteristics of each patient to classify individuals into subpopulations that differ in their susceptibility to a particular disease or their response to a specific treatment. Preventative or therapeutic interventions can then be concentrated on those who will benefit, sparing expense and side effects for those who will not".[136] Since that time, we have seen real applications in clinical practice for genetic and molecular diagnostics and therapeutics. Our growing understanding of the molecular mechanisms underlying disease has challenged the very language of medical care and taxonomy of disease. In 2011, the National Research Council in the U.S. convened an expert panel to help shape the future, in light of this explosion of knowledge. The Committee on a Framework for Developing a New Taxonomy of Disease recommended the gradual re-framing of our taxonomy of disease over a period of decades based on expanded sharing of clinical and scientific data constituting an "Information Commons."[137] They envision an infrastructure of data repositories including molecular and genetic test results, medical histories and clinical outcome information alongside research systems to be used by an integrated group of scientists and clinicians constituting a "Knowledge Network" (see Figure 9.1). Overtime, the published findings and deliberations of the knowledge network will help inform a new taxonomy of disease based on this new knowledge.

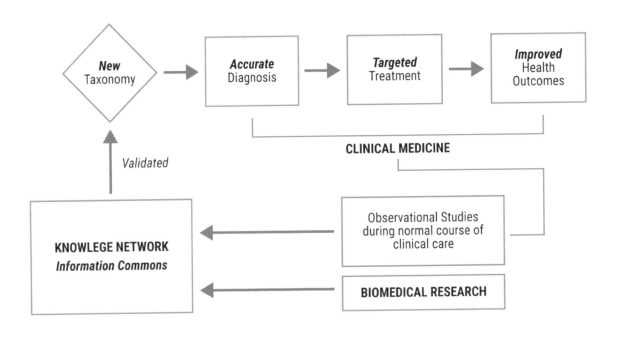

Figure 8.4: Creation of a New Taxonomy of Disease using Knowledge Networks

9.3 Precision Medicine and Genetic Makeup of a Patient

In Chapter 6, precision medicine is introduced as a clinical approach that customizes the treatment of a patient by applying all the relevant information about the disease and the patient. Precision Medicine compares biomarker and genomic data along with social and environmental factors, to important clinical outcome data such as development of a disease, enabling a customized causation model, upon which, targeted therapies can be applied.

The foundation of precision medicine is the aggregation of clinical data of all patients of a similar population. What makes precision medicine "precise" is data about the specific patient makeup and how it relates to the aggregate population. Given that almost everyone's genetic makeup is unique to the individual, then specifying the genetic makeup of the patient is certainly one of precision medicine's pillars. Assimilating the genetic complexity of each patient's data and interpreted efficiently in a meaningful way, remains one of precision medicines most significant challenges. In their viewpoint article, cardiologists Fatima Rodriquez and Robert Harrington from Stanford University summed up their optimism for what lies ahead in for their patients with cardiovascular disease. They wrote, *"Finally, the role of discovery science in developing more precise risk-predicting models cannot be overstated. By studying large, diverse populations, it should be possible to identify patients at greatest risk by incorporating information from their genes, proteins, metabolites, environment, and behaviors. In essence, these insights gained from population-based data will serve as the foundation for personalized medicine and decision making for reducing cardiovascular disease risk."* [138]

These are some of the wide-reaching mandates envisioned by the in the 21st Century Cures Act, passed by the U.S. Congress in 2016. Congress calls for expansion of scientific research programs relating to precision medicine. These programs include establishment of "The Council for 21st Century Cures," (Sec. 1141) a nonprofit corporation, to accelerate the discovery, development, and delivery of innovative cures, treatments, and preventive measures. Underscoring the need for the secondary use of health information, the act (Sec. 1124) directs that the Department of Health and Human Services (HHS) must revise health information privacy rules to allow: (1) use of protected information for research purposes to be treated as use for healthcare operations, (2) remote access to information by researchers, and (3) individuals to authorize future use of their information for research. [139]

9.3.1 Why Human Genetics is so Complicated

There is a great deal of genetic information in a human's body. So much so, if you stretched it out and laid it end to end, that cord of genetic thread would reach farther than the distance from earth to Pluto, 12 times, over 67 billion miles. Each cell in your body has a DNA strand about 6 feet long. Our genetic material is very tightly packed, yet it still allows access to each gene.[140]

An allele is one specific form of a number of alternative forms of the same gene occupying a given position on a chromosome. Genotype is the set of genes giving rise to a particular trait. A person's genotype is the information contained within their two alleles for a particular gene. It is determined by genetic testing. The "phenotype", is the observable trait or physical manifestation of genotype. Often multiple genes contribute to the phenotype such as eye color or skin tone.[141]

DNA possesses all of instructions or "blueprint" for life. It is a remarkably powerful combination of just four simple nucleotides found in pairs ("base pairs") and coiled in a double helix. Along the blue print are short segments called genes each of which provides directions to produce a protein. The sum total of an organism's entire DNA is its genome. We are most interested in DNA which codes for genes but also realize that organisms also contain some "noncoding" segments of DNA. The relative proportion of coding and noncoding DNA varies among species. In humans, only about 2% of our DNA is coding for genes leading production of proteins whereas in most bacteria, almost 98% of DNA is coding.[142] In humans, our basic blueprint guarantees opportunity for genetic variation and complexity.

Genes contain the instructions for the production of proteins in the body. Proteins provide the building blocks of cells and enzymes for carrying out the functions of growth and repair. The human genome contains approximately 20,000 protein-coding genes. Some genes are crucial for life, some are crucial for health, and some can be deleted in their entirety without apparent harm.[143] Some defects or gene mutations lead to helpful traits and can help a species evolve whereas other mutations can cause disease.

Sickle cell anemia is a condition caused by a defect in a single gene. Persons with sickle cell disease (SCD) have inherited a specific gene defect from both parents associated with the formation of the hemoglobin molecule important for red blood cell function. Patients with two copies of the defective gene produce irregular, crescent or "sickle" shaped red blood cells which can impede normal blood flow in small blood vessels causing pain (sickle cell crisis) and increase risk of infection. Persons who have inherited just one sickle gene will be "carriers" for the condition known as sickle cell trait (SCT). In the U.S. newborns are routinely screened for sickle cell so early education and treatment can begin for those affected. Today, approximately 1 in 12 African Americans carry the sickle cell trait. It is fascinating to realize that this genetic mutation which can cause disease also has a beneficial effect in other parts of the world. Carrying the sickle cell trait helps protect against the severity of malaria infection, reducing the death rate, particularly in young children.[144]

Although some diseases are caused by a single gene defect, most other "heterogeneous" genetic conditions are associated with multiple gene defects. This is particularly true of many common chronic medical conditions.. This means that inherited (germline mutations) defects in different genes, often on different chromosomes can lead to an illness such as Type 2 Diabetes. When the mutations arise during the process of cell growth in specific tissues (somatic mutations) the result can be cancer. Even though diabetes or cancer may look similar in different individual patients, it is quite likely that the specific genetic defects vary from person to person. For this reason, patients with similar looking chronic diseases or cancers may respond very differently to treatments. Testing for their specific genetic make-up can enable more precise treatment.

9.4 Machine Learning is Instrumental in Genetic Analysis

Recalling from past chapters, Machine Learning uses unsupervised methods, which infers predictions based on algorithms that analyze data sets, as opposed to other forms of Artificial Intelligence methods that are trained through heuristics, where humans code outcomes. When it comes to understanding the function of genes, the use of Machine Learning has greatly accelerated our understanding.

Consider that it is by chance that we inherit half of our genetic material from each of our parents to yield 23 pairs of chromosomes. On each chromosome is found dozens or thousands of genes, each of which has multiple possible alleles.[11] Altogether, this leads to at least 70,368,744,177,664 potential combinations. This is trillions of times more combinations than the number of people who have ever lived. This accounts for why nearly everyone, except monozygotic (identical) twins, is genetically unique.[145]

Machines employing supervised learning techniques are impractical for genetic prediction, given the combinatorial complexity of human genetics and disease outcome

---

[11] Alternate forms of a gene

possibilities. Expecting a human programmer to completely infer 70 trillion possible outcomes heuristically is impractical. Genetic outcome prediction based on unsupervised learning techniques is indicated. See the case studies for more in-depth discussions on Machine Learning methods in genetics.

9.5 Precision Medicine: The Influence of Genetic Research on Treatment

The promise of precision medicine extends into many facets of our health and well being. Understanding germline genotype[12] and somatic mutations[13] are key to unlocking the potential for new treatments. As mentioned earlier, germline mutations are inherited from an individual's parents' germ cells (sperm and egg) and are thus present in all cells of that individual's body. Germline mutations may help determine a person's likelihood of developing a disease (e.g. cystic fibrosis, diabetes). Knowing a person's genotype can help create a tailored strategy for prevention or early treatment of a disease. Testing usually occurs on a blood sample or cheek swab. Somatic mutations occur in individual cells or tissues within a person's body and may progress with abnormal growth such as the development of a tumor. Testing the genetic and cellular biomarkers of this abnormal tissue can aid in the selection of a very targeted therapy such as a monoclonal antibody or enzyme inhibitor which may kill cancer cells without harming healthy cell, minimizing side effects.

In recent years, treatment options for cancer care have been revolutionized due to advances in molecular diagnostics. Treatments tailored according to molecular diagnostics are now providing more potent therapy with fewer side effects for a variety of cancers including breast cancer, melanoma, leukemia and lung cancer. For many cancers, pathological analysis of tumors includes a molecular and genetic profile which can help in the selection of chemotherapy, immunotherapy and hormonal therapies. This rapidly advancing field of scientific and clinical knowledge has many of the characteristics envisioned by the National Research Council's committee to establish a new taxonomy for disease. Physicians, researchers and pharmaceutical manufacturers are collaborating to bring clinically relevant guidelines to the bedside using advanced clinical decision support. In order to efficiently communicate cancer treatment options, specialists have developed national consensus committees to continuously review

---

[12] Successive generations of an organism genotype. Genotype is the specific genetic makeup of an organism.
[13] Changes to the genetics of a multicellular organism which are not passed on to its offspring through the germline. Many cancers are somatic mutations.

research and clinical trial results. Through the National Comprehensive Cancer Network (NCCN) the author and update clinical guidelines in what has become a massive, yet efficient undertaking. This collaboration of oncologists, pathologists, radiation therapy specialists and researchers constitutes a "knowledge network" and is a very effective process in this dynamic era of rapid discovery. Cancer treatment guidelines are updated and re-published on an ongoing basis on the NCCN website. To a great extent, drug selection and treatment decisions which are outlined in the NCCN guidelines becomes the pre-authorization template for health insurance coverage by private and public payers. In many instances the NCCN guidelines call for use of a chemotherapeutic agent for a cancer which was not included in its original FDA approval process. In this manner, the use of cancer drugs is guided by the best possible science and clinical consensus without overburdening or being delayed by the regulatory process.

One of the greatest breakthroughs in cancer care came in 2001 with the FDA's approval of the drug Gleevac (Novartis Pharmaceuticals Corp.), also known as imatinab. This was the first drug in the class of tyrosine kinase inhibitors (TKI).[146] Gleevac inhibits the phosphorylation of certain proteins important for cell growth and other functions. Fortunately, this inhibition is active almost exclusively in cancer cells and avoids inhibition in related normal functions of closely related protein tyrosine kinases such as those found in the insulin receptor. This discrimination for a very specific enzymatic step in cancer cells is the model for "targeted therapy". Gleevac quickly became the mainstay of treatment for patients with chronic myelogenous leukemia (CML). Due to the use of Gleevac after 2001, the five year survival rate for patients with CML rose from 31% in the early 1990s to 59% for those diagnosed between 2003 and 2009.[147] The development of Gleevac spawned several related TKI drugs as well as numerous other targeted therapies. Since that time, the FDA has approved several new targeted agents along with companion diagnostic tests used to characterize tumors or other tissues which become the focus of treatment.

Some of the most challenging disease states are those caused by aberrations of the immune system. Major advances have been made in recent years in the treatment of inflammatory bowel disease, rheumatoid arthritis, multiple sclerosis, asthma and other immune-mediated conditions. With advances in proteomics[14], receptor physiology and nanotechnology[15], we are gaining insight into normal immunology and understanding

---

[14] Used interchangeably with genomics, the study of the genome.
[15] Molecular sized machines.

what happens when things go wrong. Breakthrough treatments have been introduced that dramatically improve the prognosis of patients with these conditions. Now, with drugs such as Humira (AbbVie Pharmaceuticals) and Remicade (Janssen Biotech, Inc.) for rheumatoid arthritis, patients who previously could not walk or use their hands effectively can continue very productive work and family lives. These TNF-alpha inhibiting medications were among the first monoclonal antibody drugs approved by the FDA. Similarly impressive are targeted immune modulating drugs for patients suffering from relapsing forms of multiple sclerosis. Patients who have been crippled by multiple sclerosis in the prime of their lives may be candidates for drugs such as oral Tecfidera (Biogen, Inc.).

Understanding the complexity of immune physiology and clinical response to treatment are changing the way we diagnosis and categorize disease. One exciting example is the ongoing work by the European research consortium project known as the Unbiased BIOmarkers in PREDiction of respiratory disease outcomes project (U-BIOPRED) based in England. In 2015, Dr. Ratko Djukanovic and colleagues from the University of Southampton published a groundbreaking description of 6 cohorts of asthmatic patients defined by distinct patterns of biomarkers and clinical parameters.[148] They used Machine Intelligence software to perform a comprehensive analysis of T cells, granulocytes, cytokines, and mast cell mediators across a group of 62 asthmatic patients to describe these subsets which had not been recognized before. They found reduced MAIT (mucosal invariant associated T cell) frequencies as a strong feature that is related to asthma severity, reduced regulatory-T cell frequencies in severe disease, and increased mast cell mediator levels in patients with severe disease. This provides important insight into the mechanism of disease for patients who appear to have corticosteroid-insensitive asthma. These findings are expected to pave the way for future drug development as well as new methods for studying and characterizing severe asthma. As biomarker measurement becomes more common in clinical practice we envision a time where routine Machine Intelligence analysis of clinical databases will assist physicians in selecting medications for their patients in disease management programs. Clinical researchers can use the same datasets and Machine Intelligence for advancing knowledge of medication effectiveness and safety, leading the way to new treatments.

We have learned that many cytokines, immune mediators and surface proteins are direct gene products. There is now great interest in using many of these proteins and their genetic markers for evaluating drug therapy. In 2012, the FDA approved the drug ivacaftor (trade name Kalydeco, Vertex Pharmaceuticals, Inc.) for targeted treatment of

Cystic Fibrosis (CF). The drug is effective for treating patients with the G551D mutation causing problems with salt and water transport resulting in excessively thick mucus secretions leading to recurrent lung infections. G551D is just one of hundreds of genetic defects found to cause CF and ivacaftor is effective in just 4% of the CF population in the U.S. This constitutes approximately 1,200 eligible patients. Discovery is moving quickly; in 2015 Vertex received FDA approval for a second CF drug, ORKAMBI (lumacaftor/ivacaftor) which is used to treat patients with a different gene mutation causing cystic fibrosis. The knowledge network behind this advance has been led by the Cystic Fibrosis Foundation. The foundation helped establish a tremendously productive environment for quality improvement and clinical discovery through the network of CF treatment centers participating in the national CF Registry. Although these drugs may be the priceless breakthroughs some CF patients have sought for so long, the health system at large will need to recalibrate how we plan for and allocate resources to cover the high price (>$200,000 / year/patient). The era of personalized medicine is upon us. It will challenge most all of our assumptions on how we deliver and receive care.

In 2013, Margaret Hamburg, M.D., the U.S. Commissioner of Food and Drugs released a compendium explaining the readiness of the FDA to facilitate new products and services envisioned in a new era of personalized care.[149] She mentions advances well beyond just medications including medical imaging, regenerative medicine and mobile technologies, many made possible by increased use of computers and analytics. She describes an FDA which will be innovative in the creation of new regulatory standards which will be needed to allow the field to grow and safely serve the needs of the public.

The new science is spawning new models of medical care and significantly changing relationships across the healthcare landscape. The genetic testing company called 23andMe, Inc. provides a standard set of genetic tests on saliva for just $199.[150] Consumers simply order and pay for the services online. There is no need for physician orders or insurance payments. Users receive personalized genetic test results which help in understanding their ancestry, wellness, inherited traits and carrier status for specific conditions. Pharmacogenetics is an emerging area for genetic and molecular diagnostic testing. Companies such as Genelex Corporation offer genetic testing services ordered by physicians. Panels of tests relating to metabolism of medications used for cardiovascular disease, psychiatric conditions and pain management are offered.[151] Most of the panels include testing of the cytochrome P450 liver enzyme system. Testing for CYP2C19 genetic variants helps predict an individual's metabolism of antidepressants, barbiturates, proton pump inhibitors, antimalarial and antitumor drugs.[152] Some day it may become common to test for genetic variants before putting a patient on one of these drugs or to investigate why a patient seems not to respond to a specific drug. Several well-regarded health systems are developing precision care services for patients outside of their usual referral circles. Intermountain Healthcare (Salt Lake City, UT) offers the Intermountain Precision Genomics ™ Core Laboratory service for oncologists and pathologists anywhere in the United States. They provide analysis of over 96 genomic alterations commonly associated with solid tumors. The assay looks at whole exome sequencing (WES) instead of just a hotspot mutation region.[153] The Mayo Clinic (Rochester, MN) now offers Pharmacogenetics (PGx) Profile Service including a blood test of nine important genes related to medication metabolism and a one hour consultation with a pharmacist to help interpret the results. Insurance coverage varies and does not always cover the full charge which can be close to $3,000.[154]

Many of the most common chronic diseases actually involve multiple genes found on multiple different chromosomes. Machine Intelligence is now being used to elucidate the complexity of diabetes and other diseases with multiple gene loci. In 2015, geneticists and clinicians from the Institute of Personalized Medicine at the Icahn School of Medicine at Mount Sinai in New York City published major findings related to Type 2 diabetes (T2D). They used Machine Intelligence to analyze very large data sets from over 11,000 diabetic patients. Data included genotypes based on genetic testing of patients and their phenotypes characterized by electronic medical record (EMR) information accumulated over many years of routine patient care. They successfully identified three distinct subgroups of T2D from topology-derived patient networks. Subtype 1 was characterized by T2D complications including diabetic retinopathy; subtype 2 was enriched for cancer malignancy, and subtype 3 was associated most strongly with cardiovascular diseases, neurological diseases, allergies, and HIV infections.[155] Details of these impressive findings can be found in the case study below. This work is expected to become a paradigm for unifying knowledge from research and the very large data sets already available from clinical practice. This should accelerate the translation of new insights from bench research to real world patient care.

PRECISION MEDICINE APPLICATION	CLINICAL CONDITIONS	TREATMENT EXAMPLE OR RESEARCH INSIGHT	IMPACT
Tumor Biology	Lung cancer	Imatinab (Gleevac) Tyrosine Kinase Inhibitor (somatic mutation)	Tumor specific biomarkers indicate targeted selection of chemotherapy.
Disease Subtyping	Diabetes	3 new subtypes of diabetes discovered using germline genotyping; Icahn School of Medicine, Mt. Sinai	Knowing a person's genotype may predict what diabetic complications they are prone to develop, allowing for tailored prevention and early treatment.
Pharmacogenetics	Depression	cytochrome P450 2D6 (CYP2D6) and cytochrome P450 2C19 (CYP2C19) germline genetic testing; Mayo Clinic	Select best medication to match a patient's drug metabolism profile. Minimize treatment failures and side effects.
Clinical (EHR) data + biomarker profiling	Asthma	Identification of 6 cohorts of asthma patients based on disease and treatment response profiles; University of Southampton, England	Rapid identification of specific groups of asthma patients in a large population who may benefit from specific medications and environmental prevention methods.
Drug Development	Cystic Fibrosis	ivacaftor (Kalydeco) for targeted treatment of Cystic Fibrosis (CF); effective for treating patients with the G551D germline mutation	Drug development programs can be focused on specific genetic mutations for treatment of rare diseases.

Table 8.6: Precision Medicine Applications

These examples illustrate how patients are already benefiting from the targeted use of molecular diagnostics and clinical genetics. As the cost of whole genome testing continues to fall, we are approaching the time when knowledge from each tested patient can routinely benefit all. Machine Intelligence software will continue to be a mainstay of the research and discovery process for genes and biomarkers. Additionally, we expect Machine Intelligence software will become an indispensable enabler of clinical practice for the development of tailored preventive care plans, diagnosis of disease and selection of treatments with precision.

Chapter 9

9.6 Case Study 17: Diabetes Subtypes[156]

Title: Genetic Subtyping of Type 2 Diabetes

9.6.1 Contributors:

Joel Dudley, Ph.D., Associate Professor of Genetics and Genomic Sciences and Director of the Institute for Next Generation Healthcare, Icahn School of Medicine at Mount Sinai
Li Li, M.D. Assistant Professor, Genetics and Genomic Sciences, Icahn School of Medicine at Mount Sinai

9.6.2 Case Study Highlights

- Clinical researchers created a multidimensional dataset including electronic medical records, genotype data and registry data to explore the relationship of genes to disease.
- Using the Machine Intelligence platform, they identified three distinct subtypes of Type 2 Diabetes previously undescribed.
- Knowledge of these subtypes may enable tailored prevention and treatment strategies to better care for each individual with Type 2 Diabetes.

9.6.3 Detailed Description

Mount Sinai Medical Center has been a leader in advancing precision medicine for the diagnosis and treatment of chronic diseases. Despite advances in technology and data, most patients are still diagnosed and treated using the same approach in place before the advent of the personal computer. Consequently, Mount Sinai has invested over $150 million in their electronic medical record (EMR) data and launched a biobank in 2007 for the collection of both clinical and genetic information. Mount Sinai has captured data on 27,000 patients including: genotyping, EMR, 500+ clinical variables, lab test results, ICD9 diagnoses, medications, and symptoms.

Researchers applied Ayasdi's novel TDA approach to leverage the available high-dimensional clinical and molecular data sets and enable new discoveries of the subtypes of Type 2 Diabetes. Looking at data for approximately 11,000 patients Mount Sinai identified **three subtypes** of Type 2 Diabetes with significantly specific clinical variables and genetic variants. Using TDA, Mount Sinai identified three distinct subgroups of T2D in patient-patient networks.

They hypothesized that topological analysis of patient populations in high-dimensional clinical phenotype space may identify meaningful subpopulations of T2D patients. They focused their analysis on T2D patients, who are of high clinical importance and the most prevalent disease group in the population. They identified 2551 T2D patients in their outpatient cohort as determined by the eMERGE T2D electronic phenotyping algorithm. Using their data-driven, topology-based approach, they identified three distinct subtypes of T2D.

- Subtype 1: ~30% (n = 761) of the overall T2D cases and was enriched for diabetic nephropathy and diabetic retinopathy, both microvascular complications.
- Subtype 2: ~24% (n = 617) of all T2D cases and was enriched for cancer malignancy and cardiovascular diseases.
- Subtype 3: ~43% (n = 1096) of all T2D cases and associated most strongly with cardiovascular diseases, neurological diseases, allergies, and HIV infections.

The enriched phenotypes and biological functions defined at the gene level for each subtype matched with the disease comorbidities and clinical differences that they identified through EMR-based topology data analysis (TDA). This observed agreement is likely meaningful mechanistically because the genetic data were not used to inform patient subgroup topology.

This advanced analysis could aid in designing more efficacious drugs based on more accurate patient stratification. The study's insights were published in *Science Translational Medicine*.

The team completed the phenotypic clustering first, and then overlaid the genetic information to further reinforce and validate this finding: *"With the help of Ayasdi's platform, we see our current clinical definition of type 2 diabetes may be too imprecise…these are exciting findings with potential for transforming how we approach the treatment of this major disease" -Dr. Joel Dudley.*

In the United States, Diabetes affects 29 million (9% of the population), costing $240 billion alone, according to the ADA. Further, Diabetes patients cost the health system 2-3x more than average patients, suggesting an enormous need for more effective, precise medicines. As a result of this scientific discovery, Machine Intelligence software will be used to explore ideas for more effective treatment protocols and better patient outcomes for Type 2 Diabetes patients, and advance the practice of precision medicine.

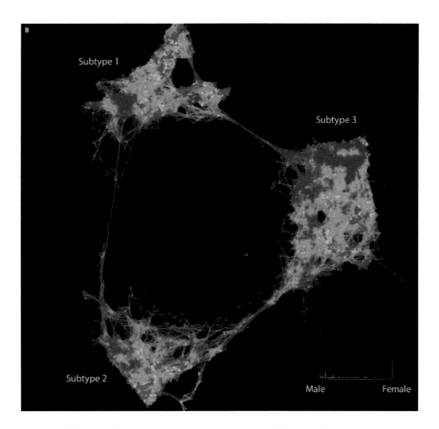

Figure CS17.1: Genetic Subtyping of Type 2 Diabetes

"Patient-patient network for topology patterns on 2551 T2D patients. Each node represents a single or a group of patients with the significant similarity based on their clinical features. Edge connected with nodes indicates the nodes have shared patients. Red color represents the enrichment for patients with females, and blue color represents the enrichment for males. The patient-patient network representation was constructed using cosine distance metric with two filter functions to assess the similarity of the clinical variables from EMRs. The clinical data set comprises more than 500 clinical variables represented in the EMRs, including patient demographics, laboratory tests, and medication orders"

9.7 Case Study 18: Patient Stratification Revealed Molecular Validation for Asthma Subtypes

9.7.1 Contributors:

Timothy Hinks MA, BMBCh, MRCP, PhD

Associate Professor, Honorary Consultant in Respiratory Medicine, University Hospitals Southampton, Wellcome Trust Postdoctoral Fellow, University of Melbourne

Ratko Djukanovic MD, DM, FRCP

Professor of Medicine, Director of the Southampton NIHR Respiratory Biomedical Research Unit, Director of the NIHR Southampton Centre for Biomedical Research

9.7.2 Case Study Highlights

- Researchers at Southampton University used Topological Data Analysis (TDA) to perform unbiased asthma patient stratification leading to improved patient classification and predictive models.
- The researchers analyzed extensive measurements of sputum inflammatory mediators, clinical findings and physiologic parameters enabling identification of 8 distinct clinico-pathobiologic endotypes of asthma not previously described.
- Severe asthma subgroups were associated with anxiety and depression, obesity, sino-nasal symptoms, decreased quality of life, and inflammatory changes including increased sputum, and matrix metalloproteinases.
- These findings will make possible the use of targeted strategies and accelerate the development of new therapies for the 150-300 million people worldwide suffering from asthma.

9.7.3 Introduction

Asthma is a collective clinical definition of a chronic airways disease where airway inflammation is the underlying pathobiological process. However, the full complexity of the illness at the molecular level is still poorly understood. It is also recognized that asthma is not a single disease but a disease comprising several phenotypes. Over the past several years Ayasdi has collaborated with researchers at the University of Southampton to apply Ayasdi Machine Intelligence software to data collected from 2 large studies involving asthmatic patients and matched control subjects. Several bio-fluids were collected from participants and multiple research methods were applied to describe the complex pathobiology within the lungs as well as the systemic circulation. These data were combined with standard clinical outcomes that are used to define disease severity.

The main challenges in analyzing these data include:

- The data is complex particularly since study participants use a wide combination of medications, and have varying co-morbidities.
- Researchers lacked tools to simultaneously analyze a diverse range of clinical and pathologic data with very different distributions.
- Classical statistics were only able to identify significant differential abundance in a low number of proteins, particularly for serum.
- Standard statistics could not easily discern sub-types of disease, other than the classical ones based on clinical severity, and could not apply the underlying molecular mechanisms to define each sub-type.
- It was difficult to pinpoint which of the many attributes are related to asthma severity and which are predictive of clinical outcomes such as asthma exacerbations.

9.7.4 Results

In their first study, Machine Learning software with topological data analysis (TDA) was used successfully to identify six patient sub-populations based on clinical testing (e.g. pulmonary function test results), allergy test results and several biomarkers.[157] Two of groups of patients with severe asthma proved to be clinically different with respect to the presence or absence of allergic sensitization to common aero-allergens like house dust mite, but were similar with respect to the activation of mast cells. This would suggest that mast cells are an important factor in diverse forms of severe asthma, and could be an important target for drug development. Many of the mechanisms identified by TDA were confirmed using alternative analysis approaches (e.g. Bayesian Network Analysis), adding confidence to the observations.

The researchers realized that this was a real breakthrough. Up to this time, many studies which attempted to define asthma endotypes had been limited by lack of robust statistical validation in replication cohorts, or had generated clusters whose identity was dominated by clinical parameters, without giving significant insight into the underlying pathophysiology. Using two distinct cohorts, TDA identified six disease clusters defined both by clinical measures and by pathological measures in blood and induced sputum.

Expanding on this work, the Southampton researchers designed a larger study with 194 asthma subjects and 21 healthy control patients. The study was funded by the Medical Research Council and Wellcome Trust. They used extensive measurements of sputum inflammatory mediators, providing the opportunity to investigate truly multidimensional clinico-pathobiologic endotypes and to investigate the mechanisms underlying these distinct endotypes. In all, 103 clinical, physiologic and inflammatory parameters were analyzed using Machine Intelligence software with (TDA). They found severe asthma subgroups were associated with anxiety and depression, obesity, sino-nasal symptoms, decreased quality of life, and inflammatory changes including increased sputum, and matrix metalloproteinases.[158]

The second study confirmed the nature of the clusters identified in previous work, while providing additional insight into the underlying pathobiology. TDA found a disconnection between clinical measures and the measures of underlying inflammation. The data also suggest that the production of an inflammatory mediator – IL-5 – is relatively resistant to standard treatment with steroids, and highlights the role of a molecule called chitinase-3-like protein 1 in neutrophilic inflammation and a class of enzymes called matrix metalloproteases in severe asthma. *"This gives a clear picture of the distinct groups of asthma we as clinicians see presenting to our severe asthma clinics, and will help with identifying subgroups for future clinical trials,"* said Dr. Timothy Hinks.

"Because asthma is a disease with a high variance in pathologies and is still not well understood, the ability to use unsupervised, multidimensional queries has been integral in accelerating our research. This progress has allowed our team to be less biased in generating hypotheses about the data. This has helped us focus on deriving data-driven hypothesis that saves time and makes our work applicable to all healthcare workers treating asthma and similarly pathologically diverse diseases. Using Machine Intelligence software, generating a network at an appropriate resolution to give significant insight takes only a few hours until insights can be gained."

Chapter 9

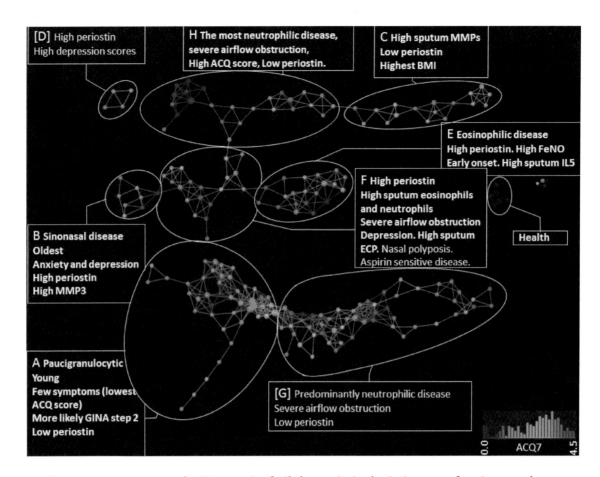

Figure CS 18.1: Topological Network of Clinicopathological Clusters of Asthma Patients

Figure CS18.1 Description: Multidimensional clinicopathological clusters in asthmatic patients in the derivation data set (Southampton cohort). A topological network generated by using 22 clinical and pathological features together identifies 1 healthy (in blue) and 8 distinct clinicopathobiologic asthma clusters (A-H). The network is colored according to ACQ7 scores, with the most symptomatic subjects in red. The TDA used 145 subjects with the most complete data: metric, variance-normalized Euclidean; lenses, principal and secondary singular value decomposition (resolution, 30; gain, 3.0/3.03, equalized) and presence/absence of asthma; node size, proportional to the number of subjects in the node. Color bars: red, highest ACQ7 score; blue, healthy participants. Features in boldface were replicated in the validation data set. GINA, Global Initiative for Asthma.

250

Chapter 10: Machine Intelligence for Revenue Cycle and Payment Integrity

"A billion here, a billion there, and pretty soon you're talking about real money."
-U.S. Senator Everett Dirksen

10.1 Chapter Preview

- Discuss how the U.S. leads the world in healthcare spending.
- Introducing healthcare administration and its role in U.S. healthcare spending.
- Discuss the various healthcare payment schemes employed in the U.S.
- Breakdown and define the components of revenue cycle management.
- Explore the claim denial structure and how it affects healthcare costs.
- Discuss how ACA and bundled payment methods are attempting to improve the administration of healthcare.
- Discuss how Machine Intelligence through the power of large numbers and similarity analysis is improving the efficiency of revenue cycle management.
- Payment integrity, fraud, waste and abuse are discussed as significant drags on healthcare costs.
- Case Studies
    - Case Study 20: Denials Management
    - Case Study 21: Detecting Medicare Overpayments
    - Case Study 22: Waste Fraud and Abuse Modeling

10.2 Introduction

Regardless of what type of healthcare system a country has, it must be paid for in one way or another. Most industrial countries, except the U.S., view healthcare as either a public utility, or an extension of the government. They reap economies of scale, and through government price controls, targeted public health programs and constraints on healthcare infrastructure, thereby being able to effectively cover all their citizens as a birthright. In contrast, the U.S. has created a complex private and public web of healthcare financial transactions which creates its own burdensome cost to the system.

Not surprisingly, all countries largely pay for their healthcare with taxes in one form or another.[159] The U.S. views healthcare as a business, governed in large part by market forces which consistently have led to high healthcare spending. Oddly enough though, the U.S. spends more government money per capita on healthcare than the United

Kingdom, Germany, Japan, France and Canada, countries most Americans refer to as having "socialized" medicine.[160]

World Bank studies of healthcare around the world show that Japan pays 10.2% of GDP, European countries pay between 9% - 12% of GDP and the U.S. pays 17.1% of GDP for healthcare.[161] From a per capita spending standpoint, healthcare costs in various nations such as UK \$3,935, Germany \$5,411, France \$4,959, Japan \$3,703, Italy \$3,258, Sweden \$6,808, and U.S. \$9,403[162]. Relative to the rest of the industrialized world, the U.S. spends a lot more for healthcare, though the U.S. doesn't seem to be getting the same health impact. Worldwide, the U.S. ranks 42nd in life expectancy;[163] three out of five U.S. personal bankruptcies are due to medical costs[164] and the U.S. ranks 37th on the quality scale of healthcare systems.[165]

Although it can be challenging to understand all the reasons for the relative high expense of healthcare in the U.S., many factors indicate that the administrative complexity of the system itself is part of the root cause. Discussed in this chapter are significant elements of that complexity, particularly how medical care is billed and revenue collected. We illustrate how Machine Learning techniques can be employed to improve business efficiency and identify cost saving opportunities of healthcare administration.

10.3 U.S. Healthcare Payment System

Though most countries enjoy economies of scale by choosing one predominant healthcare payment model, the U.S. employs five different models of healthcare payment.[166]

- Beveridge Model
- Modified-Bismarck Model
- National Healthcare Model
- Out of Pocket Model
- Charity

Most people who are not veterans, not poor or are under 65 years of age, use a Modified-Bismarck[16] payment system. The Bismarck system is characterized by private insurance

---

[16] "Modified" used in the sense that medical care is for-profit with little or no government control or regulation of pricing. Generally, in other countries, for example Germany or Switzerland, when the Bismarck model is applied, government maintains firm control over structure and pricing of healthcare.

Medicine

companies, private medical facilities, employee and employer payments and co-payments. If one is poor, or over the age of 65, the National Healthcare model applies as found in Medicaid and Medicare. If one is a veteran, there is the Beveridge model, where the government owns the hospitals and facilities, and employs the doctors and the medical personnel; an example being the Veteran's Administration healthcare system. If none of the above applies, then one is practicing either Out of Pocket model or is supported through charity.

Table 10.1 shows the distribution of payment by the various models.

BY PAYER TYPE	PERCENT	BILLIONS $
Private Insurance	32.70%	$883
Out of Pocket	11.60%	$313
Medicare	20.20%	$545
Medicaid	15.50%	$419
Other Public, Charity and Investment	20.00%	$540
Total	100.00%	$2,700

BY PAYER ENTITY	PERCENT	BILLIONS $
Federal Government	28.60%	$772
State Government	16.20%	$437
Private Employer	20.60%	$556
Household	28.00%	$756
Other Private	6.60%	$178
Total	100.00%	$2,700

Table 9.1: 2011 Breakdown of U.S. Healthcare by Payer[167]

Table 10.2 shows the percentage of healthcare costs attributed to administration for certain payer types.

BY PAYER TYPE	PERCENT	BILLIONS $
Private Insurance	18.00%	$159
Out of Pocket	NA	NA
Medicare	1.50%	$8
Medicaid	4.60%	$19

Table 9.2: Percentage of U.S. Healthcare Administrative Cost[168]

The complexity of the healthcare financing system is one of the factors driving the cost of U.S. healthcare. A simplified payment structure within the U.S. health system has the potential of saving 15% of total healthcare spending, representing approximately $350 billion per year.[169]

10.4 The Significant Cost of Administration in U.S. Healthcare

Medical administrative costs are estimated to consume one-third of healthcare spending in the U.S., a major portion of which is attributed to billing, insurance contracting and pursuit of payment.[170] Some estimates show that inefficiencies in billing and insurance related costs are bloating administration costs by anywhere from $168 to $183 billion every year.[171] Separating out hospitals, 25% of U.S. hospital costs originate from administration, which by themselves represents 1.4% of U.S. GDP.[172] The unfortunate aspect to money spent on administrative costs is they don't improve a patient's health outcome, and some suggest that healthcare administrative costs are inversely related to patient care quality.[173] As the above data suggests, understanding U.S. healthcare administration is imperative to understanding the economics of U.S. healthcare.

Because there is so much money involved, involving so many interested parties and the complexity of what is included in the calculation of administrative costs, it is often difficult to find consistent numbers regarding the actual size of administrative costs. Regardless of the exact numbers, it's safe to say U.S. healthcare administration costs are large and are a significant factor in overall healthcare costs. Further, they represent an area begging for technology that will improve efficiency, technology such as Machine Learning.[174]

For purposes of this discussion we are focused on the administrative costs associated
with the revenue cycle, including the following: [175]

- Contracting with insurers and subcontracted providers.
- Maintaining benefits databases.
- Determining patient insurance and cost sharing.
- Collecting copayments, formulary compliance, and prior authorization.
- Coding of services delivered.
- Checking and submitting claims.
- Receiving and depositing payments.
- Appealing denials and underpayments.
- Collecting from patients.
- Negotiating end-of-year resolution of unsettled claims and paying subcontracted
  providers.

10.5 U.S. Healthcare Revenue Cycle Management

Getting paid for medical services rendered is a central daily concern of medical
providers and as discussed above consumes a great deal of resources. The revenue cycle,
also called revenue cycle management or billing cycle is a multi-step process which
extends from the time the patient contacts the medical office or hospital (provider)
through the time final payment(s) are received for the services rendered. Depending on
the size of the provider group, the billing and claim preparation may be outsourced to a
3rd party. See the Revenue Cycle graphic in Figure 10.1 below.[176]

There are three primary participants in the medical revenue cycle: the patient, the
provider and the payer. The patient is the individual seeking service, the provider is the
doctor or the hospital providing medical service, and the payer is the insurance
company, government or patient, depending on the circumstance. For this discussion
the assumption is the payer is a private insurance company. As a side note, if the payer
is the patient, that means they are out of pocket for the whole medical bill and they are
left to negotiate the system on their own. Unless the out of pocket payer has
prearrangement with the provider, they will be charged the highest "chargemaster"
pricing, that no other payer will pay.[177]

The payer and provider are related by a contractual arrangement that is generally
confidential.[17] The provider is viewed as a subcontractor to the payer. The amount the

---

[17] Insurance contractual pricing is considered a trade secret by the payer and is legally protected.

provider will receive from the payer isn't known until a bill is submitted and it is paid. The payout by the payer is virtually always less than the bill presented by the provider. This is due to the fact that the bill is constructed from the "chargemaster" pricing list, which is a significantly inflated list of prices of all medical procedures and services a facility offers. In hospitals, a 10:1 ratio of chargemaster price to actual insurance payout is not uncommon.[178]

Below are descriptions of the revenue cycle based on information from the MBAA Education Center.[179]

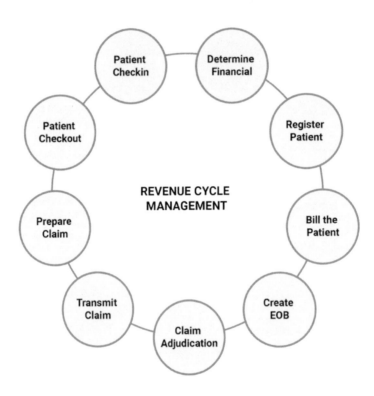

Figure 9.1: Steps in the Medical Revenue Cycle

10.5.1   Register Patients

Patient calls provider to set an appointment and provides personal and insurance information. At this point the provider verifies that an insurance contract exists between payer and provider, and notifies the patient if it does not.

10.5.2   Confirm Financial Responsibility

The payer determines which medical services are covered under the patient's insurance plan. How insurance coverage is implemented is unique to each payer, so a provider must confirm how to assign the bill correctly. Claim denials and rejections are a problem that causes resubmissions of bills with corrections, so the provider is trying to improve the odds the claim will be accepted by the payer.

10.5.3   Patient Check-in

Patient arrives at the provider's location, provides identification and insurance card, and confirms medical and personal information as necessary. The provider collects the patient's copayment.

10.5.4   Patient Check-out

After the medical service is performed the patient leaves. The provider reviews the patient visit and creates a medical report. The medical report contains the provider's information, the patient identification information, all information about the services provided, and any relevant patient history. The medical report is coded into procedure and diagnostic codes as preparation for input into the payer's claim form. This is often referred to as a superbill.

10.5.5   Prepare Claims/Check Compliance

The superbill is imported into the practice management software. Pricing is added using the provider's chargemaster as a guide. An insurance claim is created in the form the payer wishes to see. Generally, an integrity check is performed. The claim must meet specific guidelines laid out by the payer. Information privacy and data security rules of the Health Insurance Portability and Accountability Act (HIPAA) and the Office of the Inspector General (OIG) requirements also apply.

10.5.6   Transmit Claims

Since most providers are covered under HIPAA, it is required that all claims be submitted electronically, though there still are exceptions and some claims may still be submitted on paper forms. Paper forms are becoming increasingly rare. As of 2013, only 9% of claims were submitted on paper.[180] Big providers handle claims directly. Smaller providers commonly use an intermediary to process claims, called a claims clearinghouse, which formats the claim to the specification of a specific payer.

10.5.7   Claims Adjudication

Once the claim reaches the payer, it is first checked for syntax and adherence to the appropriate claim structure. If the claim is missing information or has a structural problem, it is rejected and sent back to the provider for correction.

Next the claim is evaluated by a claims adjuster to determine if it is a valid claim. At this point the claim is either accepted or denied. Larger multipart claims can be partially denied depending on the circumstances. If a claim is accepted, the payer determines the amount to pay to the provider. The payer will pay the lower of either the amount the provider is asking or the amount the payer is willing to pay. The difference between the provider's claim amount and the amount paid by the payer is called the contractual adjustment, which is written off by the provider.

The payer's payment is determined by the contractual arrangement between the provider and the payer, and is determined by the contractual arrangement between the patient and payer (insurance). Coinsurance is the percentage of the claim the patient has agreed to pay to the provider.

A denied claim is one that the payer refuses to pay for various reasons. Reasons for denial can include:

- The procedure is deemed not medically necessary
- Patient's insurance doesn't cover the procedure
- The patient's deductible reduces the payment, potentially to zero
- A referral or preauthorization was required that was not obtained
- Appropriate supporting information was not present
- Insurance coverage was not available on the date of claim
- Used an out of network provider
- Clerical mistakes, such as incorrect coding or incorrect interpretation of the codes, misspelled names, wrong addresses, etc.

10.5.8   Generate EOB

Once the claim has been adjudicated, the payer sends an explanation of benefits(EOB) or an Electronic Remittance Advice (ERA) to both the patient and the provider. The EOB details how much the payer is willing to pay for each procedure, and lists claims that were denied with reasons for the denial.

If there is more than one insurance payer involved, the claims are first submitted to the primary payer, and then the EOB and claim is submitted to the secondary, etc.

If the provider or the patient disagrees with the EOB, the aggrieved party will enter into an appeals process with the payer.

10.5.9   Bill the Patient

Coinsurance and deductible portions of payments are out of pocket expenses that are the responsibility of the patient and are billed to the patient by the provider. Depending on the provider, sometimes denied procedures are waived, but mostly they are billed to the patient. Most often patients receive the contracted price for denied payments, but sometime are charged the inflated chargemaster price, depending on the circumstances of the denial. The differences between the billed claim and the payment charged down to the contractual rate are not billed to the patient. They are written off by the provider.

10.5.10   Rejected and Denied Claims

Rejected or denied health insurance claims represent 5% to 10% of hospital revenues each year, resulting in millions of dollars in loss for a typical hospital.[181] Most hospitals and physician practices have standard methods for evaluating and re-submitting denied claims. Although improper coding is often a reason for denial, a number of other issues may be contributing.[182] As discussed above, there are many reasons claims are denied. Most providers can adequately deal with common denial reasons. However, many current analytical tools provide hospitals with only a summary-level understanding of the sources and types of denied claims. Commonly, these tools fall short when it comes to identifying the detailed, underlying reasons and characteristics of denied claims.

Physicians and hospitals face a monumental task of mastering a continually changing set of rules for billing and collecting for services rendered. Insurance carriers are offering an increasing variety of insurance products, often with high deductibles and restricted networks of providers. Some health plans are offering carve-outs, so that specific procedures and services are managed by particularly focused networks. Patient co-payments and deductibles are on the rise making actual collection of payment even more fragmented. The high cost of certain drugs, particularly related to cancer care and immunological disease has led to quite detailed and onerous prior-authorization

Chapter 10

applications to be completed by providers, and in some cases, delaying the delivery of needed care for patients. Prior authorization rules vary by insurer and can even vary between insurance plans offered by the same insurance company. Table 10.3 lists sources of billing complexity.

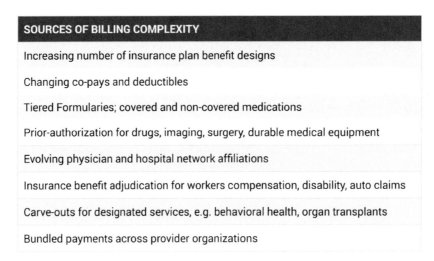

SOURCES OF BILLING COMPLEXITY
Increasing number of insurance plan benefit designs
Changing co-pays and deductibles
Tiered Formularies; covered and non-covered medications
Prior-authorization for drugs, imaging, surgery, durable medical equipment
Evolving physician and hospital network affiliations
Insurance benefit adjudication for workers compensation, disability, auto claims
Carve-outs for designated services, e.g. behavioral health, organ transplants
Bundled payments across provider organizations

Table 9.3: Source of Billing Complexity

The amount of data included in standard UB-04 billing forms along with associated 835 electronic transactions create increasingly complex scenarios for individuals to analyze. For many claims there can be close to 100 data elements needed for proper claims submission.[183] As a result, medical billing teams spend a considerable amount of time and effort investigating individual denied or rejected claims. Traditionally, researching, correcting, and resubmitting an individual claim is a manual process that does not scale easily. For these reasons, many hospitals and medical groups focus just on the largest or easiest claims to resubmit, leaving significant dollars on the table and ultimately written off as uncollectable. Coding teams often do not have the time or tools to conduct root cause pattern analysis. Even expert coders are limited to seeing patterns of 3-4 factors leading to denials. Patterns of denials with 7 or 10 factors are too complex for humans to analyze and require augmented analysis using software.

10.6 Affordable Care Act and Value Based Care

As challenging as it has been for providers to manage revenue cycle under a fee-for-service system, even more change and uncertainty await. Here we will describe the financing changes set in motion under the Affordable Care Act ("ACA") but caution readers that more change is promised by the new president's administration in Washington, D.C. Under a Donald Trump administration, it is possible that elements of the ACA will be dismantled but specific replacements have not been offered as we go to press with this book.

Fundamentally, the challenge is to efficiently care for an expanding population faced with chronic medical conditions. Rising rates of diabetes, heart failure, dementia and other neurologic diseases are resource intensive to treat and manage. Advanced surgical procedures such as hip and knee replacement, cataract removal and heart valve repair are now commonplace for patients into their 80's. Advances in infectious diseases have made chronic Hepatitis C curable and diseases like AIDs a chronic condition to be treated for decades. New disease management programs and payment models originated in the private insurance market have been embraced and expanded by Medicare and many Medicaid plans across the country. The arrangements include the sharing of financial risk by physicians and hospitals.

In 2010, the Affordable Care Act ("ACA"), commonly referred to as "Obamacare" was passed by Congress and signed into law. The bill effectively increased access to health insurance for millions of individuals who previously were uninsured. It also standardized the definition of basic health insurance plans and removed barriers to insurance for pre-existing conditions. The health insurance coverage-related components of the Affordable Care Act became effective in 2014. Between September 2013 and February 2015, the U.S. saw a net increase of 16.9 million people with health insurance. Of these, approximately 6.5 million were newly enrolled through Medicaid plans. Another 4.1 million were enrolled through the marketplace and the others through a combination of employer plans, Medicare, military plans and other state plans.[184] Many, but not all, of the 50 states have agreed to accept additional federal funding and commit to more state responsibility to expand their Medicaid programs. People now can "shop" for a commercial or public health insurance plan on their state or federal "health connector" or marketplace website.

The total impact of government sponsored health insurance continues to grow and has become the dominant driver of the healthcare marketplace in many parts of the country. As of 2014, over 55 million Americans were covered by Medicare and over 85 million were covered by Medicaid and CHIP (Children's Health Insurance Plan).[185][186] This means that almost 45% of the U.S. population of 314 million people is covered by these government health insurance plans. In 2014, Federal spending on Medicare alone was $505 billion. The drive to value-based care is seeking lower costs and more effective treatment. In order to efficiently operate under these conditions, consolidation in the provider market continues, leading to larger and larger physician and hospital health systems. Providers are rapidly adopting electronic health records and disease management programs in order to standardize care, eliminate waste and measure performance. Health system leaders are further addressing these problems by deploying new analytics tools for population and financial management, including Machine Intelligence.

10.6.1   Bundled Payments

Government and private insurers are working on ever more ways to influence efficient and effective care. Over the past 40 years, insurers have adjusted terms of payment to physicians, hospitals and other providers to drive for improved overall outcomes. In the 1980's CMS began the use of Diagnosis Related Groups (DRGs) to pay for hospital care. DRG payments are pre-determined fees for episodes of inpatient hospital care such as pneumonia, stroke, coronary bypass graft or colectomy, regardless of the length of stay or resources used. In response, hospitals across the country dramatically diminished length of stay and cost per case. Since that time, scrutiny of supplies, staffing, use of imaging, selection of medications, and almost every aspect of resource use has become standard management practice in most hospitals. DRG payment programs subsequently became popular with many private insurers. Now we are at the beginning of similar, monumental change in reimbursement with the introduction of "bundled payments" spanning inpatient and a period of post-hospital care. In 2016, Medicare began the Comprehensive Care for Joint Replacement Model of payment in 800+ hospitals as an initial test of this new method. Under the program hospitals receive a set payment for total knee and total hip replacement including the hospital phase of care and extending through 90 days of recovery.[187] Payments cover all institutional and professional fees, necessitating a high level of collaboration between hospitals, physicians, home care and rehabilitation services. Although payments for this care historically range widely from $16,500 to $33,000 across the country, payments under the new program will vary less by geography and are expected to be around $25,000.

Current practice does have a great deal of variation even within a single community. In a region with two community hospitals it's common to have upwards of 10 orthopedic surgeons performing joint replacement. There may be 5 or more home care services and potentially dozens of skilled nursing and transitional care facilities which might offer rehabilitation services. Length of inpatient stay commonly ranges from 2 – 5 days and post-hospital care regimens may include discharge directly to home with home care services or upwards of 7-10 days in a skilled nursing facility. Understanding the variation and identifying best care pathways can be facilitated with the use of Machine Intelligence.

Advanced analytics can help discern optimal combinations of surgeon, hospital length of stay and aftercare services. Pathways can be determined for specific patient types based on age, co-morbidities and social factors. Expect innovation and new partnerships as hospitals sign preferred contracts with a selected few home care and rehabilitation partners in each community. Surgical technique and technology continue to evolve accordingly. Within the past few years, some orthopedic surgeons have begun to perform "same day surgery" for total knee replacement for selected patients.[188] The safety and efficiency of this continues to be a topic of significant scrutiny.

10.7 The Power of Large Numbers and Similarity Analysis

There is a tremendous opportunity for provider organizations to manage patient care and revenue with a deeper understanding of patient flow and reasons for denied claims, using improved analytical solutions. Machine Intelligence software represents an innovative analytical approach for revenue cycle management, getting better and better with larger numbers of claims. It provides a holistic view of claims and quickly surfaces groups of similar claims that are denied, along with the key characteristics and reasons for denial. Across a large system of providers, clinics and hospitals, pattern analysis improves the opportunity to find even small instances of similar denials. Machine Intelligence software combines topological data analysis (TDA) with statistical, geometric, and Machine Learning algorithms to uncover all the patterns and relationships within a provider's claims-related data. The topological summaries, generated using TDA, visualize insights and patterns in care delivery and in claims data that conventional analytics tools cannot bring to the surface. The software rapidly correlates and analyzes thousands of attributes (such as procedure codes, physician and payer-related information, as well as provider locations) and groups claims that are similar to reveal patterns and outliers through visual networks. It automatically lists the statistically significant characteristics of these groups of claims and explains outliers. Hospitals and physicians benefit from using Machine Intelligence software to conduct a retrospective analysis of hotspots of denied claims and determine the root causes for denials. The uncovered insights help them proactively optimize their processes to prevent future denials.

The software ingests all the claims data, including UB-04 data elements and transactional information associated with the claims, and creates a visual network of all the claims based on machine algorithms of similarity. Claims with similar characteristics are clustered closer together within the network, whereas claims that are less similar are further apart. Traditional reporting using dashboards and Excel sheets may show aggregate numbers, but they are unable to show the relationships between similar claims. The network can then be colored by any attribute of interest, including the payer type, denial reason category (e.g., medical necessity, pre-certification required), diagnostic and procedure codes reported in the claim, or percent of claims denied, to surface subtle patterns in the claims data.

10.8 Identify Underlying Denial Patterns and Hotspots

Coloring the network by whether a claim was denied or rejected reveals hotspots, or dense clusters, of denied/ rejected claims within the network. These hotspots are generated without having to input any preconceived notions of the underlying reasons for denial, allowing for a true data-first methodology. It saves analysts and medical billing specialists from having to guess and check which procedures, providers, and reason codes are in common within groups of denied claims. Machine Intelligence software can efficiently identify the subtle similarities within a group of claims. It surfaces the attributes in common along with possible reoccurring mistakes. By drilling into a hotspot, an analyst can determine the characteristics that drive denials and those features that differentiate them from paid claims. The software efficiently distinguishes denied claims by surfacing the unique combination of diagnostic codes, payer, and procedure attributes that characterize these denied claims. Based on these attributes, claim analysts can not only fix individual claims, but have time to create profiles of claims known to have a high risk of denial.

10.8.1   Predicting and Preventing Denials

The average personnel cost of re-working a claim is $252. In addition to the personnel cost of re-working a claim, the medical organization loses the time value of the delayed revenue even if it is subsequently collected. Using a systematic approach to revenue cycle, providers can predict and prevent denials from occurring. If a newly denied claim is recognized to have similar attributes as the claims reviewed in a hotspot, it can be quickly categorized and prioritized for correction. The reason for denial is likely to be the same, which limits the investigation effort required to determine the root cause of the denial to fix the claim. Examples include the use of insurance-specific codes or plan-specific formulary requirements. Understanding the causes for denials, particularly those based on lack of prior authorization or clinical documentation can be mitigated by upstream work flow changes. The electronic medical record order entry system can be configured to document important information for justifying specific treatments or high cost diagnostic testing, thus satisfying prior authorization requirements. Physicians may be asked to adopt standardized documentation templates to capture both primary and secondary procedures, and patient co-morbidities to enable billing staff to properly code all important aspects of the encounter, insuring the bill is sent out properly the first time. Using the proper analytic approach and committing to improving operational aspects of care, the revenue cycle can be optimized so reimbursement is received on time and precious resources are focused on patient care.

10.8.2   Payment Integrity, Fraud, Waste and Abuse (FWA)

As the total cost of healthcare continues to grow, now past 17% of GDP, insurers and providers alike are striving to be sure that payments are proper. "Payment integrity" refers to the proper administration of insurance payments according to insurance company rules. Providers are intent on billing for and collecting for all of the services rendered. Payers are worried about over paying or paying for services not properly delivered to patients. The typical physician practice faces a bewildering set of payment rules from dozens of insurers. A typical hospital deals with hundreds of insurers and payment programs. For most practices, the risk is under-collecting with rising frustration over insurance payments denied for administrative reasons even though the patient had genuine need for the services. At a time when insurance co-payments and deductibles are on the rise, physicians are dealing with patients confused by the rules and in some cases, unable to make the payments. Insurers have put rules for prior-authorization for durable medical equipment and high-cost drugs and imaging studies which, for the most part, reflect evidence-based care, but slow down service delivery for patients and providers alike.

Unfortunately, there are those few patients and providers who have taken advantage of the complexity of the system, to inappropriately file claims, bill for and collect insurance payments. For years, private insurance companies have managed internal programs to identify fraud, waste and abuse (FWA). In 2014, the Federal Office of Inspector General described its plans to increase efforts, in conjunction with the Department of Justice, to combat FWA.[189] CMS defines *fraud and abuse* in relatively broad terms"[190]

"Fraud means an intentional deception or misrepresentation made by a person with the knowledge that the deception could result in some unauthorized benefit to himself or some other person."

"Abuse means provider practices that are inconsistent with sound fiscal, business, or medical practices, and result in an unnecessary cost (to the Medicare or Medicaid program), or in reimbursement for services that are not medically necessary or that fail to meet professionally recognized standards for healthcare.

During Fiscal Year (FY) 2015, the Federal Government won or negotiated over $1.9 billion in healthcare fraud judgments and settlements. During that time the Department of Justice (DOJ) opened 983 new criminal healthcare fraud investigations.[191]

COMMON TYPES OF FRAUD AND ABUSE
Medical Identity Theft
Billing for Unnecessary Services or Items
Billing for Services or Items Not Furnished
Upcoding
Unbundling
Kickbacks

Table 9.4: Common Types of Fraud and Abuse

For years, the program has required insurers participating in the Medicare Advantage program to take on the work of having an active FWA program. In most Medicare Advantage contracts, these payers pass some of this responsibility down to hospitals, physicians and other providers to have specific policies and procedures to safeguard against FWA. Detection of FWA typically requires analysis of paid claims data to determine if patterns suggest inappropriate billing.

Examples of Fraud, Waste and Abuse include a wide range of activities. Two examples from the 2015 Annual Report of the Department of Health and Human Services and Department of Justice were reported as follows:[192]

"In October 2014, an occupational therapist pled guilty in the Eastern District of New York to healthcare fraud conspiracy for his role in a scheme that involved the payment of cash kickbacks to elderly beneficiaries who received massages and light group exercises that were billed to Medicare and Medicaid as individual one-on-one occupational therapy and other occupational therapy services. As part of the scheme, the defendant, who was a full-time therapist for the New York Board of Education,

*signed false and fabricated patient charts and billing records for therapy that was not
actually provided. As part of the plea, the defendant agreed to restitution and forfeiture
of $1.6 million. Between February 2008 and February 2011, the defendant was the
seventh-highest biller of occupational therapy in the country."*

*"In October 2014, two owners of several Brooklyn, NY medical clinics pled guilty to
healthcare fraud conspiracy and falsification of records in the Eastern District of New
York. The medical director of one clinic pled guilty to healthcare fraud conspiracy in
March 2015. The defendants owned and operated a series of medical clinics that were
used to submit more than $14.3 million in Medicare claims, of which $5.3 million was
paid. The indictment alleged that the majority of the claims were fraudulent because
they were for services such as vitamin infusions, physical and occupational therapy, and
diagnostic tests that were medically unnecessary, not provided, or otherwise not
reimbursable. The defendants also allegedly laundered the proceeds of the fraudulent
scheme and falsified documents, which they then provided to Medicare auditors and the
FBI in order to conceal the fraudulent scheme."*

Health insurance companies typically have payment integrity programs managed by an
in-house staff of data analysts and claims specialists. A set of algorithms is used to
identify patterns of inappropriate billing activity. Certain patterns are tagged as
potential fraud cases which then require detailed review by fraud investigators. The
audit may include a request for more detail or justification from the provider. In some
cases medical record review or onsite visit to the provider is indicated. The most
common fraud "schemes" are relatively easy to detect. However, large dollar amounts
can be distributed over smaller, less frequent fraud schemes. The most determined
fraud perpetrators are constantly changing targets and tactics to defraud payers. For this
reason, more sophisticated tools of anomaly detection using Machine Intelligence are
increasingly being used. Topological data analysis along with Machine Learning
algorithms can be used to identify new patterns across very large numbers of claims and
providers. Normal and abnormal patterns within clinical specialties can be highlighted
and identified for fraud investigation work. See Case Study 21, Fraud Waste and Abuse
Modeling, for an example of work now underway at one large health insurance provider.
In this case, the Machine Intelligence platform was used to study patterns of known false
positive and false negative fraud screening tests. The Machine Intelligence system found
common patterns among these cases which can immediately be used to refine those
models. New profiles of fraud were also detected which can be used to expand the set of
tools used for fraud detection in this and other insurance plans.

10.9 Case Study 19: Denials Management

10.9.1   Contributor

A large multi-hospital health system and medical group

10.9.2   Case Study Highlights

- Machine Intelligence applied to medical claims can identify common patterns for payment denials in a multihospital system
- Systematic analysis across numerous hospitals and physicians uncovers denial patterns previously unrecognized.
- Improving best practices can improve workflows to insure billing is accurate the first time and denials are prevented.
- Network level intelligence empowers providers to negotiate better with payers and improve revenue.

10.9.3   Introduction

The General Hospital System (GHS)[18] has grown from consolidation of multiple hospitals over a period of years. Traditionally, each hospital was responsible their own revenue cycle management, employing software and personnel of their choosing. After several years of collaboration, it became apparent that the hospitals were employing significantly different workflows including variation in their acceptable levels of "write offs" in different clinical specialties and deploying varying levels of coding and billing professionals to achieve their results. The GHS chose to identify best practices for revenue cycle workflow, standardize targets and benchmark productivity of their revenue cycle staff. They realized that common problems existed across clinical disciplines and across payers and that communicating as a "system" with payers would benefit all of their hospitals and physician practices.

The GHS identified the major steps in the revenue cycle workflow and steps along the way where better intelligence was needed (Figure CS19.1). They realized that areas of low volume procedures and lower priced services were commonly not addressed at the individual hospital level, but in aggregate the write offs were substantial. In some cases,

---

[18] Reference to the "General Hospital System" is a pseudonym for the hospital system contributing the story, who wished to remain anonymous.

low volume procedures, even though costly, were not getting the attention needed to identify underlying problems in billing and collection.

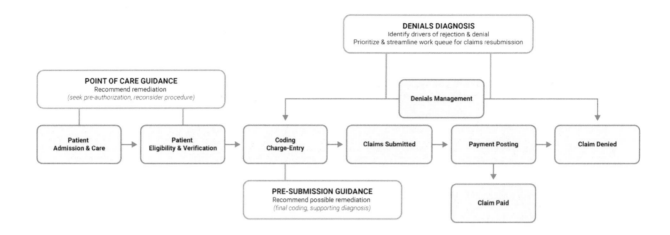

Figure CS19.1: Revenue Cycle with Opportunities for Improved Analytics

As part of the re-organization of revenue cycle management, GHS collected closed claims data in their health system data warehouse. Each hospital, ambulatory surgical center and infusion center contributed data on their claims outcomes including completed with payments, write offs and payment denials.

10.9.4   Results

Using Machine Intelligence software, GHS generated an analysis of denied claims seen in Figure CS19.2. The software provides a similarity analysis of claims and is colored to show highest incidence of denied claims in red and lowest incidence of denied claims in blue. At least nine distinct "hotspot" groups of interest with high levels of denied claims, causing financial losses, were quickly identified.

Claims that are close together in this graph or "network" are relatively similar, while claims that are far apart in the network are relatively different from each other. Given differences in payer rules and insured populations, it is common for clusters to be generated which are payer specific (e.g. Medicare vs commercial insurer). The software facilitates the discovery of similar groups of denied claims which can be quickly quantified. In Figure CS19.2, shows groups of similar cases profiled by denial rates and financial losses.

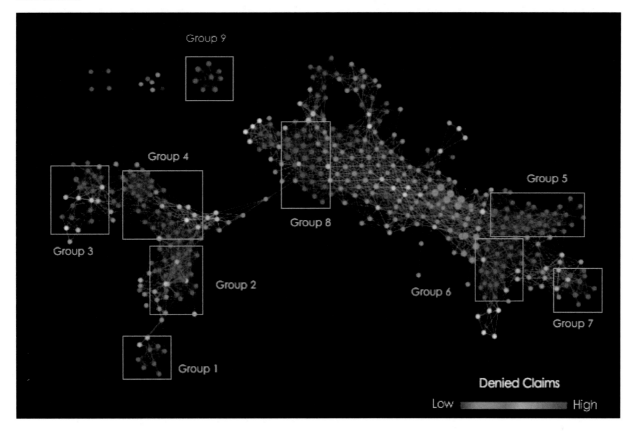

Figure CS19.2: Denied Claims Showing "Hotspots"

Using the system, GHS selected a group of 2,974 claims for patients undergoing colonoscopy with a high rate (87.89%) of payment denials. By reviewing the common HCPCS codes in this group, it became apparent that some specific coding issues were contributing to most of these denials (Figure CS19.4). Colonoscopy claims are notorious for being rejected on the grounds of lack of medical necessity and providers regularly run afoul of complex coding guidelines. A provider is typically faced with a variety of coding scenarios each of which is often susceptible to inconsistent interpretation of the guidelines by the adjudicator:

- Screening colonoscopy for Medicare patients
- Screening colonoscopy for non-Medicare patients
- Screening colonoscopy for Medicare patients that becomes diagnostic or therapeutic
- Screening colonoscopy for non-Medicare patients that becomes diagnostic or therapeutic

Features for this hotspot revealed that a major factor leading to denial involved the selection of the diagnoses codes in the claim and the selection of an inappropriate

HCPCS code for each colonoscopy scenario. The sequencing of codes triggers the screening colonoscopy as "diagnostic", thereby impacting how much of the payment is covered or deferred to the patient's out-of-pocket expense. Another group of cases had pre-existing colonic polyps which affected the subsequent coding and payment of claims. It also became apparent that there was variation in the ways in which different insurers paid claims with these coding patterns.

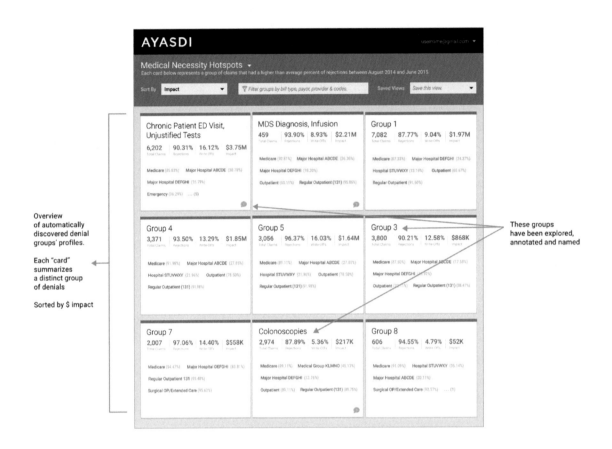

Figure CS19.3: Automatically Generated Denial Groups of Similar Cases

Identifies significant characteristics of each claim profile

Shows difference between successful and denied claims

Helps determine action plan to tackle and fix each group of denials

Figure CS19.4: Payer and Diagnosis Details of Denied Claims

General Hospital System has the opportunity to deploy Machine Intelligence software to identify and prevent over 60 percent of all denials, thus saving millions of dollars annually. Previously, their claims processing software deployed at the individual hospital level gave priority for re-working individual claims for the most egregious errors. Using Machine Learning analysis at the system level, they now have a tool for identifying significant losses in aggregate.

GHS can now systematically review patterns of denials by clinical case type and by payer. Best practices from high performing hospitals and clinics with low denial rates are shared with those sites experiencing high denial rates. Enhanced coding practices, documentation tools and provider and coder education are now being used to standardize patient care workflows. Improved awareness of their own practices with timely evidence of denials now enables the hospital system and medical group to negotiate with payers and improve collections.

273

10.10   Case Study 20: Detecting Medicare Overpayments

10.10.1   Contributor

CMS Medicare Provider Utilization and Payment Data Set

10.10.2   Case Study Highlights

- Machine Intelligence analysis of Medicare claims data can effectively identify patterns of overpayments to providers and other suspicious activities.
- Scrutiny of provider coding practices is now possible through access of large payer datasets.
- Machine Intelligence software can automate the identification of overpayments and aberrations in billing practices through comparison with provider peer groups.

Providers and payers alike are increasingly automating routine billing practices and payment patterns.

In recent years, government programs for health insurance have been expanding due to more accommodating eligibility rules for state Medicaid programs and expanding utilization of services for Medicare beneficiaries. Inevitably there are errors in billing and coding practices by providers and payment errors by payers. Now, Machine Learning analysis is being used to identify errors and overpayments.

Complexity is ever expanding with new patients and providers entering these programs on a monthly basis. Referral patterns involving physicians, hospitals, home care, durable medical equipment providers and pharmacies are in continuous flux. New medications, surgeries, medical devices and equipment are introduced on a regular basis. This change is a management and payment challenge for government insurance programs which try to make timely payments to providers. So too, it is a challenge for physicians who rarely have any comparative information on their own billing practices compared to their peers. It is common to see significant variation on the selection of codes and code combinations among same-specialty providers within the same medical group.

Beginning with The Centers for Medicare and Medicaid Services (CMS) Medicare data from 2012, the federal government greatly expanded efforts to foster transparency in its insurance programs by releasing a public data set of payment information. CMS now provides periodic releases of the "Medicare Provider Utilization and Payment Data Set: Physician and Other Supplier Public Use File." It is a treasure trove of information rolled up to the individual provider (physicians and other healthcare professionals) level enabling comparisons across specialty, procedures types and geography. This file set includes information on utilization, payment (allowed amount and Medicare payment), and submitted charges organized by National Provider Identifier (NPI), Healthcare Common Procedure Coding System (HCPCS) code, and place of service.[193]

10.10.3   Results

Figure CS20.1 is an example of an analysis conducted using CMS Medicare Provider Utilization and Payment public use file. The Machine Intelligence software creates a network of nodes and edges. Nodes are groups of similar data points and edges connect nodes with at least one data point in common. This network represents 36,000 providers and nine million claims. Each cluster represents providers that have similar utilization.

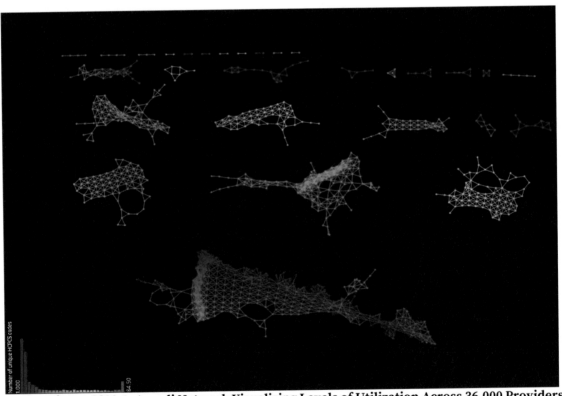

Figure CS20.1: Ayasdi Network Visualizing Levels of Utilization Across 36,000 Providers

The software helps uncover highly nuanced relationships and trends that previously went undetected. It can be used to analyze historical claims data and create a visual representation of all the information contained within them. The visual network can then be colored by an attribute that warrants further exploration, such as overpayment. The software automatically surfaces groups of claims that represent overpayment and provides a listing of the key attributes that characterize these groups. This helps business analysts rapidly find new characteristics of suspicious payment behavior.

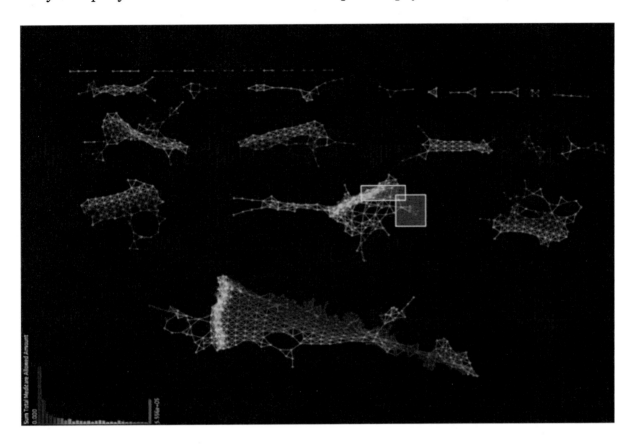

Figure CS20.2: Graph of Medicare Allowed Amounts

Figure CS20.2 Description: Coloring the network by Medicare allowed amount shows the range of payment across physicians with similar utilization. The areas of localized red nodes, highlighted above, can be identified as possible regions of overpayment warranting further investigation.

In Figure CS20.2, we have colored the network by Medicare allowed payments. As these physicians are clustered by similar utilization, the payment amounts should also be similar and this is confirmed by a fairly uniform coloring within each group. However, the cluster of physicians in the center contains red nodes indicating higher payment amounts, anomalous to the rest of the group. By selecting these red nodes, the software can surface the distinguishing characteristics of these groups of physicians. This type of analysis can help identify physicians who might be "overcoding" cases by using higher intensity evaluation and management codes than is supported by normal documentation practices. This type of pattern analysis can assist the medical group or the payer in identifying providers where further analysis is warranted such as chart review and coding practices.

CMS Medicare Provider Utilization and Payment public use file reports only Medicare claims and therefore does not represent the totality of most physicians' practices. CMS data set is not adjusted for severity of patient illness. It does enable comparison at the physician specialty level but does not distinguish variation of sub-sub specialties. For example, it will allow comparison of all family physicians, but does not specifically segregate those performing obstetrical deliveries from those not performing deliveries. Using Machine Learning software, however subgroups of interest can be appropriately identified based on procedures performed and compared.

At the same time that medical groups are increasingly focused on revenue capture, many payers are stepping up their scrutiny of provider coding practices and resource use patterns. Many providers and payers feel that it is no longer adequate to randomly audit on a once per year basis. As new providers enter an organization, new treatments are instituted, new equipment is put into service and new payer contracts signed, the likelihood of unwanted variation puts the revenue cycle at risk. Establishing an "always on" cycle of analysis and learning will enable both providers and payers to ensure accurate and timely coding, billing, collection and payment practices. Machine Intelligence software will be useful to both parties for identifying variation in a routine and systematic manner.

10.11 Case Study 21: Fraud, Waste and Abuse Modeling

10.11.1 Contributor

A large health insurance company

10.11.2 Case Study Highlights

- The health insurer found their conventional hypothesis-driven models to detect fraud were lacking in specificity and sensitivity. Machine Intelligence software is deployed to assist in the creation and continuous improvement of fraud detection models, resulting in higher rates of fraud detection.
- Allowing for continuous surveillance of the claims payment process, makes it possible to detect potential fraud prior to payment, limiting the amount of revenue leakage due to fraud.
- Machine Intelligence speeds up the deployment of fraud detection models, by enabling faster time to insight regarding new fraud profiles.

10.11.3 Introduction

Healthcare fraud, waste, and abuse (FWA) costs exceed hundreds of billions of dollars annually in the U.S., representing tens of millions of dollars wasted for each payer. Payers are consistently challenged by the limited resources at their disposal to process the growing number of claims and make timely payments. At the same time, they need to continuously monitor for suspicious claims to prevent revenue losses. Identifying new patterns of aberrant behavior is a slow process, requiring many analysts to compare reports from different sources before they can confirm a new trend. This allows sophisticated fraudsters to rapidly evolve their strategies and outpace current detection models.

Current fraud detection models are primarily rule-based and incorporate well-known indicators of fraud. For example, if a patient visits a certain hospital more than 3 times in one month or if the patient receives services from a facility more than 100 miles from their residential address, the claims can be flagged by rules that incorporate these established indicators. However, the subtler and evolving indicators of suspicious behavior are scattered throughout complex medical claims data and may be missed by traditional analytical techniques.

One large, national health insurance company found it increasingly difficult to staff the large number of fraud investigators and data scientists needed to stay ahead of a growing problem with FWA detection. This was particularly difficult as they diversified with new insurance products and as they acquired smaller insurer plan portfolios. As the number of claims increased, uncovering patterns and anomalies within them became increasingly difficult.

The fraud detection unit was charged with determining the combinations of characteristics (e.g. codes, providers, procedures and drugs) that signal fraud or overpayment. They were accustomed to using a hypothesis-driven approach and were heavily reliant on business analysts and special investigation units (SIUs) using their experience to determine the features to incorporate into their fraud detection rules and models. They had some experience using conventional Machine Learning techniques but found these models tended to be over-fit as they attempted to incorporate all the underlying claims data parameters.

To augment and replace some of their traditional methods, they selected a new paradigm of Machine Intelligence software which combines topological data analysis (TDA) with statistical, geometric, and Machine Learning algorithms to uncover all the patterns and relationships within the data. The TDA software rapidly correlates and analyzes thousands of attributes simultaneously and groups data points that are similar to reveal patterns and outliers through visual networks. The software automatically lists the statistically significant features that characterize these patterns and outliers. These features can then be used to develop more effective, localized fraud detection rules and models. The methods enabled them to:

- Validate and improve existing detection models
- Prioritize fraud leads for SIU teams
- Improve detection in the pre-payment cycle
- Identify new patterns of aberrant behavior
- Achieve faster time to insight regarding fraud activity

10.11.4 Validate and Improve Detection

Using the Machine Intelligence software to evaluate existing algorithms and models to detect fraudulent transactions, the software can identify errors in a model by comparing visual networks that represent the outcomes predicted by the existing model and the actual ground truth (i.e., were the transactions fraudulent or not). By comparing the model estimation with the ground truth, a payer can quickly focus on the subgroups of transactions in the network where the model made mistakes. The software automatically generates a list of the statistically significant variables associated with each subgroup. This helps payers identify combinations of attributes that indicate fraud that had previously gone undetected and then incorporate them into models. The TDA data-driven approach to model diagnostics and improvement also helps firms create models that can adjust as new data arrives, thereby curbing performance deterioration.

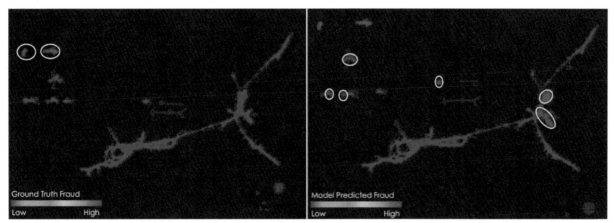

Figure CS21.1: Comparison of Ground Truth with the Model Predicted Fraud Showing Areas for Improvement

10.11.5   Prioritize Fraud Leads

The TDA based Machine Intelligence software can also help with prioritizing leads for SIU teams. As the networks are created using a notion of similarity, claims that are connected to identified regions of fraud, waste, or abuse within the generated networks, will contain similar aberrant characteristics. These leads can be grouped and ranked for the SIU teams for additional investigation. This payer is now able to source the leads in one-fifth the time compared to its previous methods. They now rank the leads by ease of recovery and potential dollars before passing the leads to their SIU. With improved lead scoring, the SIU dedicates their time and resources to investigating higher quality leads that will result in greater returns.

10.11.6 Improve Detection in the Prepayment Cycle/Identify Aberrant Behavior

Detecting fraud before claims are paid moves payers away from the unsuccessful "pay and chase" model, which is time and resource intensive. Only 5% of such claims are ever recovered. By investing in better detection methods, payers can proactively identify fraud in the pre-payment process and prevent unnecessary payments.

Machine Intelligence software can be incorporated further upstream to establish a comprehensive fraud detection and prevention framework. Not only does Machine Intelligence software help analysts improve their fraud detection models, but it also uses predictive analytics to comb through the thousands of variables that describe each claim and classifies them as suspicious if they exhibit characteristics of fraudulent claims. This helps analysts stop claims before they are paid and minimize the amount of revenue leakage.

10.11.7 Faster time to Insight Regarding Fraud Activity

This large payer typically spent 2-3 months on a single model to detect overpayment for a designated specialty. They knew that this was an unsustainable process with hundreds of specialties needing dedicated models. They found the Machine Intelligence software to be faster and more adaptable, often enabling the creation of new models in as little as two weeks. The payer is now equipped to keep pace with change in the market.

Chapter 11: The Future of Machine Intelligence

"Declare the past, diagnose the present, foretell the future..."
-Hippocrates[194]

11.1 Chapter Preview

- Discuss the public perceptions and new realities of advanced analytics.
- Describe how better models, advancement in human mimicry, and expanding on augmented human capabilities are the primary directions of Machine Intelligence development.
- Identify methods for the automation of building data driven solutions to complex problems.

11.2 Introduction

Currently, there is a lot of discussion in the media about the perils of Artificial Intelligence for future generations. The popularity of television shows such as *"Humans"* and *"Westworld"* are certainly examples of the public at large finding Hollywood dramatizations of computers running amok entertaining, if nothing else. Technical luminaries, most provocatively Steven Hawking, are raising the potential for cataclysmic outcomes, such that *"The development of full Artificial Intelligence could spell the end of the human race."* [195] Dire predictions notwithstanding, even Hawking recognizes the great positive potential for "thinking machines", with more neutral statements, such as *"either the best, or the worst thing, ever to happen to humanity"* or *"crucial to the future of our civilisation and our species"* [196]

Contrary to the more entertaining and less likely extreme views, for the most part, Machine Intelligence is being embraced as a game changing technology. A more likely future will include great progress in first world and third world countries alike, with advanced population health, medical diagnostic and therapeutic capabilities. Used wisely, Machine Intelligence will broaden human capabilities in the prevention of epidemics, discovery of new treatments and in matching care optimally for communities and individuals.

11.3 Complexity and Opportunity

It is interesting to speculate where advanced analytics and modeling will be heading in the coming years. Future deployment scenarios for Machine Intelligence may be characterized as follows:

- Model increasingly complex data types.
- Mimic increasingly complex tasks currently solved by humans, and extend the models thus constructed to situations where humans do not perform well.
- Augment human capabilities to permit the solution of complex problems by cooperation between humans and machines.
- Automate the process of building data driven solutions with the gamification of complex problems.

The beginnings of methods that will ultimately achieve these goals are becoming apparent. Here are a few examples of this notion, but there will doubtless be many others.

11.3.1   The Modeling of Complex Data Types

Often modeling is done by constructing features or coordinates, i.e. numerical values associated to an entry in a complex data base. For example, in natural language processing, a key feature attached to a single document is a vector whose entries are the counts of the various words used in the document. Working with these vectors has enabled very useful analyses of large databases of documents. Other complex data types for which one can carry out a similar strategy are databases of sessions at a website, social networks, electronic medical records, molecular structures, and more.

Machine Intelligence offers alternate methods to construct quantitative similarity measures that codify ideas we have about which data elements are similar to which other data elements. This kind of measure can be studied by many analytic methodologies, certainly including the TDA methods discussed in this volume, and does not require choices of features. Similarity measures tend to be less vulnerable to bias in how analysis is done than direct choices of features. As MI advances, these applications will increasingly move from being very ad hoc to something more systematic, where one develops classes of data types for which there are standard approaches. We are currently in the mode of doing things in a "one off" fashion, and expect that in the future there will be a smaller number of templates each of which applies to a number of distinct data types.

In medicine, using such methods, predicting and tracking infectious disease outbreaks will become a routine and automated process. Data from many sources will be harnessed to understand the annual patterns of influenza in a community or to discover the presence of a new infectious agent such as Ebola or Zika virus on a continent. Information from electronic medical records will be anonymized to facilitate reporting frequency of infectious symptoms; patterns of grammar school absenteeism will indicate trends in sick children; rates of purchase of cold and flu medicine, weather patterns and knowledge of virus mutations from field surveillance will all be tracked and integrated in a continuous learning cycle. Advanced analytic software can identify early signals of concern so that public health authorities can create an action plan to minimize the impact of illness in a state or region, physicians will be alerted to recognize the earliest symptoms of infected patients and vaccine developers will accelerate their work in a targeted manner. The early development of such a system called MDPHnet is already underway in Massachusetts. The system allows the Massachusetts Department of Public Health (MDPH) to initiate custom queries against participating practices' electronic health records while the data remain behind each practice's firewall. MDPH is using the system for routine surveillance for priority conditions and to evaluate the impact of public health interventions.[197]

11.3.2   Augmenting Human Capabilities

Augmenting human capabilities requires the development of sophisticated forms of user interactions with data. Existing methods of modeling include spreadsheets and various kinds of business intelligence software that permit certain kinds of queries of the data, and provide the ability to create visualizations such as pie charts and histograms. One existing method that accomplishes this is hierarchical clustering, which produces useful dendrogram output. These capabilities are useful, but are not sufficient for Machine Intelligence, because they require the user to determine the right questions to ask of the data. Using Machine Intelligence, with unsupervised learning, new correlations and models are quickly designed by the software for consideration by domain experts. The TDA methods we have seen accomplish this, and additionally provide interactive capability with the data. The goal should be to produce increasingly expressive outputs, with more and more extensive interactive capabilities.

Such applications of advanced analytics are already becoming standard for new drug discovery and design. Biochemists, geneticists and clinicians working together can design new molecules based on their understanding of disease mechanisms. This dramatically reduces the cycle time for discovering new drug therapies and can facilitate treatments for rare diseases.

Already machines for reading x-rays, examining the retina and mapping seizure activity are becoming commonplace. The examination of pathological specimens such as pap smears for cervical cancer screening has already become largely an automated process due to computer-aided analysis of cells. Using computational methods of deep learning, developers demonstrated a system to accurately detect diabetic retinopathy after training a convolutional neural network using a retrospective data set of 128,175 retinal images.[198] This training data set included the expert diagnoses for each image by a team of board certified ophthalmologists. In the near future, simple retinal cameras could be placed in health clinics allowing millions of diabetic patients to achieve annual eye screening and prevent blindness at a fraction of the cost of current practice.

11.3.3   Machine Intelligence and Game Playing

Traditional Machine Learning tasks typically boil down to two types, namely **classification** and **regression/estimation.** Humans, on the other hand, are capable of many more complex tasks. Based on our classification, our curiosity leads us to perform exploration and then to create predictions. For example, people are able to recognize systematic similarities between groups of data points, they are able to detect phenomena that represent "weak signal", and they can learn complicated procedures, such as playing games. It's expected that all of these capabilities will be addressed by applications of Machine Intelligence in the future. The learning of complex tasks such as game playing is being intensively studied under the heading of *reinforcement learning.* In one of its forms, a reinforcement learning systems learns to play a game by repeatedly challenging an opponent, and using the results to understand the likelihood of winning in a given position. The method has succeeded in learning tic-tac-toe (a very simple game) as well as backgammon (a much more complicated game) ultimately enabling the machine to play backgammon at the level of a reasonably experienced human.

These methods could be harnessed to create true learning machines at the population level and at the individual patient level. As we discussed in earlier chapters, we can now quickly pinpoint the most efficient ways of performing surgical procedures, identify the effects of medications and see trends across populations in large health systems. In the future we will link knowledge from health systems and health plans throughout the country and throughout the world to massively accelerate the learning cycle yet again. Within weeks of a new medication's entry into use, we will identify harmful side effects and at the same time disseminate knowledge of clinical trials to shorten the time to implementation at the bedside. This concept is already showing great promise through the Sentinel Initiative, a long-term effort to create a national electronic system for monitoring FDA-regulated medical product safety.[199] [200] At the individual patient level, we will use game technology and personal monitoring to reinforce behaviors and medication adherence to optimize treatment. Linked with their genetic biomarker profile data, patients and providers will become informed of new treatment options as soon as they are available. Based on real world safety and effectiveness data and cost information, they can make care decisions tailored for each person.

Up to now Artificial Intelligence and Machine Learning have proceeded in two stages, one a data analytic stage (when required) and a second stage of manual design of a procedural solution to a problem. Now the true automation of this second stage is possible and becoming a high priority for innovators in this area. There are some solutions to this in the case of simple tasks. For example, decision trees are a method that is effectively automatic for certain simple classification problems. Similarly, prediction tasks can be automatically solved using linear regression for straightforward problems. Machine Intelligence is now ready to take on substantially more complex problems, ready to automate observation, classification, modeling and prediction needed for the efficient building of applications which were previously impossible to achieve. In summary, the development and advancement of Machine Intelligence has been going on for several years. It is finding new applications daily, particularly to healthcare and life sciences where problems are rich in complexity and data sources are accumulating rapidly.

The collaboration of computational and mathematical disciplines with health scientists and clinicians will provide enormous value to society's collective health.

Glossary

ACA[201]	The Patient Protection and Affordable Care Act (PPACA) 2010 HR3590, or Affordable Care Act (ACA) for short, is the new healthcare reform law in America and is often called by its nickname Obamacare
Accessibility	A dimension of data quality representing the degree to which the data is in a usable form.
Accuracy	A dimension of data quality representing the degree to which the data represents the real world it is trying to predict.
Aggregation, Data	A reduction method that replaces a complicated data set with a simpler representative data set.
Allele[202]	One of two or more alternative forms of a gene at corresponding sites (loci) on homologous chromosomes, which determine alternative characters in inheritance.
Analytics	The process within data science of analyzing and modeling data by computer analysis.
Analyzing Data	The process of understanding what the data implies. Data visualization, segmentation and clustering are all aspects of this process.
APACHE II	Acute Physiology and Chronic Health Evaluation II. A widely used scoring system for severity of illness in critically ill patients. Introduced in 1985, it generates a point score ranging from 0 to 71 based on 12 physiologic variables, age, and underlying health.
APACHE III	Acute Physiology and Chronic Health Evaluation III. An improved version of the APACHE II scoring system, featuring an equation predicting hospital morality after the first day of ICU treatment.
Artificial Intelligence	A collection of mathematical and computer science techniques that mimic human intelligence for the purpose of automating tasks humans currently perform.
Believability	A dimension of data quality representing the quality of the source. Related to veracity.
Beveridge Model	Socialized medicine. A model for delivering healthcare where the government owns all medical facilities and employs all the medical personnel. An example is the Veterans Administration
Big Data	A term for data sets which are so large that traditional data management and analytic methods are inadequate; implies some degree of complexity, commonly used for trend analysis and prediction.
Binary Variable	Observations (i.e., dependent variables) that occur in one of two possible states, often labeled zero and one. E.g., "improved/not improved" and "completed task/failed to complete task."
Bundled Payments	Instead of fee for service, a payer pays the provider in terms of the episode of care. An episode of care is all the services associated with a specific illness, condition or medical event.
Capitation[203]	A fixed amount of money per patient per unit of time paid in advance to the physician or provider organization for the delivery of healthcare services.
Categorical Data Set	See Qualitative

Categorical Variable[204]	Usually an independent or predictor variable that contains values indicating membership in one of several possible categories. E.g., gender (male or female), marital status (married, single, divorced, widowed). The categories are often assigned numerical values for nominal variable used as labels, e.g., 0 = male; 1 = female. Synonym
CDA	See Confirmatory Data Analysis or Clinical Document Architecture
Center of Mass, Data	A point representing the mean position of the data. The point where the weighted position vectors of all the parts of a system sum up to zero.
Chargemaster	Is the stated listed price of every single procedure that a hospital can provide to its patients. It is often inflated and doesn't generally represent the price a contracted payer will pay.
Charity	A healthcare system where the patient's healthcare is paid for by someone else out of a altruistic motives.
Charlson Comorbidity Score[205]	A method of categorizing comorbidities of patients based on the International Classification of Diseases (ICD) diagnosis codes found in administrative data, such as hospital abstracts data. Each comorbidity category has an associated weight (from 1 to 6), based on the adjusted risk of mortality or resource use, and the sum of all the weights results in a single comorbidity score for a patient. A score of zero indicates that no comorbidities were found. The higher the score, the more likely the predicted outcome will result in mortality or higher resource use.
Claims Clearinghouse	A 3rd party intermediary between the health provider and payer who formats the claim to the specification of a specific payer.
Classification	In topology, creating simplified analogies of more complex surfaces.
Cleaning Data	The process performed on a data set of fixing formats, filling in missing values, correcting erroneous values and standardizing dimensional categories.
Clinical Document Architecture	An HL7 markup standard that specifies the structure and semantics of "clinical documents" for the purpose of exchange between healthcare providers and patients.
Clinical Pathways	Are a tool used in clinical practice that reduces variability in the approach to treatment by standardizing methods of practice.
Clinical Practice Guidelines[206]	"Systematically developed statements to assist practitioner and patient decisions about appropriate healthcare for specific clinical circumstances."
Cluster Analysis[207]	An unsupervised learning technique where the results are grouped by some similarity criterion.
Clustering	See Cluster Analysis
Coding DNA	Sequence of a gene's DNA that transcribes into protein structure, as opposed to non-coding DNA that does not create protein structures.
Coinsurance	An out of pocket expense which is percentage of the claim the patient has agreed to pay to the provider.
Completeness	A dimension of data quality representing the degree to which the data is missing or not usable.
Complexity	A superset characteristic of a data set determined by the volume, velocity, variety and veracity. Dimensionally indentified by structural and format complexity.

Confirmatory Data Analysis(CDA)[208]	Creates methods for determining whether or not a given observed phenomenon could have appeared "at random", or more precisely as a consequence of a null hypothesis; "quantifies the extent to which [deviations from a model] could be expected to occur by chance" (Gelman; 2004). Confirmatory analysis uses the traditional statistical tools of inference, significance, and confidence. Confirmatory data analysis is comparable to a court trial: it is the process of evaluating evidence.
Conformity	A dimension of data quality representing the degree to which the data is presented in an expected format.
Consistency	A dimension of data quality representing the degree to which the data conflicts with itself.
Contractual Adjustment	The difference between the provider's claim amount and the amount paid by the payer which is written off by the provider, determined by a contractual arrangement.
Copayment	A payment made by the patient in addition to any other payment a payer may make for medical services.
COPD	Chronic obstructive pulmonary disease
Data	Information that is factual used as a basis of research, reference or prediction. Characterized by volume, Varity, volume and veracity.
Data Munging	See Cleaning Data
Data Science	The study and application of the use of automation and computer analysis to analyze data, generally large and complex data sets, in order to extract insight or prediction from data.
Data Set	A collection of stored information. N-dimensional data.
Data Wrangling	See Cleaning Data
DCSI	Diabetes Complications Severity Index
Decision Tree	Is a graphical method to display all possible outcomes through the use of branches. An analogy is a tree, where each leaf is a possible outcome.
Deductible	An out of pocket expense contracted between the payer and the patient, which is the minimum amount the patient has agreed to pay a provider before the payer's financial responsibility begins.
Deep Learning	A sub-discipline of Machine Learning. DL is a particular approach to Machine Learning that involves neural networks and hierarchal analysis.
Degree of a node	Is the number of edges emanating from the node.
Dendrogram	Is a graphical method to display the clustering of data through the use of branches. An analogy is a tree, where each leaf is a data cluster.
Dependent Variable	The presumed effect in an experimental study. The values of the dependent variable depend upon a collection of other variables called the independent variables. Strictly speaking, "dependent variable" should not be used when writing about non-experimental designs.
Diagnosis Related Group(DRG)	A method, initially promoted by CMS, to standardize classification of diagnoses into product groups for billing hospital inpatient care.
Dimension, Data	A measurable property of a data sample. A feature vector of a data sample.
Dimensional Reduction	Where inputs/dimensions required to describe a result are removed or combined, with no loss of predictive conciseness. Feature selection and feature extraction are methods of dimensional reduction.

Discrete Variable[209]	Variable having only integer values. For example, number of trials need by a student to learn a memorization task.
Discretization	The process of breaking data up into manageable pieces and analyzing the pieces individually, rather than as a single complex data set.
Discriminant Analysis	The classification of data points by drawing a "decision boundary" in the space in which the data points reside and then classify them according to which side of the boundary they're on.
Dispersion, Data	The measure of the data's position relative to the center of mass of the data
Distance Function	An extension of the notion of distance in the plane to apply to other mathematical objects, such as data sets. Serves as a quantitative measure of dissimilarity.
DNA	Deoxyribonucleic acid, a self-replicating material present in nearly all living organisms as the main constituent of chromosomes. It is the carrier of genetic information.
Duplication	A dimension of data quality representing the degree to which the data is repetitive, such that the additional entries add no new or useful information
EDA	See Exploratory Data Analysis
Edge	In a topological network it is the interconnection between nodes and indicates a relationship between the data clusters.
Electronic Health Records(EHR)[210]	An electronic version of a patient's medical history, that is maintained by the provider over time, and may include all of the key administrative clinical data relevant to that persons care under a particular provider, including demographics, progress notes, problems, medications, vital signs, past medical history, immunizations, laboratory data and radiology reports The EHR automates access to information and has the potential to streamline the clinician's workflow.
Electronic Remittance Advice(ERA)[211]	An electronic data interchange (EDI) version of a medical insurance payment explanation. Created by the payer, it provides details about providers' claims payment, and if the claims are denied, it would then contain the required explanations. The explanations include the denial codes and the descriptions, which present at the bottom of ERA.
EOB	Explanation of Benefits
Epigenomic[212]	Epigenetics is the study of potentially heritable changes in gene expression (active versus inactive genes) that does not involve changes to the underlying DNA sequence — a change in phenotype without a change in genotype — which in turn affects how cells read the genes.
Episode of Care	All the services associated with a specific illness, condition or medical event.
Euclidean Distance	In any triangle the sum of any two sides is greater than the remaining one. Also known as the triangle inequality. It's popular form is described as the shortest path between two points is a straight line.
Eulerian circuit	In topological networks, when tracing a path where the beginning point is the ending point.
Eulerian path	In topological networks, when tracing a path where it visits every edge only once
Evidenced Based Medicine[213]	"...the notion that 'to the greatest extent possible, the decisions that shape the health and healthcare of Americans—by patients, providers, payers, and policy makers alike—will be grounded on a reliable evidence base, will account appropriately for individual variation in patient needs, and will support the generation of new insights on clinical effectiveness."

Experimental Research	Is a study where a researcher can modify inputs(independent variables) to observe their effect on outputs(dependent variables).
Exploratory Data Analysis	An approach to understanding the overall structure of data, often using visual methods.
Feature Extraction	Creating new features (variables, dimensions) on the data set by introducing new functions of sets of variables. It is sometimes also called `feature engineering'.
Feature Selection	Choosing the a set of variables upon which to base an analysis. Involves discarding variables thought to be irrelevant or to have minimal effect.
Feature Vector	A measurable property of a data sample. A dimension of data.
Fee-For-Service(FFS)	For every medical procedure performed, a fee is charged.
Force Directed Layout Algorithm[214]	A class of algorithms for drawing graphs in an aesthetically pleasing way. Their purpose is to position the nodes of a graph in two-dimensional or three-dimensional space so that all the edges are of more or less equal length and there are as few crossing edges as possible, by assigning forces among the set of edges and the set of nodes, based on their relative positions, and then using these forces either to simulate the motion of the edges and nodes or to minimize their energy.
Forecast Error	The difference between the predicted value and the actual value.
Format Complexity	Also known as data type complexity. Encompasses data characteristics volume, velocity and variety. Determined by the number of dimensions within a data set and the absolute number of data elements within the data set. Low format complexity (simple) is the relatively small and limited nature of the dimensions used to describe the data set.
FWA	Fraud Waste and Abuse
Genetics	The study of genes, genetic variation, and heredity in living organisms.
Genotype[215]	The set of genes giving rise to a particular trait. A person's genotype is the information contained within their two alleles for a particular gene. It is determined by genetic testing.
Germline Genotype	Successive generations of an organism genotype. Genotype is the specific genetic makeup of an organism.
Hamming distance	The minimum number of substitutions required to transform one string into another of equal length.
HEDIS	Health Employer Data Information Set
Heuristic Rule Set	A rule set based on an a priori understanding of the environment, often created by a human trainer for artificial intelligence machines.
Hierarchical Condition Category	MC-CMS-HCC model. Used since 2004 in the Medicare Advantage program to set each Medicare enrollee's monthly capitation rate.
High-dimensional data[216]	A high number (>100) different measurable properties of a data sample. A high number of feature vectors.
HIPAA	Health Insurance Portability and Accountability Act of 1996. United States legislation that provides data privacy and security provisions for safeguarding medical information.
HITECH[217]	The Health Information Technology for Economic and Clinical Health (HITECH) Act, enacted as part of the American Recovery and Reinvestment Act of 2009 to promote the adoption and meaningful use of health information technology.
Holes, Data	Missing data point values within a dimension of a data set.

Glossary

Hot Spots, Data	Within a topological representations, areas of concentration of dependent/outcome variable values.
Implementation Science	The practice of turning science driven medical evidence into every day clinical practice.
Independent Variable	The variables on which others depend. It is often assumed that there are not dependencies among these variables, but this may be hard to verify. It is also often the case that the independent variables are under experimenter control, when dealing with experimental data.
Institute of Medicine(IOM)	A non-governmental organization, congressionally chartered under the National Academy of Sciences in the United States. Effective in 2015, the IOM was renamed the National Academy of Medicine.
Integration, Data	The process of preparing data for an analytic process.
Interpretability	A dimension of data quality representing the degree to which the data is useful in making predictions.
Königsberg bridge problem	Formally, Leonhard Euler's paper, "The Solution of a Problem Relating to the Geometry of Position", where Euler published for the first time a graphical solution to a mathematical problem. The paper describes graphically why a walking path over a number of bridges across the Pregel river is not possible. Also known as the original Eulerian path.
L^2 distance	See Euclidean distance
Learning Healthcare System(LHS)	Encompasses a number of key components committed to a collaborative sharing of data and ideas across institutions and sectors of the healthcare and scientific communities. The goal is to achieve safer, more effective and higher value healthcare and health outcomes for society. A core feature is the widespread adoption and linkage of electronic health records (EHR).
Linear regression[218]	A statistical technique for predictive modeling where a dependent variable's relationship to one or more independent variables is estimated by regressions of data.
Loading, Data	Structuring the data set so that it meets the requirements of the analytic tools.
Logistic Regression	Used to describe the relationship between a dependent categorical or binary variable to one or more independent variables.
Machine Intelligence	A collection of mathematical and computer science techniques that use human intelligence as a guide for solving a variety of problems, some of which may be problems that humans solve well, and others which humans may not be proficient at. These solutions may produce automatic procedures, or they may augment human abilities.
Machine Learning	A collection of mathematical and computer science techniques for extracting information from large data sets, to be used in the construction of automated solutions to problems of importance in many different domains.
Manhattan Distance	See Taxicab distance
Mapping Thread	In topology, when replacing a complex representation of a space with a simplified analogy, it is the path relationships between the two networks.
Meaningful Use[219]	Under HITECH, meaningful use is using certified electronic health record (EHR) technology to improve quality, safety, efficiency, and reduce health disparities; engage patients and family; improve care coordination, and population and public health; maintain privacy and security of patient health information.

Metric Space	A set of distance functions describing points in space forming a topological representation.
Modeling Data	The process that provides prognostications based on analysis of data.
Modified-Bismarck Model	Private insurance based healthcare delivery. A model for delivering healthcare where patients pay private insurance companies to act as payer for healthcare costs
Multidimensional Scaling(MDS)[220]	A graphical method to display dimensional similarity by their distance from each other, creating a map of proximities between objects.
Multiple Linear Regression	Where more than one category of independent variables describe the dependent variable
Nano-materials[221]	Materials that have one dimension in the nanoscale (and are extended in the other two dimensions) are layers, such as graphene, thin films or surface coatings. Some of the features on computer chips come in this category.
National Healthcare Model	Government acting as payer for healthcare. A healthcare payer model where the government acts as the primary payer. Medicare and Medicaid are examples.
Node	In a topological network it is a cluster of data that has dimensional similarities.
Nominal Data	Data not possessing a natural order.
Non-coding DNA	Sequences of DNA that do not encode protein sequences but can be transcribed to produce important regulatory molecules such as ribosomal RNA and others. Previously referred to as "junk DNA" which is no longer considered a precise term.
Non-experimental Research	Is a study where a researcher cannot control or manipulate the predictor variable, but instead, relies on interpretation and observation to come to a conclusion. "Control" in this context means ability to exclude influence of outside variables, not under consideration.
Non-prognostic	A data set whose predictive value is not clearly understood.
Normalization, Data	Scaling the data so that it falls within a desirable range.
n-spheres	A mathematical conceptualization of a multi-dimensional sphere, where n is the number of dimensions.
Null Hypothesis	Refers to a default position that there is no relationship between two measured phenomena, or no association among groups.
Ordinal Data	Data exhibiting a natural order.
Orthodromic Distance	Measuring the distance between two points on a sphere by geodesics describing an arc length represented by the radius of the sphere and a sweep angle.
Out of Network Provider	A healthcare provider with no contract with the payer. The patient under the terms of the agreement with payer is required to seek healthcare services from those with whom the payer has contracted.
Out of Pocket Model	The payer and the patient are the same. Some or all of the payment for health services come directly from patient resources.
Outcome Variable	A dependent variable whose values are of direct interest to the analyst. It might be revenue, survival, cost, etc.
Outlier, Data	Data dispersion around the center of mass outside a boundary of exclusion at some disqualifying distance.

Overfittting[222]	Overfitting refers to a model that models the training data too well. Overfitting happens when the model learns the detail and noise in the training data to the extent that it negatively impacts the performance on the model on new data. This means that the noise or random fluctuations in the training data is picked up and learned as concepts by the model. The problem is that these concepts do not apply to new data and negatively impact the models ability to generalize.
Parametric Model	A family of probability distribution functions described by a finite number of parameters used in Machine Learning to create for the machine a family of ranked choices.
Pathobiology[223]	The branch of medicine treating of the essential nature of disease, especially of the changes in body tissues and organs that cause or are caused by disease.
Patient Reported Outcomes (PRO)	PROs are defined by the U.S. Food & Drug Administration as "Any report coming directly from patients... about a health condition and its treatment."
Payer	The payer is the organization or person paying for the medical services provided to the patient.
Personalized Medicine	See Precision Medicine
Pharmacogentics[224]	Is the study of how genes affect a person's response to drugs. This relatively new field combines pharmacology (the science of drugs) and genomics (the study of genes and their functions) to develop effective, safe medications and doses that will be tailored to a person's genetic makeup.
Phenotype	Is the observable trait or physical manifestation of genotype. Often multiple genes contribute to the phenotype such as eye color or skin tone. https://ghr.nlm.nih.gov/
Piecewise Prognostic	A data set whose predictive value is limited to isolated sections within the data set as a whole.
Population	A group of individuals subjected to study or observation; identified by boundary conditions.
Population Health	The health outcomes of a group of individuals, including the distribution of such outcomes within the group.
Population Health Management(PHM)	Is a discipline within the healthcare industry that studies and facilitates care delivery across the general population or a group of individuals. An important goal of PHM is to gather, normalize and analyze clinical data across a patient's many care settings that can reveal opportunities to improve the patient's health and the provider's financial outcomes. http://searchhealthit.techtarget.com/definition/Population-health-management-PHM
Precision	A property of the measurement which indicates how consistent various measurements of the same object are. It is not accuracy, which is closeness of a measurement to a ground truth quantity.
Precision Medicine[225]	"The use of genomic, epigenomic exposure and other data to define individual patterns of disease, potentially leading to better individual treatment."
Predictor Variable[226]	The presumed "cause" on a nonexperimental study. Often used in correlation studies. For example, SAT scores predict first semester GPA. The SAT score is the predictor variable.

Principal Component Analysis(PCA)	Is a dimensional reduction technique that attempts to explain the variation in the output variable by the least number of input variables.
Process Measures[227]	Process measures attempt to answer the question"Did this patient receive the right care?" or "what percent of the time did patients of this type receive the right care?" Such measures are typically developed based on the known relationship between a process and outcomes.
Proteomics[228]	Proteomics is the large-scale study of proteomes. A proteome is a set of proteins produced in an organism, system, or biological context.
Provider	The doctor or the healthcare organization providing the medical services to the patient
Pythagorean distance	See Euclidean distance
Qualitative Data	Insightful investigation. Measure of quality rather than quantity. Generally has no natural order. Often described as discrete and finite.
Quality, Data	Relates to the relative prognostic characteristic of the data. The dimensions are accessibility, accuracy, believability, completeness of the data.
Quantitative Data	Measurements and statistics. Hard data. Measure of the quantity rather than quality. Quantitative data can be either discrete and finite or continuous and infinite.
Reduction, Data	Removing data from a data set that is irrelevant such that the information content of the data set remains the same.
Regression[229]	A supervised learning prediction method, where the independent and dependent variables are real or integer number measurements, by which the relationship between the variables is determined. Regressions deal with measurements, such as weights or velocities.
Relevance	A dimension of data quality representing the degree to which the data is important to the stated problem.
Reliability Statistic[230][231]	Statistical reliable models are accurate, reproducible and respond consistently during testing and application. Reliability statistics are the result of a reliability measurement method, such as the Cronbach's Alpha, Spearman-Brown formula, Pearson correlation coefficient, Kullback–Leibler divergence, Kolmogorov–Smirnov test, etc.
Risk Adjustment[232]	Under ACA's risk adjustment program, it is intended to reinforce market rules that prohibit risk selection by insurers. Risk adjustment accomplishes this by transferring funds from plans with lower-risk enrollees to plans with higher-risk enrollees. The goal of the risk adjustment program is to encourage insurers to compete based on the value and efficiency of their plans rather than by attracting healthier enrollees.
Scrubbing, Data	A process within the data cleaning activity that fills in missing values, smoothing noisy data, identifying and removing outliers and resolving inconsistencies
Similarity, Data	Data dispersion around the center of mass within a boundary of exclusion at some disqualifying distance.
Somatic Mutations	Changes to the genetics of a multicellular organism which are not passed on to its offspring through the germline. Many cancers are somatic mutations.

Stochastic Methods	Using a probability model to predict outcomes. Often used to create a predictive model and rule set from a data set for a Machine Learning machine.
Structural Complexity	Refers to the nature of the mathematical interrelationships among the data points, i.e. linear, logarithmic, spherical, time dependent, etc. Structural complexity encompasses the veracity of the data set. Validity and volatility are aspects of structural complexity.
Superbill	A medical report that is coded into procedure and diagnostic codes as preparation for input into the payer's claim form
Supervised Learning[233]	Also referred to as a mapping algorithm between the independent and dependent variables. A supervised learning algorithm has been trained by a human possessing both the input variable value and the resultant expected output variable value. Classification and regression are examples of supervised learning.
Targeted Therapy[234]	Also see Precision Medicine. Drugs or other substances that block the growth and spread of cancer by interfering with specific molecules ("molecular targets") that are involved in the growth, progression, and spread of cancer. Targeted cancer therapies are sometimes called "molecularly targeted drugs," "molecularly targeted therapies," "precision medicines," or similar names.
Taxicab Distance[235]	The distance between two points in a grid based on a strictly horizontal and/or vertical path (that is, along the grid lines), as opposed to the diagonal or "as the crow flies" distance. Simple sum of the horizontal and vertical components
Taxon[236]	A taxonomic category, as a species or genus.
Taxonomy[237]	The science or technique of classification.
TDA	See Topological Data Analysis
Testing Data Set	Used to determine whether the algorithm is operating within specification, based on training and validation. Often used to determine the level of overfitting that the algorithm inherently possesses.
Timeliness	A dimension of data quality representing the degree to which the data is relevant over time.
Topological Data Analysis (TDA)	A methodology for producing models of data sets that permit both quicker and more accurate understanding of them, as well as producing operational models which automate tasks based on the outcomes of the data analysis. It proceeds by producing maps of the data set that clarify the organization and structure of the data set.
Topological Network	A collection of nodes and edges connecting some pairs of nodes. A topological network can be laid out in the plane to produce a comprehensible map of the network.
Topology	A mathematical discipline that studies shape.
Training Data Set	Refers to training the algorithm for predictive purposes. It is the means by which a predictive algorithm is accessed for it's prognostic capability. It generally, consists of input and results data and is used to train the model by pairing the input with the expected output, for supervised learning and to provide un-categorized data for unsupervised learning.
Transformation, Data	A non-lossy process of converting data from one format into another.
TREW Score[238]	A targeted real-time early warning score that predicts which patients will develop septic shock.

Unsupervised Learning[239]	Is a method where the training inputs do not have corresponding "correct" outputs. The antithesis of supervised learning that requires a human trainer. Clustering and association are examples of unsupervised learning.
Validation Data Set	Used in order to estimate how well your model has been trained (that is dependent upon the size of your data, the value you would like to predict, input etc) and to estimate model properties (mean error for numeric predictors, classification errors for classifiers, recall and precision for IR-models etc.). The validation data set is used to tune the parameters of the algorithm.
Validity, Data	Refers to the timeliness of the data. Often considered a part of veracity.
Value Based Medicine (VBM)[240]	The Center for Value-Based Medicine suggested value-based medicine (VBM) as the practice of medicine based upon the patient-perceived value conferred by an intervention. VBM starts with the best evidence-based data and converts it to patient value-based data, so that it allows clinicians to deliver higher quality patient care than evidence based medicine alone. The final goals of VBM are improving quality of healthcare and using healthcare resources efficiently.
Variety, Data	The expansive nature of the dimensions of a data set.
Vector distance	A measure of distance along a dimensional axis consisting of a magnitude and direction.
Velocity, Data	The rate of change in the values within the data set.
Veracity, Data	The accuracy of the data set. Refers to the biases, noise, continuity and abnormality in data. Also the data's relevance to the problem being analyzed.
Volatility, Data	Refers to the changeability of data. Often considered a part of veracity.
Volume, Data	The physical size of the data set.

Glossary

Index

Index

Endnotes

[1] "Data Never Sleeps: How Much Data is Generated Every Minute?" Last Modified May 30, 2014, Last Accessed December 20, 2016, https://hosting.ber-art.nl/data-created-every-minute-infographic/

[2] Mikal Khoso, "How Much Data is Produced Every Day?" May 13, 2016, Last Accessed December 20, 2016, http://www.northeastern.edu/levelblog/2016/05/13/how-much-data-produced-every-day/

[3] "Big Data, for better or worse: 90% of world's data generated over last two years," May 22, 2013, ScienceDaily, Last Accessed December 20, 2016, www.sciencedaily.com/releases/2013/05/130522085217.htm

[4] Lucas Mearian, "By 2020, "There Will Be 5,200 GB for Every Person on Earth," December 11, 2012, Computerworld, Last Accessed December 20, 2016, http://www.computerworld.com/article/2493701/data-center/by-2020--there-will-be-5-200-gb-of-data-for-every-person-on-earth.html?page=2

[5] "10 Longest Novels Ever Written", Shortlist Magazine, July 2014, Last Accessed December 20, 2016, http://www.shortlist.com/entertainment/books/the-10-longest-novels-ever-written#art

[6] Anne Trafton, "In the Blink of an Eye," MIT News, January 16, 2014, Last Accessed December 20, 2016, http://news.mit.edu/2014/in-the-blink-of-an-eye-0116

[7] Bret Nelson, "Do You Read Fast Enough to be Successful?" Forbes, June 4, 2012, Last Accessed December 20, 2016, http://www.forbes.com/sites/brettnelson/2012/06/04/do-you-read-fast-enough-to-be-successful/#2d848f4b58f7

[8] Led Zepplin, "The Crudge", Houses of the Holy, 1973

[9] J J O'Connor , E F Robertson, "History Topic: A History of Topology," MacTutor History of Mathematics, May 1996, Last Accessed December 20, 2016, http://www-history.mcs.st-and.ac.uk/PrintHT/Topology_in_mathematics.html

[10] Wikipedia, "Digital Topology," Last Modified May 29, 2016, Last Accessed December 20, 2016, https://en.wikipedia.org/wiki/Digital_topology

[11] Teo Paoletti, "Leonard Euler's Solution to the Konigsberg Bridge Problem," MAA Press, Convergence, Volume 3, 2006, Last Accessed December 20, 2016, http://www.maa.org/press/periodicals/convergence/leonard-eulers-solution-to-the-konigsberg-bridge-problem

[12] Gunnar Carlsson, "Why Topological Data Analysis Works," January 6, 2015, Last Accessed December 20, 2016, https://www.ayasdi.com/blog/bigdata/why-topological-data-analysis-works/

[13] Arthur Conan Doyle, "Adventures of Sherlock Holmes: A Scandal in Bohemia," Published online by Page by Page Books, Last Accessed December 20, 2016, http://www.pagebypagebooks.com/Arthur_Conan_Doyle/The_Adventures_of_Sherlock_Holmes/ADVENTURE_I_A_SCANDAL_IN_BOHEMIA_p3.html

[14] "Full Definition of Data," Merriam-Webster.com, November 14, 2016, Last Accessed December 20, 2016, http://www.merriam-webster.com/dictionary/data Merriam-Webster

[15] Doug Laney, "Deja VVVue, Others Claiming Gartner's Construct for Big Data," January 14, 2012, Last Accessed December 20, 2016, http://blogs.gartner.com/doug-laney/deja-vvvue-others-claiming-gartners-volume-velocity-variety-construct-for-big-data/

Endnotes

[16] Cecilia Fredriksson, "Knowledge Management with Big Data Creating New Possibilities for Organizations," XXIV Nordiska kommunforskarkonferensen Gothenburg, November 26–28th 2015, Last Accessed December 20, 2016,
http://spa.gu.se/digitalAssets/1552/1552434_fredriksson--knowledge-management-with-big-data_paper_norkom2015.pdf

[17] Kevin Normandeau, "Beyond Volume, Variety and Velocity is the Issue of Big Data Veracity," Inside Big Data, September 9, 2013, Last Accessed December 20, 2016,
http://insidebigdata.com/2013/09/12/beyond-volume-variety-velocity-issue-big-data-veracity/

[18] "Definition of Analytics," Merriam-Webster.com, Merriam-Webster, November 14, 2016, Last Accessed December 20, 2016,
http://www.merriam-webster.com/dictionary/analytics

[19] Gregory Piatetsky, "Birthdate of 'Predictive Analytics' Term," KDNuggets, Sep 26, 2013, Last Accessed December 20, 2016,
http://www.kdnuggets.com/2013/09/birthdate-predictive-analytics.html

[20] James Manyika, et al., "Big data: The next frontier for innovation, competition, and productivity," Full Report, McKinsey Global Institute, May 2011, Last Accessed December 20, 2016,
http://www.mckinsey.com/business-functions/business-technology/our-insights/big-data-the-next-frontier-for-innovation

[21] Thomas H. Davenport and DJ Patil, "Data Scientist: The Sexiest Job of the 21st Century," Harvard Business Review, October 2012, Last Accessed December 20, 2016, https://hbr.org/2012/10/data-scientist-the-sexiest-job-of-the-21st-century

[22] "What is Data Science," Data Science at NYU, November 14, 2016, Last Accessed December 20, 2016, http://datascience.nyu.edu/what-is-data-science/

[23] Joerg Ermann, Deepak A. Rao, Nikola C. Teslovich, Michael B. Brenner, and Soumya Raychaudhuri, "Immune Cell Profiling to Guide Therapeutic Decisions in Rheumatic Diseases," Nature Reviews Rheumatology 11, 541-551, 2015, doi:10.1038/nrrheum.2015.71

[24] Xiao Chen, Phil Ender, Michael Mitchell and Christine Wells, "Regression with SPSS," Institute of Digital Research and Education, 2003, Last Accessed December 20, 2016,
http://www.ats.ucla.edu/stat/spss/webbooks/reg/default.htm .

[25] John P. Klein and Melvin L. Moeschberger, "Survival Analysis: Techniques for Censored and Truncated Data", Springer, 2003.

[26] "Implementing AML Transaction Monitoring Systems," Protiviti, 2013, Last Accessed December 20, 2016, http://www.pglewis.com/en-US/Documents/POV/Implementing-AML-Transaction-Monitoring-Systems-Protiviti.pdf

[27] "Unlocking Automation in AML Investigations," Booz, Allen, Hamiliton: Commercial Solutions|Financial Crimes, 2014, Last Accessed December 20, 2016,
https://www.boozallen.com/content/dam/boozallen/documents/2015/12/AML-automation.pdf

[28] Immune cell profiling to guide therapeutic decisions in rheumatic diseases, Joerg Ermann, Deepak A. Rao, Nikola C. Teslovich, Michael B. Brenner, and Soumya Raychaudhuri, Nature Reviews Rheumatology 11, 541-551, 2015, doi:10.1038/nrrheum.2015.71

[29] John P. Klein, Melvin L. Moeschberger, Survival Analysis: Techniques for Censored and Truncated Data, Springer, 2003.

[30] Roger H. Blake, Paul Mangiameli, "The effects and interactions of data quality and problem complexity on data mining," Journal of Data and Information Quality (JDIQ), Volume 2 Issue 2, February 2011, Last Accessed December 20, 2016,
http://mitiq.mit.edu/ICIQ/Documents/IQ%20Conference%202008/papers/2C-1%20Blake%20and%20Mangiameli.pdf

[31] Joseph M. Hellerstein, "Quantitative Data Cleaning for Large Databases," EECS Computer Science Division
UC Berkeley, February 27, 2008, Last Accessed December 20, 2016,
http://db.cs.berkeley.edu/jmh/papers/cleaning-unece.pdf

[32] FHIR Resource Index, Last Accessed December 28, 2016, https://www.hl7.org/fhir/resourcelist.html

[33] Ian Spence, "William Playfair and the Psychology of Graphs," Proceedings of the American Statistical Association, Section on Statistical Graphics. Alexandria VA: American Statistical Association, pp. 2426-2436, 2006, Last Accessed December 20, 2016,
http://www.psych.utoronto.ca/users/spence/Spence%20(2006).pdf

[34] Wikipedia, "William Playfair," Last modified on November 6, 2016, Last Accessed December 20, 2016,
https://en.wikipedia.org/wiki/William_Playfair

[35] S. Marschner, J. Davis, M. Garr, M. Levoy, "Filling Holes in Complex Surfaces Using Volumetric Diffusion," First International Symposium on 3D Data Processing, Visualization, and Transmission
Padua, Italy, June 19-21, 2002, Last Accessed December 20, 2016,
https://graphics.stanford.edu/papers/holefill-3dpvt02/hole.pdf

[36] Excerpted from: P. Y. Lum, G. Singh, A. Lehman, T. Ishkanov, M. Vejdemo-Johansson, M. Alagappan, J. Carlsson & G. Carlsson, "Extracting Insights from the Shape of Complex Data Using Topology," *Scientific Reports* 3, Article number: 1236 (2013) doi:10.1038/srep01236, July 2, 2013, Last Accessed December 20, 2016, http://www.nature.com/articles/srep01236

[37] ibid

[38] Brenda Y. Torres, Jose Henrique M. Oliveira, Ann Thomas Tate, Poonam Rath, Katherine Cumnock, David S. Schneider, "Tracking Resilience to Infections by Mapping Disease Space," PLOS Biology 14(6): e1002494. doi: 10.1371/journal.pbio.1002494, June 8, 2016, Last Accessed December 20, 2016,
http://journals.plos.org/plosbiology/article?id=10.1371%2Fjournal.pbio.1002436

[39] Alexander Louie, Kyung Han Song, Alejandra Hotson, Ann Thomas Tate, David S. Schneider, "How Many Parameters Does It Take to Describe Disease Tolerance?" PLOS Biology 14(6): e1002485. doi: 10.1371/journal.pbio.1002485, June 6, 2016, Last Accessed December 20, 2016,
http://journals.plos.org/plosbiology/article?id=10.1371/journal.pbio.1002435

[40] "2001: A Space Odyssey," Dir. Stanley Kubrick, Perf. Douglas Rain, MGM, 1968

[41] Charles Dickens, "A Christmas Carol in Prose, Being a Ghost-Story of Christmas," London, Chapman & Hall, 1843

[42] "Old Farmer's Almanac," Editor Janice Stillman, Dublin, Connecticut, Yankee Publishing, Annual

[43] Linda Graham-Barber, "Ho Ho Ho, The Complete Book of Christmas Words," New York, Simon & Schuster, 1993

[44] AM Turning, "Computer Machinery and Intelligence," Mind, 59, 433-460, 1950, Last Accessed December 20, 2016, http://loebner.net/Prizef/TuringArticle.html

[45] McCarthy, J., Minsky, M., Rochester, N., Shannon, C.E., "A Proposal for the Dartmouth Summer Research Project on Artificial Intelligence, August 31, 1955," AI Magazine, Vol 27, Num 4, 2006, Last Accessed December 20, 2016, http://www.aaai.org/ojs/index.php/aimagazine/article/view/1904/1802

[46] Pat Langley, "The Changing Science of Machine Learning," Machine Learning," Volume 82, Issue 3, pp 275–279, March 2011, Last Accessed December 20, 2016,
http://www.isle.org/~langley/papers/changes.mlj11.pdf

[47] Jason Brownlee, "A Tour of Machine Learning Algorithms," Machine Learning Algorithms, November 25, 2013, Last Accessed December 20, 2016, http://machinelearningmastery.com/a-tour-of-machine-learning-algorithms/

[48] Everitt, Brian, "The Cambridge Dictionary of Statistics," Cambridge, UK New York, Cambridge University Press. ISBN 0521593468

[49] John Tukey, "The Future of Data Analysis," Annals of Mathematical Statistics , vol 33 num 1, 1962, page 13

[50] John Tukey, "Exploratory Data Analysis," Menlo Park, Cal., London, Amsterdam, Don Mills, Ontario, Sydney, Addison-Wesley, 1977, page vi.

[51] Marc Offroy, L. Duponchel, "Topological Data Analysis: A Promising Big Data Exploration Tool in Biology, Analytical Chemistry, and Physical Chemistry," Analytica Chimica Acta, Vol. 910, 3March 2016, P. 1-11.

[52] Published in: Hae Yong Yoo, Min Kyung Sung, et al, "A Recurrent Inactivating Mutation in RHOA GTPase in Angioimmunoblastic T Cell Lymphoma," Nature Genetics **vol 46**, 2014, pages 371-375, doi:10.1038/ng.2916, Last Accessed December 20, 2016, http://www.nature.com/ng/journal/v46/n4/fig_tab/ng.2916_SF8.html#auth-1

[53] Orly Alter, Patrick O. Brown, and David Botstein, "Singular value decomposition for genome-wide expression data processing and modeling," Proceedings of the National Academy of Sciences of the United States of America, vol. 97, no. 18, 10101-10106, doi: 10.1073/pnas.97.18.10101, https://www.ncbi.nlm.nih.gov/pmc/articles/PMC27718/

[54] Orly Alter, Patrick O. Brown, David Botstein, "Singular value decomposition for genome-wide expression data processing and modeling," Proceedings of the National Academy of Sciences of the United States of America, vol. 97, no. 18, 10101-10106, doi: 10.1073/pnas.97.18.10101, https://www.ncbi.nlm.nih.gov/pmc/articles/PMC27718/

[55] Condensed for space and continuity with the chapter material. For complete treatment of the subject material refer to the original paper: Mehrdad Yazdani, Larry Smarr, Rob Knight, "Using Topological Data Analysis to Find Discrimination Between Microbial States in Human Microbiome Data," International Conference on Machine Learning (ICML), June 24, 2016

[56] Institute of Medicine, "To Err Is Human: Building a Safer Health System," Washington, DC: National Academies Press, 2000, Linda T. Kohn, Janet M. Corrigan, Molly S. Donaldson, Eds., Last Accessed December 6, 2016, http://www.nationalacademies.org/hmd/~/media/Files/Report%20Files/1999/To-Err-is-Human/To%20Err%20is%20Human%201999%20%20report%20brief.pdf. Accessed November 22, 2016.

[57] Martin Makary, Michael Daniel, "Medical error—The Third Leading Cause of Death in the US", BMJ, May 3, 2016;353:i2139, Last Accessed December 6, 2016, http://www.bmj.com/content/353/bmj.i2139

[58] "Long-Term Growth of Medical Expenditures Public and Private," ASPE Issue Brief, May 1, 2005, https://aspe.hhs.gov/basic-report/long-term-growth-medical-expenditures-public-and-private#_ftn1

[59] "NHE Fact Sheet," Centers for Medicare and Medicaid Services, Page last Modified: 08/10/2016 4:51 PM, Last Accessed December 6, 2016, https://www.cms.gov/research-statistics-data-and-systems/statistics-trends-and-reports/nationalhealthexpenddata/nhe-fact-sheet.html

[60] ibid.

[61] "The Learning Health System and its Innovation Collaboratives," the IOM Roundtable on Value & Science Driven Medicine, 2011, Denis A. Cortese, Mark B. McClellan, Chair, Last Accessed December 6, 2016, https://www.nationalacademies.org/hmd/~/media/Files/Activity%20Files/Quality/VSRT/Core%20Documents/ForEDistrib.pdf

[62] Sarah Boon, "21st Century Science Overload," Canadian Science Publishing, the CSP Blog, January 7, 2016, Last Accessed December 6, 2016, http://www.cdnsciencepub.com/blog/21st-century-science-overload.aspx

[63] "Best Care at Lower Cost: The Path to Continuously Learning Healthcare in America," The National Academes Press, 2013, Committee on the Learning Healthcare System in America; Institute of Medicine, Mark Smith, Robert Saunders, Leigh Stuckhardt, J. Michael McGinnis, Editors; http://nap.edu/13444

[64] Lutz Bornmann, Ruediger Mutz, "Growth rates of modern science: A bibliometric analysis based on the number of publications and cited references," Journal of the Association for Information Science and Technology, 19 Feb 2014, Last Accessed December 6, 2016, https://arxiv.org/ftp/arxiv/papers/1402/1402.4578.pdf

[65] Christophe Van den Bulte, Gary L. Lilien , "*Medical Innovation* Revisited: Social Contagion versus Marketing Effort," American Journal of Sociology 106, no. 5 (March 2001): 1409-1435.

[66] LeighAnne Olsen, W. Alexander Goolsby, J. Michael McGinnis, "Leadership Commitments to Improve Value in Healthcare: Finding Common Ground: Workshop Summary," Institute of Medicine, Washington, DC: The National Academies Press, 2009, Last Accessed December 6, 2016, https://www.ncbi.nlm.nih.gov/books/NBK52855/

[67] ibid.

[68] "To Err Is Human: Building a Safer Health System," Institute of Medicine, Kohn LT, Corrigan JM, and Donaldson MS, eds. Washington, DC: National Academies Press; 2000. Last Accessed December 6, 2016, Available at: http://www.iom.edu/Reports/1999/To-Err-is-Human-Building-A-Safer-Health-System.aspx. Accessed February 18, 2016.

[69] "Crossing the Quality Chasm: A New Health System for the 21st Century," Committee on Quality of Healthcare in America, Institute of Medicine, Washington, DC: National Academies Press; 2001. Last Accessed December 6, 2016, Available at: http://www.iom.edu/Reports/2001/Crossing-the-Quality-Chasm-A-New-Health-System-for-the-21st-Century.aspx. Accessed February 18, 2016.

[70] "Delivery System Reform, Medicare Payment Reform: How does the Medicare Access & CHIP Reauthorization Act of 2015 (MACRA) reform Medicare payment?" CMS.gov; accessed 9/20/2016. https://www.cms.gov/Medicare/Quality-Initiatives-Patient-Assessment-Instruments/Value-Based-Programs/MACRA-MIPS-and-APMs/MACRA-MIPS-and-APMs.html

[71] LeighAnne Olsen, W. Alexander Goolsby, J. Michael McGinnis, "Leadership Commitments to Improve Value in Healthcare: Finding Common Ground: Workshop Summary," Institute of Medicine, Washington, D.C: The National Academies Press, 2009, Last Accessed December 6, 2016, https://www.ncbi.nlm.nih.gov/books/NBK52855/

[72] "Best Care at Lower Cost: The Path to Continuously Learning Healthcare in America," Institute of Medicine, Committee on the Learning Healthcare System in America, Mark Smith, Robert Saunders, Leigh Stuckhardt, J. Michael McGinnis, Editors, Washington, DC: The National Academies Press, 2013, Last Accessed December 6, 2016, https://www.nap.edu/read/13444/chapter/1

[73] "Toward Precision Medicine: Building a Knowledge Network for Biomedical Research and a New Taxonomy of Disease," National Research Council: Committee on a Framework for Developing a New Taxonomy of Disease, Washington, DC: The National Academies Press, 2011, Last Accessed December 6, 2016, https://www.nap.edu/catalog/13284/toward-precision-medicine-building-a-knowledge-network-for-biomedical-research

[74] "Guidance for Industry: E15 Definitions for Genomic Biomarkers, Pharmacogenomics, Pharmacogenetics, Genomic Data and Sample Coding Categories," HHS, FDA, CDER, CBER, April 2008, Last Accessed December 6, 2016, http://www.fda.gov/downloads/drugs/guidancecomplianceregulatoryinformation/guidances/ucm073162.pdf

[75] Image reprinted: "Paving the Way for Personalized Medicine: FDA's Role in a New Era of Medical Product Development," FDA, October 2013, Accessed February 18, 2016, http://www.fda.gov/downloads/ScienceResearch/SpecialTopics/PersonalizedMedicine/UCM372421.pdf

[76] 21st Century Cures Act, H.R.6 —114th Congress (2015-2016), Last Accessed December 23, 2016, https://www.congress.gov/bill/114th-congress/house-bill/6

[77] MS Lauer, RB D'Agostino, "The randomized registry trial--the next disruptive technology in clinical research?" N Engl J Med, October 24, 2013, 369(17):1579-81. doi: 10.1056/NEJMp1310102.

[78] HC Sox, SN Goodman, "The methods of comparative effectiveness research," Annu Rev Public Health 2012;33:425–445, PMID: 22224891. doi: 10.1146/annurev-publhealth-031811-124610.

[79] MA Hlatky, WC Winkelmayer, S Setoguchi, "Epidemiologic and statistical methods for comparative effectiveness research," Heart Fail Clin 2013;9:29–36. PMID: 23168315. doi: 10.1016/j.hfc.2012.09.007.

[80] MA Brookhart, JA Rassen, S Schneeweiss, "Instrumental Variable Methods in Comparative Safety and Effectiveness Research," Rockville, MD: Agency for Healthcare Research and Quality, 2010, Last Accessed December 6, 2016, http://effectivehealthcare.ahrq.gov/index.cfm/search-for-guides-reviews-and-reports/?pageaction=displayproduct&productid=439.

[81] NF Col, RT Chlebowski, "Risks and Benefits of Therapy with Menopausal Hormones Versus Selective Estrogen-Receptor Modulators in Peri- and Postmenopausal Women at Increased Breast Cancer Risk," Menopause, 2008 Jul-Aug;15(4 Suppl):804-9

[82] M Crump, S Gluck, D Tu, et al, "Randomized trial of high-dose chemotherapy with autologous peripheral-blood stem-cell support compared with standard-dose chemotherapy in women with metastatic breast cancer," NCIC MA.16. J Clin Oncol. 2008;26:37–43.

[83] "A randomized trial comparing lung-volume-reduction surgery with medical therapy for severe emphysema," National Emphysema Treatment Trial Research Group, N Engl J Med. 2003;348:2059–2073.

[84] John M. Boyce, Didier Pittet, "Guideline for Hand Hygiene in Health-Care Settings: Recommendations of the Healthcare Infection Control Practices Advisory Committee and the HICPAC/SHEA/APIC/IDSA Hand Hygiene Task Force," CDC, October 25, 2002 / 51(RR16);1-44, Last Accessed December 6, 2016,http://www.cdc.gov/mmwr/preview/mmwrhtml/rr5116a1.htm

[85] "Clinical Practice Guidelines: Directions for a New Program," Marilyn J Field, Kathleen N Lohr, editors, Washington, DC: National Academy Press, 1990, Last Accessed December 6, 2016, https://www.nap.edu/read/1626/chapter/1

[86] ES Fisher, SM Shortell, LA Savitz, "Implementation Science: A Potential Catalyst for Delivery System Reform," JAMA, January 26, 2016, 315(4):339-40. doi: 10.1001/jama.2015.17949, Last Accessed December 6, 2016, https://www.ncbi.nlm.nih.gov/pubmed/26813203

[87] "Comprehensive Care for Joint Replacement," cms.gov, Last Accessed December 2, 2016, https://innovation.cms.gov/initiatives/ccjr/index.html

[88] "Better Care, Smarter Spending, Healthier People: Improving Our Healthcare Delivery System," CMS Fact Sheet, cms.gov, January, 26, 2015, Last Accessed December 2, 2016, https://www.cms.gov/Newsroom/MediaReleaseDatabase/Fact-sheets/2015-Fact-sheets-items/2015-01-26.html

[89] "Better Care. Smarter Spending. Healthier People: Paying Providers for Value, Not Volume," CMS Fact Sheet, cms.gov, January 26, 2015, Last Accessed December 2, 2016, https://www.cms.gov/Newsroom/MediaReleaseDatabase/Fact-sheets/2015-Fact-sheets-items/2015-01-26-3.html

[90] Melanie Evans, "Boeing Negotiates Directly with more Health Systems," Modern Healthcare, August 4, 2015, Last Accessed December 2, 2016, http://www.modernhealthcare.com/article/20150804/NEWS/150809961

[91] Jessica L. Nielson, Jesse Paquette, et al., "Topological data analysis for discovery in preclinical spinal cord injury and traumatic brain injury," Nature Communications, 6:8581, DOI: 10.1038/ncomms9581, October 14, 2015, Last Accessed 12/5/2016, https://d1bp1ynq8xms31.cloudfront.net/wp-content/uploads/2016/01/UCSF-Nature-6.pdf

[92] M. Panella, F. Di Stanislao, "Reducing clinical variations with clinical pathways: do pathways work?" Int J Qual Healthcare. 15 (6): 509–521. doi:10.1093/intqhc/mzg057, Retrieved July 27, 2014, Last Accessed December 6, 2016, http://intqhc.oxfordjournals.org/content/15/6/509.short

[93] Gillian I. Russell, Terminology, in FUNDAMENTALS OF HEALTH LAW 1, 12, American Health Lawyers Association 5th ed., 2011.

[94] ICD-10-CM/PCS MS-DRGv33 Definitions Manual, Centers for Medicare and Medicaid Services, Last Accessed December 6, 2016, https://www.cms.gov/ICD10Manual/version33-fullcode-cms/fullcode_cms/P0011.html

[95] Formerly known as the Joint Commission for Accreditation of Healthcare Organizations

[96] KJ Zehr, PB Dawson, SC Yang, RF Heitmiller, "Standardized clinical care pathways for major thoracic cases reduce hospital costs," Ann Thorac Surg, 1998 Sep;66(3):914-9, Last Accessed December 6, 2016, https://www.ncbi.nlm.nih.gov/pubmed/9768951

[97] "Controlling the Cost of Care Through Clinical Pathways," Biotechnol Healthc, 2009 Apr; 6(1): 23–26, Bob Carlson, Contributing Editor, Last Accessed December 6, 2016, https://www.ncbi.nlm.nih.gov/pmc/articles/PMC2702812/

[98] Eugene D. Kreys, Jim M. Koeller, "Documenting the Benefits and Cost Savings of a Large Multistate Cancer Pathway Program from a Payer's Perspective," DOI: 10.1200/JOP.2012.000871 Journal of Oncology Practice 9, no. 5, September 2013, e241-e247, Last Accessed December 6. 2016, http://jop.ascopubs.org/content/9/5/e241.full

[99] Care Process Models. Intermountain Healthcare, web link, https://intermountainphysician.org/clinical/Pages/Care-Process-Models-(CPMs).aspx

[100] Clinical Pathways. The Children's Hospital of Philadelphia, web link, http://www.chop.edu/pathways#.V-GDFZMrJmA

[101] "Pectus Excavatum Repair Care Pathway" - The Hospital for Sick Children, Toronto, CA, 2012, Image reproduced with permission of the copyright owner. Use of the referenced Clinical Practice Guideline in any setting must be subject to the clinical judgment of those responsible for providing care. Last Accessed December 10, 2016, http://www.sickkids.ca/clinical-practice-guidelines/clinical-practice-guidelines/

[102] "A National Framework for Healthcare Quality Measurement and Reporting: A Consensus Report," Washington, D.C., The National Forum for Healthcare Quality Measurement and Reporting, 2002, Last Accessed December 6, 2016, http://www.qualityforum.org/Publications/2002/07/A_National_Framework_for_Healthcare_Quality_Measurement_and_Reporting.aspx

[103] "About HL& International," Health Level Seven International, Last Accessed December 8, 2016, http://www.hl7.org/

[104] "Vocabulary Specifications," Health Level Seven International, Last Accessed December 8, 2016, http://www.hl7.org/implement/standards/product_brief.cfm?product_id=78

[105] "Introducing HL7 FHIR," Health Level Seven International, Last Accessed December 8, 2016, https://www.hl7.org/fhir/

[106] eCQM Value Sets for eReporting for 2016 Reporting Period," Value Set Authority Center, U.S. National Library of Medicine, May 1, 2015, https://vsac.nlm.nih.gov/

[107] Nicole Gray Weiskopf, Chunhua Weng, "Methods and Dimensions of Electronic Health Record Data Quality Assessment: Enabling Reuse for Clinical Research," J Am Med Inform Assoc, 2013 Jan-Feb; 20(1): 144–151. doi: 10.1136/amiajnl-2011-000681, https://www.ncbi.nlm.nih.gov/pmc/articles/PMC3555312/

[108] Intermountain Healthcare Care Process Model: Enhanced Recovery after Intestinal Surgery (ERAS), June 2014. https://intermountainhealthcare.org/ext/Dcmnt?ncid=520451354

Endnotes

[109] Donald M. Berwick, Thomas W. Nolan, John Whittington, "The triple aim: Care, Health and Cost. Health Affairs," 27, no.3 (2008):759-769. doi: 10.1377/hlthaff.27.3.759, http://content.healthaffairs.org/content/27/3/759.full.pdf+html

[110] David Kindig, Greg Stoddart, What is population health?" American Journal of Public Health, March 2003;93(3):380–3. Retrieved 2008-10-12, http://ajph.aphapublications.org/doi/abs/10.2105/AJPH.93.3.380

[111] Brian W. Ward, Jeannine S. Schiller, Richard A. Goodman, "Multiple Chronic Conditions Among US Adults: A 2012 Update," Prev Chronic Dis 2014;11:130389. DOI, Last Accessed December 12, 2016, http://dx.doi.org/10.5888/pcd11.130389

[112] Mark Stanton, "The High Concentration of U.S. Healthcare Expenditures: Research in Action," Agency for Healthcare Research and Quality, Rockville, MD Issue 19. June 2006, Last Access December 12, 2016, http://www.ahrq.gov/research/findings/factsheets/costs/expriach/index.html#diff1

[113] Jong-Myon Bae, "Value-based medicine: concepts and application," Epidemiol Health. 2015; 37: e2015014.
Published online 2015 Mar 4. doi: 10.4178/epih/e2015014, Last Accessed December 12, 2016, https://www.ncbi.nlm.nih.gov/pmc/articles/PMC4398974/

[114] Bernadette Keefe, "Defining Population Health and Social Determinants of Health," Mayo Clinic Center for Innovation, Transform Conference, Population Health: Our Lives, Our Data, Last Accessed December 12, 2016, http://blog.centerforinnovation.mayo.edu/2015/09/17/population-health-our-lives-our-data/

[115] Sheetal Sawardekar, "Population health analytics: combatting challenges: The efficiency of any population health program relies on the ability of caregivers and stakeholders to leverage population data," Healthcare IT News, September 14, 2015, Last Accessed December 12, 2016, http://www.healthcareitnews.com/news/population-health-analytics-combatting-challenges

[116] ibid.

[117] "What is a Clinical Data Registry?" AMA, National Quality Registry Network, 2014, Last Accessed December 12, 2016, http://www.abms.org/media/1358/what-is-a-clinical-data-registry.pdf

[118] "Registries for Evaluating Patient Outcomes: A User's Guide [Internet]. 3rd edition," R. Gliklich, N. Dreyer, M. Leavy, eds., HHS, Agency of Healthcare Research and Quality, Last Accessed December 12, 2016, https://www.ncbi.nlm.nih.gov/books/NBK208643/

[119] "What is a Clinical Data Registry?" AMA, National Quality Registry Network, 2014, Last Accessed December 12, 2016, http://www.abms.org/media/1358/what-is-a-clinical-data-registry.pdf

[120] "CMS Quality Measure Development Plan: Supporting the Transition to the Merit-based Incentive Payment System (MIPS) and Alternative Payment Models (APMs)," Centers for Medicare & Medicaid Services. Baltimore, MD: Centers for Medicare & Medicaid Services; May 2, 2016. Last Accessed December 12, 2016, https://www.cms.gov/Medicare/Quality-Initiatives-Patient-Assessment-Instruments/Value-Based-Programs/MACRA-MIPS-and-APMs/Final-MDP.pdf

[121] "2016 Cardiology Preferred Specialty Measure Set," U.S. Centers for Medicare & Medicaid Services, Last Accessed February 1, 2017, https://www.cms.gov/Medicare/Quality-Initiatives-Patient-Assessment-Instruments/PQRS/Downloads/Potential_Cardiology_Preferred_Specialty_Measure_Set_06_30_2014_508.pdf

[122] Cynthia Cox, Ashley Semanskee, Gary Claxton, Larry Levitt, "Explaining Healthcare Reform: Risk Adjustment, Reinsurance, and Risk Corridors," The Henry J. Kaiser Family Foundation, Issue Brief, August 2016, Last Accessed December 12, 2016, http://kff.org/health-reform/issue-brief/explaining-health-care-reform-risk-adjustment-reinsurance-and-risk-corridors/

[123] BA Young, E. Lin, M. Von Korff, et al. "Diabetes Complications Severity Index and Risk of Mortality, Hospitalization, and Healthcare Utilization," The American Journal of Managed Care. 2008;14(1):15-23.

[124] WA Knaus, EA Draper, DP Wagner, JE Zimmerman, (1985)"APACHE II: a severity of disease classification system," Critical Care Medicine 13 (10): 818–29.doi: 10.1097/00003246-198510000-00009 PMID 3928249

[125] WA Knaus, EA Draper, DP Wagner, JE Zimmerman, M. Bergner, PG. Bastos, CA. Sirio, DJ. Murphy, T Lotring, A. Damiano, et al. (1991). "The APACHE III prognostic system. Risk prediction of hospital mortality for critically ill hospitalized adults". Chest 100 (6): 1619–36.doi:10.1378/chest.100.6.1619 PMID 1959406.

[126] G. Pope, J. Kautter, M. Ingber, S. Freeman, R. Sekar, C. Newhart, "Evaluation of the CMS-HCC Risk Adjustment Model," RTI International, CMS Contract No. HHSM-500-2005-000291 TO 0006, March 2011, Accessed 03/11/2016, https://www.cms.gov/Medicare/Health-Plans/MedicareAdvtgSpecRateStats/downloads/evaluation_risk_adj_model_2011.pdf

[127] ibid.

[128] "HealthNumerics-RISC® Predictive Models: A Successful Approach to Risk Stratification (white paper)," Optum-UK.com, downloaded March 10,2016, https://www.optum.com/content/dam/optum/resources/whitePapers/Optum_HNRISC_White%20Paper.pdf .

[129] "ASA Physical Status Classification System," American Society of Anesthesiologists, October 15, 2014. Accessed March 1, 2016, http://www.asahq.org/resources/clinical-information/asa-physical-status-classification-system

[130] E. Ben-Chetrit, et al., "A simplified scoring tool for prediction of readmission in elderly patients hospitalized in internal medicine departments,". Isr Med Assoc J, 2012. 14(12): p. 752-6.

[131] CW. Seymour, MR. Rosengart MR. "Septic shock: Advances in diagnosis and treatment," JAMA. 2015; 314(7):708-16.

[132] KE. Henry, DN. Hager, PJ. Pronovost, S.A.Saria "targeted real-time early warning score (TREWScore) for septic shock," Science Translational Medicine; Aug 2015: 299RA122.

[133] High Value Healthcare Collaborative, Current Projects, accessed Sept. 23, 2016, https://www.highvaluehealthcare.org/how-we-do-it/current-efforts/

[134] "Tracking Parkinson's Disease," The Michael J. Fox Foundation for Parkinson's Disease, The Fox Focus on Parkinson, Fall 2014 Newsletter, Last Accessed December 12, 2016, https://www.michaeljfox.org/files/foundation/2014%20Fall%20Newsletter%20FINAL.pdf

[135] Syria Polio Vaccine Campaign. SumAll.org. (original posting, 2014). http://www.sumall.org/project-overview/syria-tracker/

[136] "Priorities for Personalized Medicine," President's Council of Advisors on Science and Technology, September 2008, Last Accessed December 14, 2016, https://www.whitehouse.gov/files/documents/ostp/PCAST/pcast_report_v2.pdf

[137] "Toward Precision Medicine: Building a Knowledge Network for Biomedical Research and a New Taxonomy of Disease," National Research Council: Committee on a Framework for Developing a New Taxonomy of Disease, 2011, Washington, DC: The National Academies Press.

[138] F. Rodriguez F, R. Harrington R, "Cholesterol, Cardiovascular Risk, Statins, PCSK9 Inhibitors, and the Future of LDL-C Lowering," JAMA. 2016,316(12):1967-1968.

[139] H.R.6 -21st Century Cures Act, 114th Congress, 2015-2016, Last Accessed December 26, 2016, https://www.congress.gov/bill/114th-congress/house-bill/6

[140] Chelsea Toledo, Kirstie Saltsman, "Genetics by the Numbers," National Institute of General Medical Science: Inside Life Science, June 11, 2012, Last Accessed December 15, 2016, https://publications.nigms.nih.gov/insidelifescience/genetics-numbers.html

Endnotes

[141] Help Me Understand Genetics. Genetics Home Reference series. National Institutes of Health: Lister Hill National Center for Biomedical Communications. December 21, 2016. https://ghr.nlm.nih.gov/

[142] *Ananya Mandal* "What is DNA Junk?" News: Medical-Life Science, Last Updated Nov 17, 2014, Last Accessed December 14, 2016, http://www.news-medical.net/life-sciences/What-is-Junk-DNA.aspx

[143] Michael K.K. Leung, Andrew Delong, Babak Alipanahi, Brendan J. Frey, "Machine Learning in Genomic Medicine: A Review of Computational Problems and Data Sets," Proceedings of the IEEE, Vol.104, No.1, January 2016, Last Accessed December 14, 2016, http://ieeexplore.ieee.org/stamp/stamp.jsp?arnumber=7347331

[144] M. Aidoo, DJ Terlouw, MS Kolczak, PD McElroy, FO ter Kuile, S. Kariuki, BL Nahlen, AA Lal, V. Udhayakumar, "Protective Effects of the Sickle Cell Gene Against Malaria Morbidity and Mortality,". Lancet 2002; 359:1311-1312.

[145] Dennis O'Neil, "Recombination and Linkage," Palomar College, website, Last Accessed December 14, 2016, http://anthro.palomar.edu/biobasis/bio_3.htm

[146] F. Stegmeier, M. Warmuth, WR Sellers, M. Dorsch,"Targeted cancer therapies in the twenty-first century: lessons from imatinib," Clin. Pharmacol. Ther. 87 (5): 543– 52.doi:10.1038/clpt.2009.297. PMID 20237469, May 2010, Last Accessed December 14, 2016, https://www.ncbi.nlm.nih.gov/pubmed/20237469

[147] "Leukemia - Chronic Myeloid - CML: Statistics | Cancer.Net," Last Accessed December 14, 2016, http://www.cancer.net/cancer-types/leukemia-chronic-myeloid-cml/statistics

[148] T. Hinks, X. Zhou, K. Staples, et al, "Innate and adaptive T cells in asthmatic patients: Relationship to severity and disease mechanisms," J Allergy Clin Immunol 2015;136:323-33.

[149] "Paving the Way for Personalized Medicine," Silver Spring, MD, U.S. Food and Drug Administration, October 2013, Last Accessed December 14, 2016, http://www.fda.gov/downloads/ScienceResearch/SpecialTopics/PersonalizedMedicine/UCM372421.pdf

[150] 23andMe, Inc., Last Accessed December 14, 2016, www.23andme.com

[151] Genelex Corporation, Last Accessed December 14, 2016, http://genelex.com/about/

[152] Malik Nassan, et al. "Pharmacokinetic Pharmacogenetic Prescribing Guidelines for Antidepressants: A Template for Psychiatric Precision Medicine," Mayo Clinic Proceedings , 2016; 91(7): 897 – 907, Last Accessed December 14, 2016, http://www.mayoclinicproceedings.org/article/S0025-6196(16)30002-7/abstract

[153] Intermountain Website, Last Accessed December 26, 2016, https://intermountainhealthcare.org/services/cancer-care/precision-genomics/for-health-professionals/

[154] "Pharmacogenomic PGx Profile Service," Mayo Clinic Center for Individualized Medicine, Last Accessed December 14, 2016, http://mayoresearch.mayo.edu/center-for-individualized-medicine/pgx-profile-service.asp#pgx-profile-service

[155] L. Li, W.Cheng, B. Glicksberg, et al, "Identification of type 2 diabetes subgroups through topological analysis of patient similarity," Science Translational Medicine. 7 (311), 311ra174. (October 28, 2015). [doi: 10.1126/scitranslmed.aaa9364]

[156] Li Li, Wei-Yi Cheng, Benjamin S. Glicksberg, et al, "Identification of type 2 diabetes subgroups through topological analysis of patient similarity," Science Transitional Medicine, Vol 7 Issue 311 311ra174, October 28, 2015, Last Accessed December 15, 2016, https://d1bp1ynq8xms31.cloudfront.net/wp-content/uploads/2016/01/mtsinai.pdf

[157] Timothy S. C. Hink, Xiaoying Zhou, Karl J. Staples, et al, "Innate and adaptive T cells in asthmatic patients: Relationship to severity and disease mechanisms," J Allergy Clin Immunol, Volume 136, Number 2, August 2015, Last Accessed December 15, 2016, http://www.jacionline.org/article/S0091-6749(15)00104-9/pdf

[158] Timothy S. C. Hinks, Tom Brown, Laurie C. K. Lau, et al, "Multidimensional endotyping in patients with severe asthma reveals inflammatory heterogeneity in matrix metalloproteinases and chitinase 3–like protein 1," J Allergy Clin Immunol, Volume 138, Number 1, July 2016, Last Accessed December 15, 2016, http://www.jacionline.org/article/S0091-6749(15)03117-6/pdf

[159] Bruce Bartlett, "What Your Taxes Do (and Don't) Buy for You," Economix: Explaining the Science of Everyday Life, New York Times, June 7, 2011, Last Accessed December 16, 2016, http://economix.blogs.nytimes.com/2011/06/07/health-care-costs-and-the-tax-burden/

[160] D. Squires and C. Anderson, "U.S. Healthcare from a Global Perspective: Spending, Use of Services, Prices, and Health in 13 Countries," The Commonwealth Fund, October 2015, Last Accessed December 16, 2016, http://www.commonwealthfund.org/publications/issue-briefs/2015/oct/us-health-care-from-a-global-perspective

[161] "Health expenditure, total (% of GDP)," The World Bank, Last Accessed December 16, 2016, http://data.worldbank.org/indicator/SH.XPD.TOTL.ZS

[162] "Health expenditure per capita (current U.S.$)," The World Bank, Last Accessed December 16, 2016, http://data.worldbank.org/indicator/SH.XPD.PCAP

[163] "Country Comparison: Life Expectancy at Birth," World Fact Book, CIA, Last Accessed December 16, 2016, https://www.cia.gov/Library/publications/the-world-factbook/rankorder/2102rank.html

[164] Christina LaMontagne, "NerdWallet Health finds Medical Bankruptcy accounts for majority of personal bankruptcies," Nerd Wallet, June 19, 2013, Last Accessed December 16, 2016, https://www.nerdwallet.com/blog/health/managing-medical-bills/nerdwallet-health-study-estimates-56-million-americans-65-struggle-medical-bills-2013/

[165] "World Health Organization's Ranking of the World's Health Systems," The Patient Factor, Last Accessed December 16, 2016, http://thepatientfactor.com/canadian-health-care-information/world-health-organizations-ranking-of-the-worlds-health-systems/

[166] "Healthcare Systems - Four Basic Models," PNHP, Last Accessed on December 16, 2016, http://www.pnhp.org/single_payer_resources/health_care_systems_four_basic_models.php

[167] "Healthcare Costs: A Primer," Henry J. Kaiser Family Foundation, May1, 2012, Last Accessed December 16, 2016, http://kff.org/report-section/health-care-costs-a-primer-2012-report/

[168] Aliya Jiwani, David Himmelstein, Steffie Woolhandler, James G Kahn, "Billing and insurance-related administrative costs in United States' healthcare: synthesis of micro-costing evidence," BMC Health Serv Res. 2014; 14: 556, Published online 2014 Nov 13. doi: 10.1186/s12913-014-0556-7, Last Accessed December 16, 2016, https://www.ncbi.nlm.nih.gov/pmc/articles/PMC4283267/

[169] ibid.

[170] James G. Kahn, "Excess Billing and Insurance-Related Administratitve Costs,"Institute of Medicine (U.S.) Roundtable on Evidence-Based Medicine; Yong PL, Saunders RS, Olsen LA, editors. The Healthcare Imperative: Lowering Costs and Improving Outcomes: Workshop Series Summary. Washington (DC): National Academies Press (U.S.); 2010. 4, Excess Administrative Costs., Last Accessed December 15, 2016, https://www.ncbi.nlm.nih.gov/books/NBK53942/

[171] ibid.

[172] D. U. Himmelstein, M. Jun, R. Busse et al., "A Comparison of Hospital Administrative Costs in Eight Nations: U.S. Costs Exceed All Others by Far," Health Affairs, Sept. 2014 33(9):1586–94., Last Accessed December 16, 2016, http://www.commonwealthfund.org/publications/in-the-literature/2014/sep/hospital-administrative-costs

[173] "Excess Administrative Costs," Institute of Medicine (U.S.) Roundtable on Evidence-Based Medicine; Yong PL, Saunders RS, Olsen LA, editors. The Healthcare Imperative: Lowering Costs and Improving

Endnotes

Outcomes: Workshop Series Summary. Washington (DC): National Academies Press (U.S.); 2010. 4, Last Accessed December 16, 2016, https://www.ncbi.nlm.nih.gov/books/NBK53942/

[174] "2013 U.S. Healthcare Efficiency Index: Electronic Administrative Transaction Adoption and Savings," Council for Affordable Quality Healthcare, May 5, 2014, Last Accessed December 16, 2016, http://www.caqh.org/sites/default/files/explorations/index/report/2013Index.pdf

[175] "Excess Administrative Costs," Institute of Medicine (U.S.) Roundtable on Evidence-Based Medicine; Yong PL, Saunders RS, Olsen LA, editors. The Healthcare Imperative: Lowering Costs and Improving Outcomes: Workshop Series Summary. Washington (DC): National Academies Press (U.S.); 2010. 4, Last Accessed December 16, 2016, https://www.ncbi.nlm.nih.gov/books/NBK53942/

[176] "The Medical Billing Process," MedicalBillingAndCoding.org, Last Accessed December 16, 2016, http://www.medicalbillingandcoding.org/billing-process/

[177] Last Accessed December 16, 2016, https://en.wikipedia.org/wiki/Chargemaster#cite_note-NYT-20130731-1: *Henderson, James W. (2008). Health Economics & Policy. South-Western College Pub. pp. 269–271. ISBN 978-0324645187, Kongstvedt, Peter (2009). Managed Care: What It Is and How It Works. Jones & Bartlett Publishers. p. 212. ISBN 978-0763759117.*

[178] Pat Palmer, "How Does Medical Billing Really Work?," MBAA Education Center, Last Accessed December 16, 2016, https://billadvocates.com/medical-billing-really-work/

[179] "The Medical Billing Process," MedicalBillingAndCoding.org, Last Accessed December 16, 2016, http://www.medicalbillingandcoding.org/billing-process/

[180] "2013 U.S. Healthcare Efficiency Index: Electronic Administrative Transaction Adoption and Savings," Council for Affordable Quality Healthcare, May 5, 2014, Last Accessed December 16, 2016, http://www.caqh.org/sites/default/files/explorations/index/report/2013Index.pdf

[181] Asia Blunt, "Evaluating Your Practice's Revenue Cycle: Denial Rate," American Academy of Family Physicians, Last Accessed December 27, 2016, http://www.aafp.org/practice-management/administration/finances/denial-rate.html

[182] Susan Morse, "CMS says 10% ICD-10 claims rejected, but only a fraction due to coding issues," Healthcare. Finance News, October 29, 2015, Last Accessed December 16, 2016, http://www.healthcarefinancenews.com/news/cms-says-10-icd-10-claims-rejected-only-fraction-due-coding-issues

[183] ibid.

[184] K. Carman , C.Eibner, S. Paddock,. "DATAWATCH: Trends In Health Insurance Enrollment, 2013–15," Health Aff June 2015 34:61044-1048;published ahead of print May 6, 2015.

[185] ibid.

[186] MACStats: Medicaid and CHIP Data Book. Washington, D.C.: Medicaid and CHIP Payment and Access Commission. December 2015, Last Accessed December 16, 2016, https://www.macpac.gov/publication/macstats-medicaid-and-chip-data-book-2/

[187] "Comprehensive Care for Joint Replacement Model," CMS, Last Updated October 3, 2016, Last Accessed December 16, 2016, https://innovation.cms.gov/initiatives/ccjr/index.html

[188] E. Thienpont, P. Lavand'homme, H. Kehlet, "The constraints on day case total knee arthroplasty: the fastest fast track," Bone Joint J. 2015 Oct;97-B(10 Suppl A):40-4. doi: 10.1302/0301-620X.97B10.36610, Last Accessed December 16, 2016, https://www.ncbi.nlm.nih.gov/pubmed/26430085

[189] Work Plan. Office of Inspector General. 2014. https://oig.hhs.gov/ Last Accessed 4/10/2016

[190] "Common Types of Healthcare Fraud. (fact sheet)," Washington, D.C.: Centers for Medicare and Medicaid Services, July 2016, Last Accessed December 16, 2016, https://www.cms.gov/Medicare-Medicaid-Coordination/Fraud-Prevention/Medicaid-Integrity-Education/Downloads/fwa-factsheet.pdf

[191] "Healthcare Fraud and Abuse Control Program Annual Report for Fiscal Year 2015," Washington, DC: U.S. Department of Health and Human Services and the Department of Justice. February 2016, Last Accessed December 16, 2016, http://www.oig.hhs.gov/publications/docs/hcfac/FY2015-hcfac.pdf

[192] ibid.

[193] "Medicare Provider Utilization and Payment Data: Physician and Other Supplier," Centers for Medicare and Medicaid, Last Accessed October 25, 2016, https://www.cms.gov/research-statistics-data-and-systems/statistics-trends-and-reports/medicare-provider-charge-data/physician-and-other-supplier.html

[194] *Epidemics I, xi.* Translated by WHS Jones. Cambridge: Harvard University Press, 1995

[195] Rory Cellan-Jones, "Stephen Hawking warns Artificial Intelligence could end mankind," BBC News, December 2, 2014, Last Accessed December 19, 2016, http://www.bbc.com/news/technology-30290540

[196] Alex Hern, "Stephen Hawking: AI will be 'either best or worst thing' for humanity," The Guardian, Wednesday, October 19, 2016, Last Accessed December 19, 2016, https://www.theguardian.com/science/2016/oct/19/stephen-hawking-ai-best-or-worst-thing-for-humanity-cambridge

[197] J Vogel, JS Brown, T Land, R Platt, M Klompas. "MDPHnet: secure, distributed sharing of electronic health record data for public health surveillance, evaluation, and planning." Am J Public Health.2014; 104(12):2265-70. Pubmed ID 25322301.

[198] V Gulshan, L Peng, M Coram, et. al. Development and Validation of a Deep Learning Algorithm for Detection of Diabetic Retinopathy in Retinal Fundus Photographs. JAMA. 2016;316(22):2402-2410.

[199] "Report to Congress: The Sentinel Initiative - A National Strategy for Monitoring Medical Product Safety," Department of Health and Human Services, Food and Drug Administration. August 19, 2011. http://www.fda.gov/downloads/Safety/FDAsSentinelInitiative/UCM274548.pdf (accessed 1/10/2017.)

[200] S Schneeweiss, HG Eichler, A Garcia-Altes A, et al. "Real World Data in Adaptive Biomedical Innovation: A Framework for Generating Evidence Fit for Decision Making: Healthcare Databases with Rapid Cycle Analytics to Support Adaptive Biomedical Innovation." Clin Pharmacol Ther. 2016 Dec;100(6):633-646

[201] "Affordable Care Act Summary: What is the Affordable Care Act?", Website, Last Accessed January 5, 2017, http://obamacarefacts.com/affordablecareact-summary/

[202] Definition of an Allele, Website, Last Accessed January 5, 2017, http://medical-dictionary.thefreedictionary.com/allele

[203] "Understanding Capitation," American College of Physicians, Last Accessed January 5, 2017, https://www.acponline.org/about-acp/about-internal-medicine/career-paths/residency-career-counseling/understanding-capitation

[204] Excerpted and directly quoted from: http://www.indiana.edu/~educy520/sec5982/week_2/variable_types.pdf, Last Accessed December 20, 2016,

[205] "Concept: Charlson Comorbidity Index, Manitobe Centre for Health Policy, Last Updated on January 22, 2016, Last Accessed January 5, 2017, http://mchp-appserv.cpe.umanitoba.ca/viewConcept.php?conceptID=1098

[206] MJ Fields, KN Lohr, "Clinical Practice Guidelines:Directions for a New Program," Washington DC 1990, National Academy Press, Pg38, Last Accessed January 5, 2017, https://www.nap.edu/read/1626/chapter/4#37

[207] Jason Brown Lee, "Supervised and Unsupervised Machine Learning Algorithms," Machine Learning Algorithms, March 16, 2016, Last Accessed January 5, 2017, http://machinelearningmastery.com/supervised-and-unsupervised-machine-learning-algorithms/

[208] Exploratory and Confirmatory Data Analysis, SAS Website, Last Accessed January 5, 2017, http://support.sas.com/documentation/cdl/en/imlsug/64254/HTML/default/viewer.htm#imlsug_ugintro_sect003.htm

[209] Excerpted and directly quoted from: http://www.indiana.edu/~educy520/sec5982/week_2/variable_types.pdf, Last Accessed December 20, 2016,

[210] Electronic Health Records, CMS.gov, Last Accessed January 5, 2017, https://www.cms.gov/Medicare/E-Health/EHealthRecords/index.html?redirect=/EhealthRecords/

[211] "HIPAA EDI Document Standard," EDI Basics, GXS, Inc, Wikipedia Last Accessed January 5, 2017, https://en.wikipedia.org/wiki/Electronic_remittance_advice

[212] "What is Epigenetics?" Epigenetics: Fundamentals, Last Accessed January 5, 2017,Ehttp://www.whatisepigenetics.com/fundamentals/

[213] Leadership Commitments to Improve Value in Healthcare: Finding Common Ground: Workshop Summary, Institute of Medicine (US) Roundtable on Evidence-Based Medicine, Washington (DC): National Academies Press (US), 2009, Last Accessed January 5, 2017, https://www.ncbi.nlm.nih.gov/books/NBK52855/

[214] Stephen G. Kobourov, Spring Embedders and Force-Directed Graph Drawing Algorithms, (2012), arXiv:1201.3011, Wikipedia, Last Accessed January 5, 2017, https://en.wikipedia.org/wiki/Force-directed_graph_drawing

[215] "Genetics Home Reference," U.S. National Library of Medicine, Last Accessed January 5, 2017, https://ghr.nlm.nih.gov/

[216] Robert Clarke, Habtom W. Ressom, Antai Wang, et al, "The properties of high-dimensional data spaces: implications for exploring gene and protein expression data," Nature Reviews Cancer 8, 37-49 (January 2008) | doi:10.1038/nrc2294, Last Accessed January 5, 2017, http://www.nature.com/nrc/journal/v8/n1/full/nrc2294.html

[217] "HITECH Act Enforcement Interim Final Rule," HHS.Gov, Last Accessed January 5, 2017, https://www.hhs.gov/hipaa/for-professionals/special-topics/HITECH-act-enforcement-interim-final-rule/index.html?language=es

[218] "What is Linear Regression?" Statistical Solutions, Last Accessed January 5, 2017, http://www.statisticssolutions.com/what-is-linear-regression/

[219] "Meaningful Use Definition & Objectives," HealthIT.gov, Last Accessed January 5, 2017, https://www.healthit.gov/providers-professionals/meaningful-use-definition-objectives

[220] Stephen P. Borgatti, Multidimensional Scaling, Website, Last Accessed January 5, 2017, http://www.analytictech.com/borgatti/mds.htm

[221] "Defining Nanomaterials," Nano Werk, Last Accessed January 5, 2017, http://www.nanowerk.com/nanotechnology/introduction/introduction_to_nanotechnology_3.php

[222] Jason Brownlee, "Overfitting and Underfitting with Machine Learning Algorithms," Machine Learning Algorithms, March 21, 2016, Last Accessed January 5, 2017, http://machinelearningmastery.com/overfitting-and-underfitting-with-machine-learning-algorithms/

[223] Pathobiology, The Free Dicitionary, Last Accessed January 5, 2017, http://medical-dictionary.thefreedictionary.com/pathobiology

[224] "What is pharmacogenomics?" The U.S. National Library of Medicine, Last Accessed January 5, 2017, https://ghr.nlm.nih.gov/primer/genomicresearch/pharmacogenomics

[225] Committee on a Framework for Development a New Taxonomy of Disease; National Research Council, "Toward Precision Medicine: Building a Knowledge Network for Biomedical Research and a New Taxonomy of Disease," Washington D.C. National Academies Press, Last Accessed January 5, 2017, https://www.nap.edu/catalog/13284/toward-precision-medicine-building-a-knowledge-network-for-biomedical-research

[226] Excerpted and directly quoted from: http://www.indiana.edu/~educy520/sec5982/week_2/variable_types.pdf, Last Accessed December 20, 2016

[227] Process Measures, Evaluating the Quality of Healthcare, Office of Behavioral & Social Sciences Research, Last Accessed January 5, 2017, http://www.esourceresearch.org/Default.aspx?TabId=808

[228] "What is proteomics?" EMBL-EBI, Last Accessed January 5, 2017, http://www.ebi.ac.uk/training/online/course/proteomics-introduction-ebi-resources/what-proteomics

[229] Jason Brownlee, "Supervised and Unsupervised Machine Learning Algorithms," Machine Learning Algorithms, March 16, 2016, Last Accessed January 5, 2017, http://machinelearningmastery.com/supervised-and-unsupervised-machine-learning-algorithms/

[230] Matjaˇz Kukar, Igor Kononenko, "Reliable Classifications with Machine Learning," University of Ljubljana, Faculty of Computer and Information Science, Trˇzaˇska 25, SI-1001 Ljubljana, Slovenia, Last Accessed January 5, 2017, http://citeseerx.ist.psu.edu/viewdoc/download?doi=10.1.1.14.176&rep=rep1&type=pdf

[231] Rob Eisinga, Manfred te Grotenhuis, Ben Pelzer, "The reliability of a two-item scale: Pearson, Cronbach or Spearman-Brown?" Department of Social Science Research Methods and Department of Sociology, Radboud University Nijmegen, PO Box 9104, 6500 HE Nijmegen, The Netherlands, October 8 2012, Last Accessed January 5, 2017, https://www.researchgate.net/profile/Manfred_Grotenhuis/publication/232610246_The_Reliability_of_a_Two-Item_Scale_Pearson_Cronbach_or_Spearman-Brown/links/00b4951759c45468bf000000.pdf

[232] Cynthia Cox, Ashley Semanskee, Gary Claxton, Larry Levitt, "Explaining Healthcare Reform: Risk Adjustment, Reinsurance, and Risk Corridors," The Henry J. Kaiser Family Foundation, August 17, 2016, Last Accessed January 5, 2017, http://kff.org/health-reform/issue-brief/explaining-health-care-reform-risk-adjustment-reinsurance-and-risk-corridors/

[233] Jason Brownlee, "Supervised and Unsupervised Machine Learning Algorithms," Machine Learning Algorithms, March 16, 2016, Last Accessed January 5, 2017, http://machinelearningmastery.com/supervised-and-unsupervised-machine-learning-algorithms/

[234] "Targeted Cancer Therapies," National Cancer Institute, Last Accessed January 5, 2017, https://www.cancer.gov/about-cancer/treatment/types/targeted-therapies/targeted-therapies-fact-sheet

[235] Manhattan Distance, Wikipedia.org, Last Accessed January 5, 2017, https://en.wiktionary.org/wiki/Manhattan_distance

[236] Taxon, dictionary.com, Last Accessed January 5, 2017, http://www.dictionary.com/browse/taxon

[237] Taxonomy, dictionary.com, Last Accessed January 5, 2017, http://www.dictionary.com/browse/taxonomy

[238] Katharine E. Henry, David N. Hager, et al, "A targeted real-time early warning score (TREWScore) for septic shock," *Science Translational Medicine* 05 Aug 2015: Vol. 7, Issue 299, pp. 299ra122 DOI: 10.1126/scitranslmed.aab3719, Last Accessed January 5, 2017, http://stm.sciencemag.org/content/7/299/299ra122

[239] Jason Brownlee, "Supervised and Unsupervised Machine Learning Algorithms," Machine Learning Algorithms, March 16, 2016, Last Accessed January 5, 2017, http://machinelearningmastery.com/supervised-and-unsupervised-machine-learning-algorithms/

[240] Jong-Myon Bae, "Value-based medicine: concepts and application," Epidemiol Health. 2015; 37: e2015014, Published online March 4, 2015, doi: 10.4178/epih/e2015014, Last Accessed January 5, 2017 https://www.ncbi.nlm.nih.gov/pmc/articles/PMC4398974/

38081006R00192

Made in the USA
Middletown, DE
05 March 2019